INFORMATION TECHNOLOGY and INDUSTRIAL POLICY

Jill Hills

CROOM HELM
London & Canberra

©1984 Jill Hills
Croom Helm Ltd, Provident House, Burrell Row,
Beckenham, Kent BR3 1AT
Croom Helm Australia Pty Ltd, 28 Kembla St,
Fyshwick, ACT 2609, Australia

British Library Cataloguing in Publication Data

Hills, Jill
   Information technology and industrial policy.
   1. Technology — Information sources
   I. Title
   607   T10.5

ISBN 0-7099-3701-6

Printed and bound in Great Britain

CONTENTS

List of Tables & Figures
Preface

INTRODUCTION   1

1. EXPANDING MARKETS, THE INTERNATIONAL FRAMEWORK
   & INDUSTRIAL POLICY

   1.1 Expanding Markets...................   7
   1.2 International Industrial Structure..   11
   1.3 Industrial Strategies & the Inter-
       national Scene......................   12
       1.31 Protection through Tariffs...   12
       1.32 GATT & the EEC   13
       1.33 Definition of 'Industrial Policy' 16
   1.4 Industrial Policy & Technology.....   19
   1.5 Strategies Towards Technology & Markets 22
   1.6 What Kind of Industrial Policy?   27

2. IDEOLOGY, STATE CONTROL & BRITISH INDUSTRIAL
   POLICY

   2.1 Conflict Between Ideology & State
       Control.............................   48
   2.2 The British Industrial Policy Community 49
   2.3 British Industrial Policy...........   55
   2.4 Conclusion..........................   68

3. MARKETS: TELECOMMUNICATIONS, COMPUTERS & MICRO-
   ELECTRONICS
   3.1 Introduction........................   76
   3.2 Telecommunications.
       3.21 The Evolution & Structure of the
            Market.........................   77
       3.22 The International Structure of
            the Industry...................   80
       3.23 The British Market............   83

CONTENTS

      3.24 International markets......... 86
  3.3 Computers.
      3.31 Features of Computer Markets.. 89
      3.32 Technological & Historical
           Development................... 91
      3.33 International Structure....... 92
      3.34 Structure of British industry. 94
      3.35 British Domestic Markets...... 97
  3.4 Microelectronics
      3.41 Historical Development........ 99
      3.42 International Structure....... 102
      3.43 Structure of British Industry. 104
      3.44 Conclusion.................... 105

4. TELECOMMUNICATIONS
  4.1 Introduction....................... 109
  4.2 Post Office Organisation & Monopoly 111
  4.3 Cartel versus Competition 123
  4.4 Politics & Public Exchange Technology 130

5. COMPUTERS
  5.1 Introduction....................... 151
  5.2 Imports & R&D...................... 153
  5.3 Public Procurement................. 156
  5.4 Public Procurement - Minis......... 166
  5.5 Public Procurement - Software...... 170
  5.6 Conclusions on Public Procurement.. 172
  5.7 Research, Development & Investment.. 174
  5.8 Rationalisation & Foreign Technology 175
  5.9 Conclusion......................... 184

6. MICROELECTRONICS
  6.1 Introduction....................... 197
  6.2 Imports, Tariffs & Multinationals... 198
  6.3 Domestic Technology or Inward
      Investment......................... 203
  6.4 Battle for Inmos................... 212
  6.5 Creating Demand.................... 217
  6.6 Conclusion......................... 219

7. COMPARATIVE STRATEGIES AND ALTERNATIVE
   MODELS OF INDUSTRIAL POLICY.
  7.1 Introduction....................... 225
  7.2 Mainframe Computers................ 225
  7.3 Minicomputers & Peripherals........ 231
  7.4 Microelectronics................... 233
  7.5 Telecommunications & Office
      Technology......................... 236
  7.6 Strategies Compared................ 240
  7.7 An Alternative Model for Industrial
      Policy
      7.71 The American Model....... 245

CONTENTS

        7.72 The Japanese Model....... 245
    7.8 The Alternatives Available to Britain 253

8. CONCLUSION 263

   SELECT BIBLIOGRAPHY...................... 280

   INDEX.................................... 289

TABLES AND FIGURES

Tables

2.1	Governments, Policies & Institutions.	60
3.1	Market Shares of World Telecommunications Equipment............	81
3.2	Share of Total Sales in Telecommunications Equipment by Main Manufacturing Firms Outside Their Country of Origin................................	82
3.3	UK Market Share of Major Manufacturers in PABx..................	86
3.4	World Market Share in 1965	94
3.5	Computers Installed by US Firms and Computers Manufactured by European Firms Under Licence as a % of Total Computer Installations..................	94
3.6	US and UK Controlled Computers in the UK as a % of Total Computer Installations...........................	97
3.7	Top Firms in the Data Processing Industry in 1978......................	98
3.8	Acquisitions in the US Semi-conductor Industry.....................	102

Figures

1.1	Markets included within the Information Technology Sector of Industry.	8
1.2	The Relationship Between Ideology Towards Markets & Centralisation of States	35
1.3	The Relationship Between Ideology Towards Markets, Centralistion of States & Policy Instruments.....................	36
3.1	Major Telecommunications Manufacturers in UK Market..............	84
3.2	Concentration in the British Mainframe Computer Industry	96
5.1	Some Negotiations between Mainframe Manufacturers & Foreign Owned Companies.....	177

To Tonya,Patrick and Christina

PREFACE

This book was finished during the year which I spent as a Hallsworth Research Fellow at Manchester University and I am very grateful to those who made that time possible. Because it has been a long time in the making, too many people have contributed to the book to thank by name. I would like to say a general thankyou to friends, to colleagues, to those who agreed to be interviewed and to those who have commented on previous drafts and papers. But there are those who must be thanked personally. In particular, I would like to thank Bo Sarlvik for his long-distance support and numerous late-night telephone discussions, Jean Blondel for his interest in Japan, when others thought him and me mad, Tony King for his many-sided knowledge, Geraint Parry and Hugh Ward for their sharp, constructive criticism, Barry Evans for his lay-person's guide to satellites, Steve Kennedy for advice on redrafting and Sue Read of Harrington Computer Services for help with the word-processing. To my ex-husband, Mike, must go gratitude for my socialisation into the world of information technology and my introduction to Japan. To Mike Hopkins of Loughborough University and to NTT and its personnel in London I would like to express my thanks for their willingness to find material. Needless to say, all responsibility for shortcomings and inaccuracies are mine. Finally my grateful thanks to Gwynneth Osborn and my three children, Tonya, Patrick and Christina, for their good humour and endless cups of coffeee.

Jill Hills

INTRODUCTION

This book is concerned with the way in which the British government has responded to the growth market of information technology. It was conceived in 1977, before that term had become part of everyday vocabulary. In fact, until the very late 1970s, there was no term to express the converging technologies of computing, telecommunications and microelectronics. It was not until 1979 that political awareness of the microchip developed. The microchip has provided the enabling technology for the convergence of the three industries, and together they represent a world growth market fought over by the industrialised West.

This study falls within the area of government-industry relations, an under-researched area of policy-making with a tendency towards the descriptive. David Steel, in his survey of the literature, points out that the coverage is patchy, with emphasis upon general surveys, case-studies of particular industries, discussion of public enterprise and studies of business associations predominating.[1] Of those articles and books not covered by Steel, Wyn Grant's <u>The Political Economy of Industrial Policy</u> is an overall review of British government intervention since the 1970s.[2] But, despite its comparisons with West Germany and Ireland, even Wyn Grant's detailed coverage of industrial intervention does not explain why British policy should differ from those of other nations. In general 'industrial policy' is seen as a domestic issue, in a way which financial policy is not.

Three recent books have placed national industrial policies into an international context. <u>International Trade and Industrial Policies</u> edited by S.J.Warnecke raises the problem of the way in which industrial policies of national governments subvert the GATT code on subsidies.[3] The

INTRODUCTION

second, Industrial Policy as an International Issue, by William Diebold Jr., addresses the methods by which GATT could encompass the elements of national industrial policies.[4] Neither completely addresses itself to the problem that diminution of tariff barriers and increased capital liberalisation have made 'industrial policy' the most effective mechanism through which governments may alter the rate of change within domestic economies. The approach adopted by John Pinder in National Industrial Strategies and the World Economy, which he edited, is perhaps the nearest to that adopted here.[5] Pinder acknowledges industrial policies as mechanisms of political control over economies increasingly subject to external world threats and argues the case for limited protection towards certain markets within Europe.

This study differs, however, from the above works in that it attempts to relate the detail of British policy in the growth market of information technology to the broader questions of British industrial policy and to the still wider questions of that policy within an international framework. As the failure of the GATT talks in 1982 indicated, the world market is gradually moving from an international trading system based upon markets to one based upon politics. If, as Warnecke suggests:

> ..trade liberalisation has depended upon social, political and economic pluralism in the major members of the GATT system,[6]

then the gradual transfer of the international trading system from one based on markets to one based on politics has implications for the political control of domestic economic structure. It is to those implications that this book addresses itself.

It argues that changes in the international structure, brought about by increasing interdependence among the industrialised countries, and by the weakening of the American economy, have led to all industrialised countries adopting forms of industrial policy. These industrial policies are necessary because interprenetration of capital through multinational companies and the lowering of tariff barriers by GATT have made national economies vulnerable to external factors. World market forces have undermined the efficacy of national government actions in relation to their domestic economies, whilst public opinion in the Western industrialised world has increased expectations of governments. Not only the British government, but the American and

INTRODUCTION

others,are faced with the problem of balancing protection and support for domestically owned industries with their international obligations. The problem in Europe is greatest in expanding high technology markets. The world division of labour has made it likely that the industrialised countries will have to increasingly rely on these expanding markets in order to create the exports from which domestic employment in service industries can be expanded.

Given the wide range of other factors which must be taken into account, it is clearly not possible to give an assessment of the extent to which industrial policy per se contributes to economic growth. Japan's success has been attributed to widely disparate factors ranging from its young population,its seniority based wage structure, its educational system and high levels of numeracy, to its higher capital investment,low defence spending,its productivity increases,its weak trade unions and the stability of one party in power almost continuously since the Second World War.[7] Other product related factors such as better design and marketing, quality control and targeting of world markets are also mentioned. A similar range of economic,political and market related factors have been cited to account for Britain's decline,[8] with the additional explanation put forward by Samuel Beer,which revolves around the erosion of the cultural base of consent.[9]

The purpose here is not to examine the macroeconomic reasons for Britain's decline, although that decline has been more precipitous than that of other industrial countries. Rather the purpose is to point out that an 'industrial policy'adopted by any one government makes sense only within the context of international markets and an international trading system in which comparative advantage between countries has shifted over the past two decades. A rational industrial policy could be defined as one which cushioned or slowed the social dislocation involved in industries where a country has lost its comparative advantage to others and which supported those markets in which it either had or sought that advantage.[10] In that context we are concerned here with an explanation of how in certain growth markets,in which Britain might be expected to have an advantage, she has come to a position where her exports are matched,or more than matched, by imports. But the explanation has to go further than mere consideration of policy towards those specific markets:it has to take in British industrial policy in general, the industrial policies of other

INTRODUCTION

countries and the trends in the international economy.

The question no longer is whether countries should adopt an 'industrial policy', but, given that all governments in the industrialised West do support their domestic industry in order to give it market advantage, what is the best method of organisation of an industrial policy for any one political system? By examining the 'fit' of ideologies towards markets and differing political systems an attempt is made here to answer that question. In particular, in the case of Britain, the 'core' liberal ideology towards markets, which characterises much of British industrial policy, is at odds with the British centralised political system. The clash between the two, exacerbated by the fragmented nature of the British state, leads to confusion of objectives and incoherent strategy towards growth markets. Policy towards the markets of telecommunications, computing and microelectronics illustrates this confusion, as also does comparison with the strategies of other governments. The conclusion is that Britain cannot afford a liberal ideological approach to these markets because it allows the international market to be replicated within the domestic economy.

The book begins with a discussion of changing international industrial structure, tariff and non-tariff barriers and flows of technological know-how. The first chapter contains a discussion of the variables which are important in the determination of industrial policies and the 'fit' between ideologies towards markets, political systems and the instruments of industrial policy. Moving from the international plane to the case of Britain the conflict between the 'core' ideology and political control of markets by the British state is illustrated in a general review of British industrial policy in Chapter Two. Because industrial policy towards any one market is affected by the international and domestic structure of that market, Chapter Three reviews these structures for telecommunications, computers and microelectronics, now coalescing into the one market of information technology. Chapters Four, Five and Six present an historical analysis of policy towards these markets since 1964, once more illustrating the conflict between ideology and state control. In Chapter Seven, British policy towards these markets is contrasted with that of other countries in Western Europe and with Japan and the USA. The alternative models presented by American and Japanese style industrial

INTRODUCTION

policies are discussed, and the possible ways forward for British industrial policy. Finally, the concluding chapter argues that although the economic costs of Britain's attachment to a 'core'liberal ideology cannot be quantified, unless action is taken by the national government at this time to control the flows of capital and technology, then the options open to future governments will have foreclosed. If the present incoherent policies towards growth markets continue, then Britain is set to become a technological dependency of America. And, as America's economy weakens, so that technological power is likely to be translated into political power. The major concerns of British governments must be how to develop effective non-tariff barriers in the form of 'industrial policy' so as to minimise the political and economic costs of technological dependence.

NOTES AND REFERENCES.

1. David R.Steel,"Review Article:Government and Industry in Britain",British Journal of Political Science,Vol.12,October 1982,pp.449-503.
2. Wyn Grant,The Political Economy of Industrial Policy(London,Butterworths,1982).
3. S.J.Warnecke ed.,International Trade and Industrial Policies . Government Intervention and an Open World Economy(London,Macmillan,1978).
4. William Diebold Jr.,Industrial Policy as an International Issue(New York,McGraw Hill,1980).
5. John Pinder ed.,National Industrial Strategies and the World Economy(London,Croom Helm,1982).
6. S.J.Warnecke,"Introduction.Government intervention and an open global trading system"in S.J.Warnecke ed.,p.12.
7. Of a large number of books and articles see: Ezra Vogel,Japan as Number One . Lessons for America.(New York & London,Harper Row,1979);Hugh Patrick and Henry Rosovsky,Asia's New Giant (Washington D.C.,Brookings,1976);Johny K.Johannson,Japanese Export Management . The Organisational , Institutional and Market Factors behind a World Force (Stockholm,Marknadsteknisk-centrum,1981).
8. Of a number of books on British economic decline see for instance: F.T.Blackaby ed., British Economic Policy 1960-74 (Cambridge,Cambridge University Press,1978);R.Caves and L.B.Krause eds.,Britain's Economic Performance(Washington

INTRODUCTION

D.C.,Brookings,1980);Andrew Gamble, *Britain in Decline* (London,Macmillan,1981).

9. Samuel H.Beer,*Britain Against Itself* (London,Faber and Faber,1982). Beer points to the number of books targeting the British political system for attack, see: p.xiii.

10. An extended definition of a 'rational'industrial policy is given by Brian Hodges,"Industrial Policy. A Directorate General in Search of a Policy" in Helen Wallace,W.Wallace and C.Webb eds.,*Policymaking in the European Communities*(London,Wiley,1977),pp.113-136.

Chapter One

EXPANDING MARKETS, THE INTERNATIONAL FRAMEWORK AND INDUSTRIAL POLICY

1.1 EXPANDING MARKETS

Over the past twenty years the growth rates of industrialised countries have varied dramatically. Whereas Japan and Germany have achieved fast growth, the USA and Britain have achieved little or none. Although North Sea Oil has enabled Britain to maintain a balance of payments surplus in the latter 1970s and early 1980s Britain's proportion of world trade in terms of volume of manufactured goods declined from roughly one third at the beginning of the century to less than one tenth now. Each year Britain's growth in export trade has been slightly less than that of her main industrial competitors. Yet Britain's dependence on exports has increased to over 30% of GNP, compared to the 5% dependence of the USA or 10% of Japan.[1]
  Britain's industrial decline has gradually deepened. From 1978,when full employment was abandoned as an official goal, politicians have referred to ' structural unemployment' in Britain. The term is used to describe an economy in which older industries, such as shipbuilding and textiles still play an important role in employment; an economy in which medium technology industries, such as automobiles face a loss of competitiveness against imported products; an economy in which high technology industries, such as aerospace, nuclear power and computers, struggle to maintain a foothold in world markets and even to maintain solvency itself.
  The American and British economies now display similar characteristics.[2] For both, growth in volume of exports over the period 1968 to 1978 was less than the world average.[3] The process of decline in America is slower, partly because of its huge

7

THE INTERNATIONAL FRAMEWORK & INDUSTRIAL POLICY

Figure 1.1 Markets included within the information technology sector of industry.

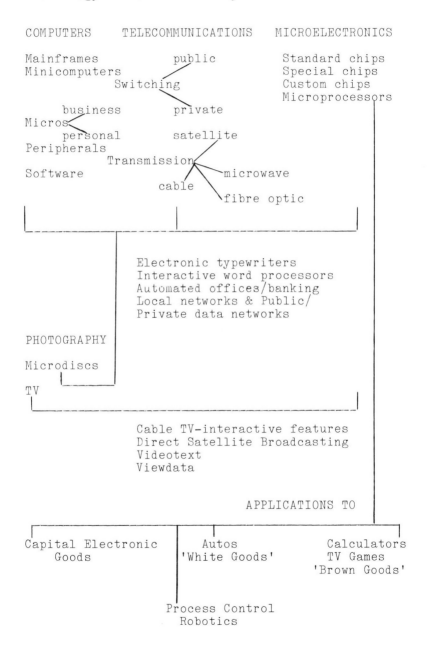

domestic market, and partly because of heavy defence spending.But the gradual weakening of that economy has become increasingly evident.[4] Hence it becomes of importance for each of these countries to consider the experience of others.

    The primary concern in this book is the expanding market of information technology.That market comprises the products and markets of three industries -those of computers,telecommunications and microelectronics. The three markets have traditionally been separate,although now linked by the office technology market.With technological advance in electronic components, the three traditional markets have coalesced, so that computers and such office products as interactive word processors both use microchips within themselves and communicate with each other via telecommunications links which are computer controlled.(See Figure 1.1) Changing technology has also produced rapid alterations in markets within which newer markets have given greater opportunities than older,more mature ones.For instance, microcomputers were a faster growing market in 1982 than were large mainframes. The output of the three traditional industries is expected to have a major influence on both industry and society in general.[5] At the time of writing market forecasts predict a growth of between 13% and 15% per annum in the world wide demand for information technology products.[6] In addition microprocessor based products are expected to have a compound growth of 32% between 1980 and 1985.[7] Products incorporating microelectronics include those where basic chips are packaged, such as calculators, watches, TV and video games, and products in which microprocessors are applied to driving machinery, such as cars and consumer durables.In addition, on the process control side, microprocessors have been applied to a wide range of machine tools, spawning the robotics industry. These various applications of microprocessors are outside the ambit of this study, which is primarily concerned with the three original industries of computers, telecommunications and microelectronics, out of whose technological convergence has come the possibility of information flowing quickly from place to place and from machine to machine.However, because British government information technology policy also includes policy on applications, these initiatives are briefly discussed later.

    To quantify the past importance of the three industries to the British economy is of some difficulty because the classification of the three

industries' products has varied over the years,and import/export figures are muddied by reimports and re-exports, mainly attributable to foreign multi-national enterprises. But these are all industries in which Britain could be exporting at least as much as it imports. In fact Britain's export/import ratio in telecommunications which stood at 2.98 in 1965, fell to 0.9 in 1974,recovered to 1.3 in 1979,falling to 1.0 in 1981.The same ratio for computer hardware systems in 1980 was 0.9 with computer parts and peripherals contributing the heaviest item of imports. For electronic components, in 1980, the ratio was 0.9 and for office technology the export /import ratio stood at 0.8, with imports centred mainly on word processors and other electronic goods and exports mainly in lower value added goods.[8]

Within a British economy which is concentrated (62 firms accounted for 56% of exports in 1980),these industries are particularly so. In 1978 the largest five firms were responsible for 85% of employment and 84% of output in telecommunications; for 69% of employment and 81% of output in computers; for 47% of employment and 47% of output in radio and electronic components . In office machinery, the largest five accounted for 54% of output and 61% of employment.[9]

The three major industries employed about 260,000 people in 1981, a drop of 24,000 from 1975.[10] A decrease of eleven thousand jobs in the tele-communications industry came as it switched from heavy engineering to electronics. In the computer industry, between 1980 and 1982, 5000 jobs disappeared.[11] And, in the office technology sector, employment dropped from 27,000 in 1973 to 14,000 in 1979. With the change in telecommunications technology, a further loss of jobs is scheduled as computerisation of telephone exchanges reduces numbers of both operators and maintenance engineers in British Telecom. The Information Technology Working Party of the National Economic Development Council (NEDC)expects employment in the sector to be less in 1985 that in 1970.[12]

These figures and other evidence suggest that the technology of microelectronics may itself displace jobs in manufacturing, service and commercial sectors.[13] This view is not shared in British government reports or by the leaders of the major parties. Their argument is two fold. They suggest that the new technology, particularly within the service sector,has freed staff for other work or has created new possibilities, rather than displaced jobs.Second,in the manufacturing sector, they argue

that companies must modernise their products and production processes in order to become competitive with overseas suppliers.[14] From this concern with relative productivity and with the upgrading of products came the 1979 Thatcher Government's concern with the diffusion of the technology of microprocessors.[15] According to this view, increased employment will be generated through increased competitiveness to which the new technology will contribute.

1.2 INTERNATIONAL INDUSTRIAL STRUCTURE

Of concern in the debate on whether Britain should concentrate on production in expanding markets,such as information technology, is its position in the changing international economic order. The developing countries need access to international markets and,in particular, to the high purchasing power of the already industrialised countries of the West. But in the process of gaining this access the penetration of exports from the developing countries into the domestic markets of the industrialised nations causes readjustments in the structure of those markets.[16]

Ease of global access and communication has brought the reality of a worldwide division of labour. This world division of labour is itself the product of massive overseas investment by the industrialised West. Just as the proportion of trade between the industrialised countries themselves has grown,so also has the proportion of overseas investment, as companies have set up local manufacturing units to cater for local markets, to reduce transport costs or to evade tariff and non-tariff barriers to imports.[17] Whilst the stock of American overseas investment remains the largest (and Britain's the second largest), such investment is no longer a one-way flow from the USA. The pace of Japanese and West German investment quickened during the 1970s, particularly into the USA.[18]

In an international trading system in which the hegemony of the United States has given way to increased pluralism and instability, and in which many of the industrialised nations are dependent on supplies of energy from the Third World, industrialised domestic economies have become more sensitive to external events. The industrialised compete with each other. And it is this competition as much as that from developing countries which has fuelled industries into job

11

displacing technical change.[19] For each country the benefits of free trade have been balanced by the costs of economic adjustment. For those with the greatest reliance on exports the problems have been the greatest.

1.3 INDUSTRIAL STRATEGIES AND THE INTERNATIONAL SCENE

The majority of governments in the industrialised nations have accepted the thesis that they can influence markets. Even the most ideologically liberal, such as the USA, adopts measures of protectionism to maintain certain markets for national producers, allows localities to compete with subsidies for industrial investment ,provides government funding to offset large-scale R&D costs in high-technology industry, and subsidises exports through tax incentives.[20] Both protective tariffs and industrial subsidies (whatever called) attempt to give market advantage to domestically owned, or domestically based companies within a particular industrial sector.

1.31 Protection through tariffs
Traditionally market advantage to domestic industries has been given by tariffs.That market advantage may come through the maintenance of the existing form of industrial structure, or come by means of altering it. In the latter case protection via tariffs or quotas may be used as a temporary instrument whilst alterations in the structure take place. For instance, in 1981, the rationale for import restrictions on Japanese cars into America was that it would give a breathing space to allow the restructuring of the American automobile industry. Similarly the 'Alternative Economic Strategy' proposed by the Labour Party in Britain in 1981 supported the use of both selective import controls and financial aid to industry.[21] The EEC has itself linked protection to its'industrial policy' by imposing a heavier than normal tariff on microchips whilst at the same time seeking to develop a European presence in the industry.[22]

Demand for protection comes from those industries suffering the effects of international competition within the domestic economy.[23] But whether action is taken aginst imports will depend, both on the amount of political clout which can be amassed by producers and labour in any particular industry,and,what John Zysman calls the extent of

THE INTERNATIONAL FRAMEWORK & INDUSTRIAL POLICY

the autonomy of the State from interest group pressure.[24] Stephen Krasner makes the point that American multinational companies have lost much of their assets abroad to nationalisation and that therefore their interests and those of domestic producers have coalesced around protectionism.[25] As America has lost its productivity and technological advantage over the industrialised West, so trade policy has shifted from the province of specialised Congressional committees onto the political agenda of individual Congressmen.[26] Countervailing tariffs have been increasingly used against products which the United States considers to be subsidised by other governments.[27]

The USA can use such tariffs, partly because it had protective legislation already in force when it became a signatory to the General Agreement on Trade and Tariffs (GATT), but also because it has a relatively small proportion of its capital owned by foreign enterprises. With a huge domestic market, it relies on exports for less than 10% of its GNP. For other industrialised countries, a greater reliance on exports, the provisions of GATT and the EEC and progressive penetration of foreign capital make protective tariffs difficult to sustain.

1.32 GATT and the EEC

The present problems facing the British economy were not evident in the immediate post-war period. The majority of exports were to the old colonies whilst manufactured imports came mainly from the USA. Bilateral trade agreements ensured cheap food from the Commonwealth, whilst its markets provided captive recipients for Britain's manufactured goods. In the immediate post-war period Britain was forced to give up her Commonwealth preferences in return for American aid, and in 1947 joined GATT to work towards liberalised world trade.

GATT was a child of the Americans. It aimed at:

> reciprocal and mutually advantageous arrangements directed to the substantial reduction of tariffs and other barriers to trade and to elimination of discriminatory treatment in international commerce.[28]

The method of implementation of free trade was to be the principle of non-discrimination under which:

> any advantage, favour, privilege or immunity

granted by any contracting party to any product originating in or destined for any other country shall be accorded immediately and unconditionally to the like product originating in or destined for the territories of all other contracting parties.[29]

To this general rule the only exceptions were to be those related to existing preferential systems and to future customs unions and free trade associations. Above all free trade was expected to benefit the USA with its undamaged post-war economy and technological lead over other countries. Between 1947 and 1967 six multilateral trade negotiations took place, the final negotiations being known as the Kennedy round when unilateral tariff reductions of about one third took place on non-agricultural products. Since then, the Tokyo round has produced further decreases in the tariffs of certain categories of manufactured goods. Several studies have demonstrated that the importance of tariffs on manufactured goods as a mechanism limiting world trade has decreased.[30]

Attention has swung to the protection of the industrialised nations from those lesser developed, through discriminatory trade negotiations. These are themselves contrary to the spirit of GATT. These negotiations have been both conducted through GATT, as in the case of the MFN Agreement, and outside GATT in bi-lateral agreements between countries on quotas of imports for certain manufactured products. Such bi-lateral agreements have extended in recent years to agreements between the industrialised countries themselves.

By the 1970s, the rising volume of trade between countries and the increased dependence on exports of all the industrialised nations, in turn produced protectionist pressures within domestic economies. These pressures were particularly acute in the USA. In 1971 the economy showed a deficit on overseas trade for the first time and the international monetary system went into crisis. In 1974 Congress passed the Trade Balance Act which allowed the imposition of higher tariffs whenever an import reached its 'peril point'- a certain proportion of domestic sales.[31]

In addition the USA maintained its Buy America Act. Regulations passed in 1954 updated that Act, which was originally passed in 1933 to deal with the Great Depression. Under the Act, American manufacturers receive public sector preference with products 5% more expensive than foreign competition,

up to 12% more expensive,if produced in a depressed area, and up to 50% more expensive for the defence market. This Act has effectively closed the public sector to overseas suppliers. Further protective legislation has been passed in recent years and the International Trade Commission has been established to act as a watchdog over import penetration. In 1981 Congress threatened to act against any country whose market did not seem as open to American exports as it would have liked. Through these various protective Acts ,Western European countries have been explicity excluded from certain markets in the USA.[32]

In contrast, members of the EEC have their own tariff barriers controlled by membership of that body and in turn through its membership of GATT. Britain joined the EEC in 1973. In as much as it is a regional free trade grouping maintaining preferential terms of trade between member countries, the EEC exists in contradiction to the spirit of free trade between all nations espoused by GATT. However,EEC rules are intended to harmonize with GATT and have the force of law in member countries. EEC directives may be enforced by the European Court.

GATT attentions have increasingly turned to non-tariff barriers to trade. Within GATT there has been concern to attempt to replace such non-tariff barriers with visible restrictions on specific products.The restrictions would legitimately operate where the domestic industry of importing countries was suffering from an increase in imports. These moves have been resisted by the Japanese. The breakdown in GATT talks in 1982 indicates the unwillingness of governments to forego their freedom to utilise non-tariff barriers in favour of free trade.[33]

But acting along these lines,in 1981,GATT regulations on public sector contracts came into force.Public sector contracts have been used by governments within their industrial policies to favour domestic industry and to provide a home base of assured demand from which companies may export. Under the GATT and EEC rules, member countries may no longer discriminate against foreign companies in the disbursement of public sector contracts of over 150,000 Units of Account(about £130,000).Within the EEC this rule has the force of law and governments can be challenged by multinational companies in the European Court.

The result is that the domestic policies of EEC member nations are now out of balance with those of

Japan and the USA. Those who are members of the EEC are bound by law, whilst for the others the GATT rules remain no more than international agreements. For them, breaking the rules is a subject of negotiation, not legal recourse. Hence the concept of free trade is acting to the detriment of members of the EEC as they attempt to maintain domestic employment and domestically owned industry.

Supposedly, governments have had to be careful not to offend against EEC rules of fair competition in the aid that they have given to industry. However, as the recession of the late 1970s gained momentum, the EEC was itself forced to bow to internal national pressures towards protection. Although lamenting national propensity to take protective action in support of domestic industries many of those measures have not been challenged by the Commission. Nations belonging to the EEC therefore operate industrial policies which conflict with the interests of other member states.[34]

To some extent, such an outcome was inevitable in a common market without political unity, and in which member states betrayed divergent growth patterns. Areas on the periphery of the EEC have fared worse in terms of growth than have areas at the centre. To combat this problem of divergent growth the EEC has developed a regional policy, but as divergencies increase, so that policy has been insufficient to level incomes between areas. EEC policy also limits regional aid to forms of aid which will alter the structural characteristics of employment in a region. Supposedly, subvention which preserves the status quo in dying industries is not allowed. But political pressures on national governments have demanded otherwise. Hence part of national policy is geared to getting around EEC regulations. Membership of that body has increased the international constraints on domestic governments in their pursuit of an industrial policy.

1.33 Definition of 'Industrial Policy'
Political scientists have achieved no agreement on the definition of the term 'industrial policy'. As Grant points out, the programmes contained within any one industrial policy may overlap with others such as Manpower Planning.[35] It is therefore difficult to delineate where industrial policy begins and ends. What such a policy is expected to contain in the way of programmes will depend on the legitimacy which is attached to the term itself. It is a term which is culturally and ideologically defined. In those

countries of liberal ideological persuasion – that is where there is a belief in a distinct division between state and industry where there is a belief in the supremacy of markets over politics – although policy mechanisms may be used to finance industry, they go under names different from that of 'industrial policy'. The definition adopted in this book attempts to circumvent these problems of cultural and ideological bias by defining 'industrial policy' as a system of tariff and non-tariff barriers. In other words, instead of looking at industrial policy as purely domestic policy, this book sees it as part of domestic adjustment to international trade.[36]

We are concerned with the mechanisms by which a government attempts to preserve or alter industrial structure in the face of international pressures, and the way it seeks to gain advantage for domestic industries in the international market place. In our definition, industrial policy consists of those mechanisms used by government to pursue structural adjustment, either in declining industries, or in expanding industries. These mechanisms may be intended to slow down change, maintain the status quo, or hasten change. They may be industry specific, product specific, or company specific. They may include tariff barriers, quota arrangements, bilateral agreements, overseas aid to procure resources, or to procure low wage manufacturing bases. They may include encouragement of inward investment, or that of direct investment overseas. In the domestic market they may include indirect methods of support, such as tax relief, or direct methods, such as public procurement preferences. They may include rationalisation of industrial sectors, and the provision of grants and loans or finance for R&D. They may also contain the creation of institutions to reform the market or mediate between it and the government. And they may also contain the control of imports and exports of technology.

Up to the end of the 1950s the major European countries tended towards tariff based protectionism on the one hand, and, on the other, regional aid to those geographic areas suffering from decline. The 1960s witnessed the Kennedy Round of GATT with its reductions in import tariffs on most manufactured goods and, following the formation of the EEC, a massive penetration of American multi-national capital into Europe. From the 1960s Britain, France and West Germany all developed forms of governmental intervention at the level of the firm.[37] It may be

17

no coincidence that just at the time that tariff barriers on manufactured goods were reduced, they were actually becoming obsolete as a mechanism of control over structural change. The penetration of foreign-owned subsidiaries into European economies meant that their manufactured goods escaped any tariff protection - an important factor in those industries where it was considered necessary to have a domestically-owned presence. Indeed, it can be argued that tariff barriers are most useful in those industries, or in those product markets, where there is little foreign capital penetration.They are particularly useful against manufactures from the Third World, and in those countries where foreign capital accumulation, as a proportion of national capital accumulation, is minimal - the USA and Japan being the most obvious examples.

Non-tariff barriers in the form of industrial subsidies have had the advantage that they do not offend against GATT and can be more specific in terms of companies or sectors than tariffs. Their disadvantage is that they place greater pressure on central institutions and decisionmakers to pick sectors or companies to benefit from aid. The central government bureaucracy plays a crucial role in the effectiveness of an 'industrial policy' in a way which it does not when a generalised tariff is in operation.

If the policy is not to become a mere handing out of money to whoever shouts loudest, some cohesive goal is necessary amongst government actors. Hence the statement by a Vice Minister of the Ministry of International Trade and Industry in Japan:

> Businesses introduce new products and develop export markets on their own initiative. The main role of MITI is to come up with a vision to serve as a policy target and to persuade and guide industry towards that vision

epitomises the type of overriding view which an industrial policy demands of bureaucrats.[38]

If such a policy is to succeed then the fewer layers of linkages and the more direct the feedback from manufacturer to government, the better. It seems reasonable to suppose that the more indirect the aid - the more in terms of tax allowances rather than direct loans - and the less the industry/ bureaucracy contact, the less likely it is that aid will be utilised for the purpose envisaged. Hence the institutionalisation of direct

THE INTERNATIONAL FRAMEWORK & INDUSTRIAL POLICY

which only came to light through American Congressional hearings several years later.[47]

Multinational subsidiaries themselves may have problems adapting to the changing demands of host governments, or may wish to align themselves with the host country, only to be brought up sharply by decisions taken overseas. The fundamental problem was accentuated by the 1982 Soviet gas pipe-line issue, when the Reagan administration used legal powers to enforce compliance with its decision that American technology should not be exported by British or American owned firms. That problem is how can two countries - the home and the host - claim loyalty from one corporation? And in world recessionary times, how can host countries retain sovereign control over operations of multinationals when national governments vie with each other to attract inward investment, employment and technology?[48]

1.5 STRATEGIES TOWARDS TECHNOLOGY AND MARKETS

Faced with both a gap in technology and possible inward investment in the product market, governments have had the choice of several strategies:

1) <u>To allow a free market in technology and hand over the product market to multinationals.</u>
In certain high technology sectors this strategy may be the only viable one for smaller countries without the necessary resources to fund their own research programmes. In Belgium, Spain, Portugal and Norway over 90% of telecommunications manufacture is done by foreign firms. In Italy, in 1974, foreign owned firms accounted for all the data processing installed. Similarly the Benelux countries had no domestic mainframe computer manufacturer. IBM (US) alone took 60% of the Benelux market.[49]

In other countries the strategy may be adopted by default. France in the early 1960s took a laissez faire attitude towards its mainframe computer industry with the result that in 1964 Machines Bull, the leading French company was taken over by General Electric of America.[50]

Today Ireland, Holland and Belgium are the most obvious examples of Western European countries embracing the strategy over the range of markets discussed in this book. They seek to attract inward investment from both American and Japanese firms. In Britain, the Department of Industry's policy in the 1980s towards microcircuit standard chip production

Relying on imported technology also implies that countries are prepared to rely for economic growth on technology which is not up to date. In order to keep their lead in innovation, companies maintain control over new technology and license only that which will not compete. Although in the 1970s the cash-strapped position of many American companies moved the terms of trade in technology in favour of the buyer, for industrialised countries to rely on licensing agreements for their technology implies that they will either improve that technology through R&D, or will accept their position in the market as uncompetitive compared to that of American companies. Problems of technological transfer are both helped and exacerbated by multinational companies. On the credit side, multinationals may bring to a country technology which would otherwise not be available, and may develop technology within the host country. But there are good reasons why the corporation may retain R&D decisions in its home country, which in turn may lead to uncertainty as to how much technological diffusion is taking place. For instance in the case of Britain, figures for 1975 showed that foreign companies undertook 17% of R&D in British industry, which is actually less than one might expect from their 30% holding in industry at that time.[44]

For governments planning an industrial policy, the multinational corporation provides problems of control. The practice of transfer pricing makes it difficult for national governments to quantify the value of foreign investment to the national economy or to control the activities of firms.[45] One study has shown that one third of gross direct investment into the EEC between 1967 and 1975 was repatriated to home countries through disinvestment of multinationals.[46] Inward investment by trans-national corporations may provide employment in the host country, but with that provision they also become political actors. They may constrain domestic policy by threatening to withdraw employment. Ford and Chrysler have provided examples in Britain. When times are hard, multinationals may actually withdraw labour - as British Leyland withdrew from Belgium. Multinationals may also use their formidable public relations resources to persuade political decision takers that they are indeed 'domestic' and have the 'national interest' at heart. They may also use those same resources to undermine any domestic manufacturer in competition with them. For instance, International Business Machines (IBM) maintained an anti-ICL knocking team in Britain,

exploitation of new technology. For instance, in 1978, a report from ACARD suggested that Britain had been good at innovation, but less good at developing that innovation into marketable products.[40] Twelve years previously a report from the OECD also pointed to the higher rate of innovation in the United States compared to that in Western Europe and Japan. That report concluded that several factors contributed to the supremacy of the United States and the 'gap in technology' between it and the rest of the world.

The American government spent four and a half times the amount of that spent by Western European countries and eight times the amount of EEC countries in support of R&D. In the electrical and electronics industries, the American government supplied 63% of the funds spent on R&D compared to the 36% supplied by the British government, 37% by the Swedish government, 5% by the German government and 0.5% by the Japanese government. The majority of American funding came through the Space programme.

The report also pointed to the relative advantage enjoyed by large companies in R&D. They could amortise capital costs, could spread risks, could avoid duplication of research, could cover the costs of 'lead times' for a product to become economically attractive to the market and could take advantage of large-scale production. This technological advantage offered to large firms was augmented by their ability to invest overseas and to market technologically new products in Europe, which were already established on the American home market.[41] In a review conducted in 1975, the OECD concluded that only four companies (two British, one German, one Japanese) outside America had contributed to the most important technological innovations in the field of electronic components. American companies had a considerable lead.[42]

The technological gap between the USA and the rest of the world has been maintained through the international system of patents, in which registered inventions are protected from usage by other companies unless the authorisation of the innovatory company is obtained and payment of royalties made. Technological know-how is therefore expensive for developing countries or less innovatory developed countries to gain access to. Licensing agreements between companies vary in their nature but may exclude certain markets in which the innovating company is present. The importation of technology under licence may thereby limit the possibility of exports in growth industries.[43]

THE INTERNATIONAL FRAMEWORK & INDUSTRIAL POLICY

government/industry contact, of direct (i.e. company specific) aid rather than indirect aid, of agreements specifying expected outcomes and of government monitoring, are of immense importance to the operation of industrial aid.

To summarise,'industrial policy' needs institutions to co-ordinate the goals of government and industry. It needs mechanisms for the distribution of aid and it requires the monitoring of that aid. To be effective, it requires a strong bureaucracy and either co-optation of industry into government or institutions which mediate between industry and state.

When viewed from a competitor's standpoint a disadvantage to industrial policy is its lack of transparency. Whereas protective tariffs are obvious to all concerned, a non-tariff barrier may exist for many years before other countries become aware of what is going on. The components of industrial aid may not all be labelled 'industrial policy', particularly when an ideologically liberal government is in power. In Britain, for instance, regional aid, has gradually become intertwined with sectoral aid. Indirect policies of industrial aid are evident in other countries. Energy and defence policy in the USA, energy policy in France and West Germany and policies of R&D support have been identified by competitors as non-tariff barriers to free international trade. Each fulfills a similar function in allowing the distribution of monetary resources to industry. In Britain, defence policy, particularly under the 1979 Thatcher Government, can also be seen as part of an industrial policy.

1.4 INDUSTRIAL POLICY AND TECHNOLOGY

In high technology industries disparities between industrialised countries in both innovation and access to technology have demanded some form of 'industrial policy' from governments. In particular, European governments have been called upon to respond to the dominant position of the United States in technology. They have had to marry the conflict between their domestic industrial need for access to that technology and the inward investment and market dominance of American multinational corporations. A combination of these factors has led European governments to finance high technology industries.[39]

Countries vary in their technological capacity, their ability to innovate, and their rate of

has also followed this line.

There are however dangers to this strategy.
a) If a technology is new then the innovating firm is likely to export it rather than set up local manufacture. Political strings may attach to exports. For instance, the French altered their laissez faire attitude towards their computer industry in 1965 when the Americans hesitated about allowing the installation of American computers in French nuclear research establishments.[51]
b) Multinationals may have a differential pricing policy for product markets at home and abroad. For instance the Austrian government complained in 1978 that IBM charged more for its computers in Austria than in the USA. IBM argued that costs were higher for manufacture in Austria.[52]
c) When demand for a product is high in the American home market shortages may result elsewhere. That was the case with microcircuits in Britain in 1979. The opposite can also happen, with the market flooded when demand slackens in the USA. That also happened in 1967.[53]
d) In components, multinationals aim at world markets. They may not be interested in business with small manufacturers needing small quantities of microchips. That problem has already manifested itself in Britain.[54]
e) Local subsidiaries of multinationals may not be interested in exporting to markets in which they would compete with the parent company.
f) Although entering into local manufacture the multinational may centre R&D in the home country. The technological gap between the American market and the host country may be increased. (Ironically today American manufacturers are using this argument about Japanese multinationals).

In defence of this strategy, it is possible to argue that governments do not aid the inward investment of companies unwilling to bring with them the latest technology. But no government can force a firm to transfer its latest innovation, once that firm is established. The French government, in its microchips policy, has attempted to circumvent these problems by allowing the American firms only 49% of equity in joint ventures with French firms. The Japanese adopted a similar mechanism of control after the Second World War.

THE INTERNATIONAL FRAMEWORK AND INDUSTRIAL POLICY

2) To borrow foreign technology for domestic manufacture and allow a free product market.
This strategy holds similar dangers to the first. Registered patents are protected for seventeen years and all the problems occur that have been previously mentioned.However,borrowing technology has the advantage that it is often cheaper than developing domestic technology. It may allow an industry to catch up quickly with existing technology. A striking example of the use of this strategy was the Venture Capital Fund designed to bring American technology to Britain,inaugurated by the National Enterprise Board (NEB) under the 1979 Thatcher Government.

3) To borrow foreign technology for domestic manufacture and exclude foreign investment and imports.
It has proved possible for the Japanese to successfully borrow foreign technology whilst excluding imports and inward capital investment. After the Second World War they strictly controlled the licensing of foreign technology, borrowed necessary technology and used it as a temporary expedient whilst developing their own. Radio Corporation of America (RCA) was allowed to manufacture within Japan, because it had done so before the war.IBM was allowed to set up independent manufacture as the price it demanded for a licensing agreement,but the computer market was not liberalised to imports until 1975.[55] However the strategy has caused some problems in Japan. The seven computer manufacturers which existed in the 1950s were allowed each to reach agreement with a different American licensor. These agreements led to differing standards and specifications for computers. Later,when it became evident that the number of manufacturers needed rationalisation, these differing standards stood in the way.

4) To develop domestic technology whilst excluding foreign investment and imports.
The Japanese are the obvious proponents of this fourth strategy. In the computer industry, in particular, government support has gone to developing domestic technology. Fujitsu, the only computer company not to rely on licensing of American technology has been particularly favoured by R&D contracts from MITI. In 1981,National Electronic Corporation (NEC) announced its impending

independence of Honeywell (US) technology as a matter of pride.

The telecommunications markets in Japan, Germany,France,Britain and Sweden have all been heavily protected, with the market in public exchange equipment mainly reserved for domestic suppliers. Although some multinationals with local manufacturing subsidiaries have been let into the market,government monopoly of the telecommunications network has allowed imports to be kept to a minimum. However,this strategy is open only to those markets not covered by GATT regulations.

5) To buy foreign companies with a lead in technology and to diffuse it to the home country.
This strategy was followed by the Japanese. In 1972 cash starved Amdahl (US) was bought into by Fujitsu, who then gained access to Amdahl's technology and manufacturing. The manufacture of Amdahl's computers was subsequently shifted to Japan.[56]

6) To develop domestic technology whilst allowing foreign investment and imports.
This strategy has been used by the British, French, German and Swedish governments in the mainframe computer market since the mid 1960s and by the Japanese since 1975. The Japanese use the strategy in electronic components.But once foreign licensing has been allowed the issue is not clear cut. At times domestic manufacturers in technological industries in Western Europe have been in competion with one group of multinationals whilst, at the same time, dependent on others for their technology. For instance in Britain, in the 1960s International Computers Limited (ICL) was in competition with IBM and Honeywell (US) but dependent on Univac (US) for an agreement to market Univac computers and dependent on Radio Corporation of America for its technology.

In practice, the support of indigenous firms within a free market for technology may also entail support of American technology. To define what is 'British',or what is 'French', becomes increasingly difficult when a British owned firm may have more foreign made components within its products than a multinational with a local manufacturing subsidiary. The problem of defining a 'domestic' company becomes of practical importance when policies of public procurement are used to favour 'domestic' companies. In several countries this difficulty of definition has been solved through reference to domestically

owned manufacturers. In the USA this has been done by law, in Britain through administrative regulation and in Japan and France through a variety of direct and indirect mechanisms. But, as discussed earlier, the possibility of public procurement preference has been made more difficult by EEC regulations.

There are problems however with the development of domestic technology.The cost may be considerable. R&D is expensive for companies to pursue and technological diffusion takes place so quickly that companies need to have a substantial share of a market to gain sufficient returns on their investment. These problems in turn lead to requests for government help with the subsidisation of R&D and for protected markets in which to develop products as a base for export.

The policies of most of the industrialised countries towards their computer, telecommunications and microchip industrial sectors can be categorised into one or two of these strategies. Strategies change over time within markets and may differ between markets. In the case of Britain, we shall see that government agencies may be found pursuing different strategies for the same market at the same time.

The policies of Western European governments towards these technological industries have clearly been affected by the American domination of technological innovation. But that pattern of dominance is changing. With the weakening of the American economy the American administration is faced politically with similar decisions on inward investment and Japanese multinationals as those faced previously by European and Japanese governments over American investment.[57] In 1981, American newspapers carried a series of concerted demands from electronics manufacturers both for protection from Japanese imports and for a constructive 'industrial policy'. But the Reagan Administration's initial reaction displayed its ideological adherence to market liberalism.It demanded that other countries cease to hide their high-technology industry behind the non-tariff barriers of industrial policy. Concomitantly both the EEC and the USA brought economic pressure to bear on Japan to abolish non-tariff barriers to imports.In other words, rather than construct an industrial policy based on non-tariff barriers,the Reagan Administration preferred to bring political pressure to bear on the Japanese to liberalise trade. Subsequently it introduced controls on the export of technology, banning the export of

'critical' technology - technology which might be used in defence products - monitoring software exports and stopping the presentation of conference papers.[58] So what determines how governments will construct an 'industrial policy'?

1.6 WHAT KIND OF INDUSTRIAL POLICY?

The argument presented so far has been that all governments of the industrial West have intervened in their domestic industries, at least since the 1960s. Intervention has been forced upon them by the increasing openness of the world economy, by increasing concern for the contribution of exports to GNP, for the performance of particular industries and as a result of concern for domestic employment. The argument is close to that of David Cameron, who, after looking at a variety of explanations for the growth in public expenditure in Western economies, concludes that the best predictor of such growth is the extent of the openness of the domestic economy. It is not possible, however, to argue that national industrial policies reflect the openness of the various domestic economies. Britain with a more open economy that Japan seems to have a less developed industrial policy. It seems that although membership of GATT has produced the public espousal of 'free trade', how far that concept has been carried into domestic practice has depended not only on the levels of adjustment necessary within the domestic economy, but on several other factors.[59]

In this section it will be suggested that the mechanisms of a government's industrial policy are related to four factors, which may themselves vary over time. These variables are: ideology towards markets, the political system of the country (reflecting centralisation/decentralisation and bureaucratic fragmentation), the relationship between industrial capital and finance capital within the domestic economy, and the structure of particular markets (often reflecting their particular technology).

These factors are themselves often historical products. The amount and extent of government intervention in industry is contained to some degree by general perceptions of its legitimacy. That perception of legitimacy will itself reflect the articulation of interests within the domestic economy over time by such actors as political parties, the bureaucracy, interest groups and the media. And this articulation of interests and their

perception will in turn reflect historical conditioning to more or less close relations between government and industry, as well as the immediate interests of certain sections of the domestic polity. Hence, perception of the legitimacy of government intervention at any one point in time will reflect both long and short-term elements, the long-term being provided by the historical and the short-term by economic and political interests.

Writing in the 1960s Andrew Shonfield contrasted the historical development of government /industry relations in France with those in Britain. Whereas in France, the government had historically been involved in industry, in Britain, Shonfield argued, greater importance had been given to the concept of individual freedom and thus to the autonomy of companies as private actors.60 To use R.N.Berki's dichotomy, in Britain 'society'had taken precedence over 'state'.61 Similarly, Shonfield pointed out, in the USA the concept of the autonomy of the firm had placed limitations on the possibilities of American government action.62

It is possible to contrast this historical development of capitalism built on liberalism, particularly within Britain and the USA, with its development in Japan, where it has been built upon a particular brand of Confucianism. As Morishima explains, Japanese Confucianism, unlike Chinese Confucianism, emphasised the virtues of loyalty to one's lord. Shintoism, the alternative Japanese religion, inspired 'patriotism and Emperor worship'.Morishima concludes:

> It is therefore not surprising to find that Japanese capitalism was - and still is - nationalisitc, paternalistic, and anti-individualistic... In spite of her economic success in the post-war era,the prospects of individualism and liberalism blossoming and maturing in Japan are extremely remote.'63

Within Japan the emphasis on the autonomy of the firm is negligible (although growing). Instead the emphasis tends to be on the 'national interest' as defined by the political and bureaucratic elites in conjunction with industry. There has been a strong relationship between bureaucracy and industry since the Meiji era, beginning in 1868, and industry may legitimately be harnessed to the political and economic aspirations of the government.

One can think of these two contrasting historical traditions as providing the 'core' of

present day ideology towards markets. The 'core' of
the liberal approach towards markets is a belief in
the supremacy of economics over politics and a
belief that the autonomous actions of individuals
and firms will produce harmoniously the maximisation
of welfare for society. The 'core' of mercantilist
ideology emphasises the opposite. To the
mercantilist, politics determines economics and it
is conflict between nation states which will achieve
the goal of the maximisation of welfare for the
nation. In the one, the autonomy of the firm is
paramount, in the other, the subordination of the
firm to the 'national interest' as defined by
politicians.[65]

These 'cores' of ideology cannot be used to
predict the actions of any one government at any one
time, but they represent parameters to government
action. They are, however, parameters always under
attack - the liberal by the mercantilist and the
mercantilist by the liberal. These attacks come from
policy decisions which, themselves, either reflect the
present interests of sections of industry or capital
within the domestic economy, or reflect specific
political priorities.[66]

One could argue that in a 'liberal' economy the
interests of all companies would be served best by
gaining financial support from the government and
retaining autonomy over themselves. But, in fact,
interests differ as to the amount of political
control over markets which companies desire. The
interests of a foreign company newly investing in a
country are in gaining financial support from the
government, in retaining autonomy over such matters
as technology, overseas production and withdrawal,
and gaining access to the domestic market. If they
are large and strong international companies, then
their interests will be in a free domestic market.
In contrast, the interests of domestically owned and
producing firms may best be served by gaining
financial support from the government, in retaining
autonomy and in having access to the market
restricted in their favour. In particular, small
businesses are likely to see their interests best
represented through mechanisms of protection for
their share of markets.

In contrast, outward investing domestically
owned multinationals may wish to retain as free a
market as possible at home, so as to limit the
possibility of reprisals in their overseas
manufacturing bases. This concern is likely to be
particularly relevant to those with bases in the
USA. But, in certain products, or markets,

particularly where they wish to build up sales at home or expertise in manufacture before exporting products, their interests may mirror those of companies producing within, and selling to, the domestic market. Foreign multinationals which already have a large share of the host country market may well have similar interests to those of domestic companies - for government intervention to protect markets from newcomers. The one set of interests is best represented by a liberal ideology towards markets: the other set by mercantilism and protection.[67]

In a similar way, in a country with a 'core' mercantilist ideology, one would expect domestic capital with large export markets and hence dependent on free access to other countries, or in the process of multinationalising, to find their best interests served by liberalism rather than mercantilism. These conflicts of interest provide the motor for a pulling away from the 'core' ideology. Although they are hardly yet developed in Japan, demands for autonomy of industry can be heard.[68] In Britain, conflict between the two competing concepts of the role of the state has not simply been a conflict between Conservative and Labour Parties. In fact it is only in the 1980s that the Labour party has espoused a mercantilist ideology. During the 1970s it accepted the benefits of free trade, at least with the industrialised West and accepted the autonomy of the firm. Rather the competition between the two concepts has been part of the thread of development of the Conservative Party.[69] Proponents of one or the other have triumphed at different times, or even at the same time. (Sir Keith Joseph at the Department of Industry and Peter Walker at Agriculture provide examples within the 1979 Thatcher Government.)

If ideology were simply the representation of industrial interests and governments their representatives, then one would expect political priorities to reflect the particular capital structure of the domestic economy. Hence a country with a large number of inward and outward investing multinationals could be expected to emphasise the importance of 'free' markets in government policy. The USA (until the 1970s), Britain and West Germany provide examples. On the other hand, where domestic capital (i.e. located and manufacturing for the domestic economy) is dominant, then one would expect government policy to veer towards protection. The obvious example is Japan (until the mid 1970s). One would also expect government policies to change as

THE INTERNATIONAL FRAMEWORK AND INDUSTRIAL POLICY

the structure of capital changed. If outward investment became less important, or domestic capital began to multinationalise, then one would expect government policy to change. Krasner suggests that American policy towards protection can be explained by the failing importance of multinationals to the American economy and the increased importance of domestic capital. Japanese moves towards free trade could be explained by the entry of domestic companies into global production from the mid 1970s.[70] The argument has been taken further in Britain. There the particular interests of the City have been seen as the determining factor in the actions of consecutive governments to support sterling at the expense of industrial capital.[71]

But such explanations tend to overlook the importance of political priorities, both in determining policy and in reaffirming ideology. One may as easily explain the ideological importance of 'free' markets to West Germany, Britain and more recently, Japan, in terms of their defence dependence upon the United States and their subjugation to American interests.[72] Or, in the case of Britain, one may turn to the political importance given to foreign policy and the defence of Britain's diminishing world role, or to the national salience of employment as an issue from 1967.[73] These political priorities may conflict with the particular interests of sections of capital within the domestic economy. For instance, writing in the mid 1970s, Robert Gilpin suggested that, at times, the American government had seen its interests as separate from those of its multinationals and had acted against them.[74] Some microelectronics companies greeted the news that the Carter administration intended to finance their industry through defence R&D with the opinion that it was a mechanism by which the state could reassert control over the market.[75] The Reagan administration's action in 1982 on the Soviet pipe-line and its embargo of 'critical' technology are two further examples of the same phenomenon.

It seems that current ideology on the legitimacy of government intervention in markets will reflect the workings out of conflict between economic and political interests around the 'core' ideology. The perceived illegitimacy of President Reagan's action in subordinating the interests of companies to his conception of the 'national interest' may well have had as much to do with the invasion of the autonomy of private actors as to the conflicting interests of Western European

states. The events of the last ten years seem to indicate that the industrialised countries have shifted their ideological positions. The United States has moved closer to mercantilism and Japan has moved towards the espousal of free trade and liberalism. Yet both have retained their 'core' ideology. Writing in 1983, one could not convincingly argue that American industry and government sees the 'national interest' defined by politicians to be above the self-interest of autonomous actors. Nor could one argue the opposite about Japan - yet. Hence, when, in a moment, an attempt is made to represent two of the factors relevant to the mechanisms of industrial policy in a diagrammatic form, it should be remembered that there is a shifting time dimension which cannot be represented. What is being represented is the 'core' ideology.

Working with this ideological spectrum along which nations can be ranked according to the legitimacy with which government intervention in industry is regarded, Peter Katzenstein has suggested that the USA, Britain and West Germany fall at the most liberal end of the spectrum. At the other, neo-mercantilist, end he places Japan. Italy is seen to have some affinity to the Anglo-Saxon pattern and France to share 'some resemblance to Japan'. He relates these ideological differences between states to the policy instruments used by governments to alter their domestic economy, the most liberal ideological states tending to use macro, rather than micro-economic measures. He acknowledges also that the differences in mechanisms used are not simply the product of ideological differences, but also reflect differences in the domestic structure of the six states.

Katzenstein goes on to point out that the policy process in Japan and France favours bureaucrats, whilst in the USA, Britain and to some extent, West Germany, the coalition between business and the state tends towards a business/elected politician axis.[76] On a more basic level Shonfield also emphasised the differences between states, but drew attention to the impact of institutional differences between political systems on the arrangements and possibilities of government/industry consensus.[77] Taking this simple approach we can say that states differ in their centralisation of power. Although, as Katzenstein argues, the process by which political decisions are taken may differ between France, Britain and Japan, all three states share a similarity in the power which accrues

to central government. In all three states elected parliaments tend to act as an adjunct to, rather than in competition with, the central bureaucracy and heads of state. In the final analysis, in each, power rests with the bureaucracy and its political heads. In contrast, in the USA, the President and bureaucracy share power with a Congress which often competes or conflicts with Presidential policy proposals. A bargaining relationship exists between the two, whilst the individual States themselves represent semi-autonomous collations of power. West Germany, with its decentralised political system, falls between the USA on the one hand and the centralised policy making system of Britain on the other. These differences, in turn, are likely to be reflected in the extent of aid to industry and the mechanisms of that aid. Cameron found that a high degree of centralisation (measured by the proportion of all government revenues generated by the central government) was correlated with increases in public spending. On the other hand, federalism had a dampening effect on that spending.[78] It seems likely that a decentralised system allows more room for officials' discretion and is likely to produce competition, conflict and bargaining between functionally and geographically differentiated and, often, autonomous units.

Because of these factors, in decentralised states one would expect an 'industrial policy' based on a coherent strategy of non-tariff barriers to be more difficult to operate than in centralised states. Where non-tariff barriers are used, then they are likely to be given generalised application through the force of law, rather than involving the bureaucracy in picking sectors or companies for subsidisation. Tariffs and quotas also have the benefit of generalised application and are therefore suitable to decentralised political systems, and one would expect to find these used more in those decentralised states where producer pressure can be brought to bear on the legislature. The USA is the obvious example of this process.

In centralised states one would expect ministerial and bureaucratic decisions to be directed at retaining control by the state. One would expect strong decision-taking on industrial matters, whether these be tariffs or quotas or non-tariff barriers. One would expect large sections of industry to be controlled by the state and one would expect indirect control of industry through public sector purchasing practices. But, in contrast to the decentralised state, where the public sector

preference would come through legal methods of control, in the centralised state one would expect the extension of state control of industry to come through bureaucratic regulation.

To talk of a centralised state suggests that it is both unitary and reified. Neither is true. If we take Eric Nordlinger's definition of the state as 'made up of and limited to those individuals who are endowed with society wide decision making'of both high and low levels, then, although the formal responsibility for the conception of policy may be centralised in Britain, France and Japan, its actual conception and implementation may be widely dispersed.[79] In these terms the bureaucratic fragmentation of Britain makes it less centralised than France or Japan.

In even suggesting that the centralised state would wish to retain control over its economy and markets, one is implicity agreeing with Nordlinger's argument that the state can be autonomous of societal constraints. Nordlinger takes further the concepts of the environmentalist school of organisational analysis.These suggest that organisations attempt to control their environment in order to increase their own stability.[80] According to this view, the state is not one organisation but a multitude of organisations, each staffed by people who may develop a view of the organisation's interests concerned with the maintenance and extension of its existence and territory. An internally pluralist organisation, the state contains numbers of differentiated units between which conflict and bargaining may occur, both units and individuals wielding that power which accrues to their position in the structure and seeking to dominate their environment.[81]

Yet the state is crucially different from other organisations. Although state units may bargain, or set up formal mechanisms to promote stable relationships with sectors of society which are important to themselves,in the final analysis the state has the power to enforce compliance. Because of this structural power, because there are no autonomous organisations of equal power to challenge it in their interests, the centralised state is more likely to extend its control over larger sectors of the economy than the federal state.Using this train of analysis one can explain Cameron's findings that the more open the economy, and the more centralised the structure, the more public expenditure by the state. Concomitantly one may expect that the more unstable the economic

THE INTERNATIONAL FRAMEWORK AND INDUSTRIAL POLICY

Figure 1.2 The Relationship Between Ideology Towards Markets and Centralisation of States.

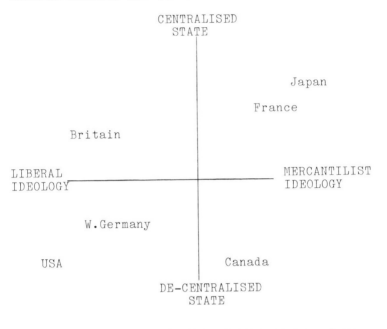

environment, the more the differentiated units of the state will seek to control that part of it over which they have power. In turn, where the centralised state is bureaucratically fragmented, as in Britain, these initiatives by different units of the state may lead to conflicting policies.

If we look at the two possible ways of categorising countries - the ideological plane according legitimacy to government intervention in industry, and the extent of centralisation of the political system, it is possible to present the categorisations diagrammatically. From Figure 1.2 we can see that the USA and West Germany have both a de-centralised political system and a liberal ideology towards industry. Japan and France have a predominantly mercantilist ideology and a centralised political system. Britain has a centralised political system and a predominantly liberal ideology.

We have just discussed the policy mechanisms of industrial aid which might be expected in centralised and decentralised states. Similarly, one

THE INTERNATIONAL FRAMEWORK AND INDUSTRIAL POLICY

Figure 1.3 The Relationship Between Ideology Towards Markets, Centralisation of States and Policy Instruments.

POLICY INSTRUMENTS

MERCANTILIST IDEOLOGY	CENTRALISED STATE
Direction of investment	Direction of investment.
Public sector purchasing	Public sector purchasing.
'Corporatist' State	State control of large sections of industry.
Cartelisation	
Close relations between government and industry.	Close relations between government and industry.
Industrial aid via other than industrial policy.	Tariff barriers.
Company autonomy.	Public sector purchasing through legal mechanisms.
Weak links between government & industry.	Weak links between government & industry.
Free market	
LIBERAL IDEOLOGY	DE-CENTRALISED STATE

would expect policy mechanisms to vary according to the legitimacy attached to that government intervention. In states with a 'core' liberal one would expect the autonomy of the firm to be respected. One would expect 'industrial policy' based on non-tariff barriers to be legitimised through other policies, such as defence and regional

aid. Companies, even, where subsidised through these indirect policies, would be expected to operate with a minimum of regulation. One would expect competition to be emphasised and there to be strong anti-monopoly regulation. One would expect inward capital investment to be welcomed and few barriers to be placed against outward investment. One would expect a free trade in technology.

In contrast, in mercantilist states one would expect either an incorporation of industry into government or at least strong industry/government linkage. An emphasis on exports would lead one to expect government resources to be placed at the disposal of exporting industry, whilst tariff and non-tariff barriers would be used to decrease import penetration. One would expect barriers to foreign capital penetration of the domestic economy and control of overseas investment. A lack of emphasis on competition would lead one to expect considerable cartelisation between companies. One would expect the export of technology to be encouraged and the import of technology to be contained by government policies.

It is interesting that when we present these divisions in a diagrammatic form (Figure 1.3), then the instruments of a centralised state 'fit' with the instruments of a neo-mercantilist philosophy. Both Japan and France have a philosophy accorded to government intervention in industry, which is in accord with their centralised states and strong bureaucracies. Canada has a neo-mercantilist philosophy which clashes with its de-centralised political system.[82] In the case of the USA and West Germany, a liberal ideological approach to industrial intervention and a belief in 'free' markets, clashes with a decentralised state's major instrument of control - that of protective barriers, such as tariffs and quotas. Similarly, the ideological approach of those states clashes with the need for decentralised systems to have legalised preferences for public sector purchasing. In fact, the position of the USA on an 'industrial policy' is possible because the separation of powers allows the President to uphold the ideals of free trade and the 'core' ideology whilst the Congress passes protective legislation. In Britain's case, a predominantly liberal ideology towards markets clashes with a centralised state's predisposition to direct affairs.

There is however a third factor which may influence the mechanisms by which a government constructs an 'industrial policy' in favour of

domestic industry. Both a decentralised state and a liberal ideological state may still be able to carry out such an 'industrial policy' if it can use private sector agencies as its instrument. Where the bureaucracy itself is subject to political and parliamentary pressure, it may use the banks or investment institutions to carry out long-term objectives. The mechanism depends upon the linkage (often historical) between those investment institutions and the market for industrial capital. West Germany and Sweden provide examples of government usage of banks to provide industrial finance, despite a liberal ideology.

In contrast, the fragmentation of the banking system in the USA has prevented this mechanism from being used. In Britain the banking sector has been predominantly linked to international finance and not to industry.[83] There has been considerable argument as to whether the City and its linkage to international finance has been responsible for high interest rates to defend sterling, resulting in the decline of British industrial investment. As Keith Middlemass concludes, the arguments between economists will probably continue for some time.[84]

Leaving aside the arguments over whether high exchange rates have contributed to British industrial decline, what the evidence on bank loans seems to indicate is that in comparison to their counterparts in West Germany, France or Japan, British banks have been relatively uninvolved in the industrial sector. In February 1983, the proportion of total advances and acceptances accruing to manufacturing industry was 21%. Almost 60% of bank lending in 1982 was to individuals.[85]

According to Michael Moran, between 1961 and 1971, the clearing banks were the "recipients of 'requests'(which virtually meant instructions) to allocate the quantity and direction of credit in accordance with various policies".They were involved in a "number of schemes to provide cheap credit for such politically favoured activities as exports and shipping". But, as Moran explains, the diversification of the financial community,with the growth in importance of such institutions as insurance companies and building societies, undermined the credit control functions of the banks, and the system was dismantled in 1971. Even when in force, the arrangements for credit control favoured loans to other than manufacturing industry and were not specific as to sectors of exports.

Later the Labour Government of 1974-1979 included the banks in its sector working parties set

up under the auspices of the NEDC to bring into effect its industrial strategy, but, as we shall see later, these moves were overtaken by other events.[86] The role of the banks has been undermined by the channelling of private savings into insurance and pension institutions. These attempt to minimise risk in their investments and take only 1% or 2% of equity in companies, and little managerial interest in investments.[87] The policy of the Thatcher Government has been to involve these private sector institutions, in a limited manner, in schemes to finance industrial regeneration within inner cities (under environmental policy) and in selective schemes for small business, but they have not played a major part in any British government's industrial policy.

One final factor influences the mechanisms of governments' industrial policies - the structure of international and domestic markets. In discussing policies towards technological markets earlier, it was pointed out that the international structure of markets will have an impact upon domestic policy. One can expect that if governments do not intervene in a market, then the structure of the international market will replicate itself within the domestic economy.[88] Government policy will be constrained at any one point in time by the extent to which the domestic structure of an industry mirrors that international structure.

High import penetration of a specific market may lead to pressure for tariff barriers to be erected, or to government fostering domestic industry for the purpose of import substitution. But the greater the proportion of a market taken by multinational companies manufacturing locally, the less the room for manoeuvre for a government wishing to support nationally owned industry. Quotas and tariffs are only effective against imports, not in markets where there is considerable foreign capital penetration. So, for instance, because there is already considerable Japanese capital investment in the electronics industry in the USA, tariffs and quotas cannot be effectively used by the American government to protect its microchip industry. In contrast, the Japanese have been able to use tariff barriers because there is relatively little foreign capital penetration into that country. If domestically owned industry is to be supported by government in a market where there is considerable local presence of multinational companies, non-tariff barriers discriminating in favour of domestic companies have to be used.

These mechanisms, such as preferential public sector purchasing, suffer the disadvantage that, if publicised, they are likely to attract the hostility of multinationals manufacturing locally. And, in some markets, where the share of multinationals is very large, it may either be too costly for government to intervene, or, if it does so, the market available for domestic suppliers may be too limited to produce a viable company. Obvious examples of this problem occurred in the French government's intervention in the mainframe computer market and in the British government's abortive intervention in the 1980s in the automated office technology market. To some extent the Japanese have surmounted this problem by strict anti-monopoly legislation which limits the market shares of foreign owned enterprises, but for EEC countries, in particular, the situation is further complicated by GATT and EEC regulations. Further problems inevitably arise also in weaker economies, when local manufacture by overseas companies creates considerable employment.

Domestic market structure limits the possibilities of government action and may preclude certain policy mechanisms from use. A fragmented market may make the formulation of supportive mechanisms difficult. A highly concentrated market structure may face government with one or two powerful companies opposed to discrimination in favour of the other. It is because of the importance of market structure in determining whether an industrial policy based on non-tariff barriers can be successful that the second chapter discusses the international and domestic markets in information technology products.

There is one further problem related to market structure which may exercise governments. If a market is protected in favour of domestic suppliers through public sector preferences, there is a danger that the industry may become dependent upon that source of demand and may not seek export markets. Zysman documents this dependency in the case of French electronics manufacturers and the point has been emphasised in Britain by the Electronics Committee of the NEDC.[89] Dependency may lead to stagnation. We shall be looking at this aspect of policy in relation to computers and telecommunications.

To conclude this chapter, it has been argued that all governments of the industrialised West have been forced to intervene in the industrial structure of their domestic economies because of the

increasing openness of the world economy. The mechanisms which they use to deal with this new found necessity differ according to the 'core'ideology of the country, the political system (according to its centralisation of power, its bureaucratic fragmentation and its autonomy from societal constraints) and the structure of domestic financial markets. Which markets are chosen for intervention will depend to some degree upon both national and international market structure. One may expect that without the intervention of governments, the international market structure will be replicated within the domestic economy and that this aspect of the workings of the international economy will provide the motor to action on the part of national governments in particular sectors of industry. These actions of governments then reaffirm or contradict the 'core' ideology.

One may see the tensions in both British and American industrial policy as the products of battles between opposing interests to 'shift' the 'core' ideology, either towards liberalism or towards mercantilism. In addition, the state itself, defined as 'those individuals who are endowed with society wide decision making', and its sub-units may develop their own priorities concerned with the extension and autonomy of their power. These priorities, justified as being in the 'national interest' have the effect of either confirming or undermining the 'core'ideology and producing shifts in the expectations of the role of the state in industrial intervention.

NOTES AND REFERENCES

1. John Black,The Economics of Modern Britain, 2nd edition,(London,Martin Robertson, 1980),pp. 224-228,259; David T.Jones,"British Industrial Regeneration:the European dimension" in William Wallace ed.,Britain in Europe,(London,Heinemann, 1980),p.118.

2. On the relation of concentration to innovation see: Andrew Shonfield,"Does Government have a role?" in Charles Carter ed.,Industrial Policy and Innovation(London,Heinemann,1981), pp.11-12.

3. John Black,p.259;Anatole Kaletsky, "World economies dance to a US tune", Financial Times,8th June 1981.

4. Samuel Brittan,"Clues to world stagnation,"Financial Times,22nd July 1982.

5. On this influence, see for example, Sir Ieuan Maddock,"The future of work",New Scientist, Vol.78,23rd November 1978,pp.592-5.
6. On the European market see :Financial Times,12th January 1981.
7. Computer Weekly,25th December 1980.
8. Business Monitor PQ363,PQ330,PQ350,PQ338, PQ364,PQ366 (London,HMSO,various years).
9. Business Monitor MA4,(London:HMSO,1980).
10. S.J.Prais,The Evolution of Giant Firms in Britain. A study of the growth of concentration in manufacturing industry in Britain 1909-1970, (Cambridge,Cambridge University Press,1976),pp.8-9; Gareth Locksley and Terry Ward, "Concentration in manufacturing in the EEC",Cambridge Journal of Economics,1979,Vol.3,pp.91-97.
11. Gareth Locksley,A Study of the Evolution of Concentration in the UK Data processing Industry with some International Comparisons,(Brussels, Commission of the European Communities,1981),passim. Business Monitor PA363,PA366,PA364,PA350,PA338, various years.
12. Roy Rothwell and W.Zegveld,Technical change and employment(London,Frances Pinter,1979), pp.152-3.
13. See for instance: J.R.Besant,J.A.E.Bowen, K.E.Dickson,J.Marsh,The impact of micro-electronics(London,Frances Pinter,1981); J.Haslam, "An appraisal of microelectronics technology", National Westminster Bank Review,May 1979,pp. 55-63;Clive Jenkins and B.Sherman,The Collapse of Work (London,Eyre Methuen,1979);SPRU Women & Technology Studies,Micro-electronics and women's employment in Britain,(Sussex,SPRU,1982).
14. See for instance:CPRS,Social and employment implications of microelectronics (London,HMSO,1978); J.Sleigh,B.Boatwight,P.Irwin,R.Stanyon,The manpower implications of micro-electronics technology (London,HMSO,1979);Interview with Patrick Jenkin, Secretary of State for Industry, British Business, 11th March 1983,p.424;Speech by Jim Callaghan, reported in, The Guardian,24th January 1979.
15. Microelectronics the options (London,Dept.of Industry,1979);Microelectronics - the new technology(London,Dept. of Industry,1978).
16. OECD,The impact of the newly industrialising countries on production and trade in manufacturing (Paris,OECD,1979);North-South: a programme for survival,Report of the Independent Commission on International Development Issues (London,Pan,1979).
17. On motives for foreign direct investment

see: Ann D.Morgan,"Foreign Manufacturing by UK Firms",in F.Blackaby ed.,De-industrialisation, (London,Heinemann,1980),pp.88-89.

18. Survey of Current Business,August 12th 1982,p.36.

19. L.Soete,"International competition, innovation and employment". Six countries workshop,Paris, November 1978, quoted in R.Rothwell,Technical change and employment,pp.24-5.

20. On the US Trade Act of 1974 see: Stephen Cohen,"Coping with the new protectionism",National Westminster Bank Quarterly Review ,November 1978,pp.2-15.

21. London CSE Group,The Alternative Economic Strategy(London,CSE Books,1980).

22. On EEC policy towards IT see:House of Lords, Report of the Select Committee on the European Communities,New Information Technologies(London, HMSO,1981).

23. On US non-agricultural protection see: W.Diebold Jr., Industrial Policy as an International Issue ,pp.17-21;William R.Kline, N.Kawabane,T.O.M.Kronsjo & T.Williams,Trade Negotiations in the Tokyo Round,(Washington D.C., Brookings,1978),pp.189-206.

24. John Zysman,"The French State in the International Economy",in P.J.Katzenstein ed.,Between Power and Plenty Foreign Economic Policies of Advanced Industrial Societies(Madison,Wisconsin, University of Wisconsin Press,1978),pp.255-295.

25. Stephen D.Krasner, "US Commercial and Monetary Policy. Unravelling the Paradox of External Strength and Internal Weakness",in P.J.Katzenstein ed.,p.81.

26. Financial Times,12th February 1982.

27. Economic Survey of Japan 1980/81, (Tokyo,Japan Times,1981),p.201,gives a list of twenty separate appeals on dumping and countervailing tariffs between 1970 and 1980.

28. Joan Edelman Spero,The Politics of International Economic Relations(New York,St Martin's Press,1977),p.68.

29 Ibid.

30. A.Olechowski and G.Sampson,"Current trade restrictions in the EEC,USA and Japan",Journal of World Trade Law,Vol.14,May 1980,pp.220-230.

31. William R.Cline et al., p.3

32. Sunday Times,14th August 1983.

33. K.Kojima,"Japan and Multilateral Trade Negotiations", Oriental Economist,Tokyo,Vol.43,April 1975,pp.32-40;Financial Times,10th June,12th June,27th July 1982.

34. D.T.Jones,"British Industrial Regeneration: the European Dimension", in William Wallace ed., Britain in Europe,pp.130-131;Brian Hodges, "Industrial Policy. A Directorate General in Search of a Policy"in H.Wallace,W.Wallace and C.Webb eds.,Policymaking in the European Communities (London,Wiley,1977),pp.113-136.

35. Wyn Grant,The Political Economy of Industrial Policy,(London,Butterworths,1982), pp.1-5.

36. On the arguments for managed trade and an alternative exchange rate policy see: R.R.Nield, "Managed Trade between Industrial Countries" and Deepak Lal,"Comment"in R.Major ed.,Britain's Trade and Exchange Rate Policy(London,NIESR,1979), pp.5-36.

37. See: Guy de Carmoy,"Subsidy Policies in Britain,France and West Germany, an overview"in S.J.Warnecke ed., International Trade and Industrial Policies ,pp.35-43.

38. Quoted in Eugene Kaplan, Japan:The Government-Business Relationship(Washington D.C.,US Dept. of Commerce,1972),p.16.

39. The following section relies on:Jill Hills, "Political Response to Growth Markets: a Comparative Analysis of the Information Technology Market." Public Administration Bulletin,No.38,April 1982,pp. 66-79.

40. ACARD,Industrial Innovation(London,HMSO, 1978),p.13.

41. OECD,Gaps in Technology(Paris,OECD,1968), pp.13,24,34-5.

42. OECD,Electronic Components(Paris,OECD, 1968),p.43.

43. On international transfer of technology see: Raymond Vernon,"International Investment and International Trade in the Product Cycle",Quarterly Journal of Economics ,Vol.80,1966,pp.190-207;John B.Granger,Technology and International Relations(San Francisco,W.H.Freeman,1979),pp.40-63;Jack Baranson, Technology and the Multinationals. Corporate Strategies in a Changing World Economy(Lexington, D.C.Heath,1978).

44. "Industrial R&D in 1975"Trade and Industry,Vol.35,April 1979,pp.325.

45. For reviews of the literature see:Roger Williams,"The Multinational Enterprise.A 1977 Perspective",in J.Hayward & R.Berki ed.,State and Society in Contemporary Europe(Oxford,Martin Robertson,1979),pp.237-52;Michael Moran,"The Politics of International Business",British Journal of Political Science,Vol.8,April 1978,pp.217-36.

46. D.Van Deb Buelcke et al.,Investment and Disinvestment Policies in Europe(Farnborough,Saxon House,1979),p.32.
47. New Statesman,Vol.95,12th May 1978,p.630.
48. For a discussion of the problems of MNCs in Britain see: Electronics EDC,Policy for the UK Electronics Industry in Britain (London,NEDO,1982), pp.16-18.
49. Select Committee on Science & Technology, Minutes of Evidence,6th December 1973, to UK Computer Industry Sub-committee,(London,HMSO,1972-3),Appendix pp.30-1.
50. John Zysman,"French Electronics Policy:the Costs of Technological Independence"in S.J.Warnecke & E.N.Suleiman ed.,Industrial Policies in Western Europe(New York & London,Praeger,1975),pp.227-45.
51.The Economist,Vol.220,13th August 1966,p.659.
52. Ibid.,Vol.267,24th June 1978,p.93.
53. Giovanni Dosi,"Institutions and Markets in High Technology" in Charles Carter ed., Industrial Policy and Innovation(London,Heinemann,1981),p.195.
54. Jim Northcott,J.Marti & A.Zeilinger, Micro-processors in Manufactured Products,(London, PSI,1980),p.20.
55. On Japanese Industrial Policy towards computers see: Ira C.Magaziner & T.M.Hout;Japanese Industrial Policy(London,PSI,1980),p.20,Computer White Paper(Tokyo,JIPDEC,1976);MITI,Current State of the Information Industry in Japan(Tokyo,MITI, 1980),roneo.
56. Jack Baranson,pp.71-84.
57. New York Times,20th August,21st August 1980.
58. Jill Hills,"Foreign Policy and Technology the Japan-US,Japan-Britain & Japan-EEC Technology Agreements"Political Studies,Vol.31,June 1983, pp.205-233.
59. David R.Cameron,"The Expansion of the Public Economy: A Comparative Analysis"American Political Science Review,Vol.72,1978,pp.1243-1253.
60. Andrew Shonfield,Modern Capitalism (Oxford,Oxford University Press,1965),passim.
61. R.Berki,"State and Society:an Antithesis of Modern Political Thought"in Jack Hayward & R.Berki,pp.1-20.
62. Andrew Shonfield,p.338.
63. Michio Morishima,Why Has Japan 'Succeeded'?Western Technology and the Japanese Ethos(Cambridge,Cambridge University Press,1982), pp.18-19.
64. Among a large number of books touching on

this subject see: John W.Dower,Origins of the Modern Japanese State. Selected Writings of E.H.Norman(New York,Random House,1975);Robert E.Ward ed.,Political Development in Modern Japan(Princeton,Princeton University Press,1968);Richard Story,A History of Modern Japan(Harmondsworth,Penguin,1972).

65. Robert Gilpin,US Power and the Multinational Corporation(London,Macmillan,1975),p.27.

66. I am indebted to Hugh Ward for many of the ideas in this section.

67. Andrew Gamble,Britain in Decline(London, Macmillan,1981) identifies a conflict of interest between 'industrial'and 'finance'capital,as does Michael Moran,"Finance Capital and Pressure Group Politics",British Journal of Political Science,Vol.11,1981,pp.381-404, and Frank Longstreth,"The City,Industry and the State" in Colin Crouch ed.,State and Economy in Contemporary Capitalism(London,Croom Helm,1979),pp.157-191. I am suggesting here that a greater degree of distinction is needed in relation to industrial capital, depending on existing market structure and the company's place within it.

68. Jill Hills,"Government Relations with Industry:Japan and Britain. A Review of Two Political Arguments."Polity,Vol.XIV,No.2,1981, pp.222-249.

69. Nigel Harris,Competition and the Corporate Society.British Conservatives ,the State and Industry,1945-64.(London,Methuen,1972),Robert Leach, "Thatcherism,Liberalism and Tory Collectivism", Politics,Vol.3,No.1,pp.9-14.

70. For instance,the Economic Survey of Japan 1980/81(Tokyo,Prime Ministers Office,1981),states: "In order to make use of the vitality of the national economy and further develop it,Japan has to defend the free economic system of its own accord, not by request from other countries",p.148.

71. On the relationship between the Bank of England and government see: Michael Moran,"Monetary Policy and the Bank of England",Public Administration,Vol.59,1981,pp.47-61.

72. This argument is put forward by Mary Kaldor,The Disintegrating West(Harmondsworth, Penguin,1978);Tony Benn Arguments for Democracy (London,Cape,1981).

73. The former argument is put forward amongst others by Susan Strange, Sterling and British Foreign Policy(Oxford,Oxford University Press,1971); Andrew Gamble,pp.108-116;Andrew Shonfield,British Economic Policy Since the War(Harmondsworth,Penguin, 1958).

74. Robert Gilpin,pp.138-150.
75. See Jill Hills,"Foreign Policy ..",p.214.
76. P.J.Katzenstein,"Introduction:Domestic and International Forces and Strategies of Foreign Economic Policy",in P.J.Katzenstein ed.,pp.20-22.
77. Andrew Shonfield,Modern Capitalism,passim.
78. David Cameron,p.1253.
79. Eric A.Nordlinger,On the Autonomy of the Democratic State,(Cambridge,Mass.,Harvard University Press,1981),p.11.
80. On the environmentalist school of thought see: Charles Perrow,Complex Organisations. A Critical Essay(Glenview,Illinois,Scott & Foreman, 1979),pp.200-48;Nicos Mouzelis,Organisation and Bureaucracy. An Analysis of Modern-Theories (London,Routledge & Kegan Paul,1975),Chaps.6 & 7.
81. On power relations within and between organisations see, for instance: Stephen Lukes, Power. A Radical View(London,Macmillan,1974); R.A.Rhodes,Control and Power in Central Local Relations(Farnborough,Hants,Gower/SSRC,1981); Michael Crozier,The Bureaucratic Phenomenon (Chicago,University of Chicago Press,1964).
82. On Canadian Industrial Policy see: William Diebold Jr,"Past and Future Industrial Policy in Canada" in J.Pinder ed.,pp.206-235.
83. Michael Moran,"Banks and Politics:An Anglo-American Comparison",Paper to the Annual PSA Conference,Newcastle, 1983.
84. Keith Middlemass, Politics in Industrial Society. The Experience of the British System since 1911(London,Deutsch,1979),p.434.
85. Economic Trends(London,HMSO,April 1983), pp.64-5.
86. Michael Moran,"Finance Capital..",passim.
87. Wilson Committee to Review the Functioning of Financial Insitutions,Cmnd 7937(London,HMSO, 1980),Chap.19.
88. Gareth Locksley,p.46.
89. John Zysman,Political Strategies for Industrial Order(Berkeley,University of California Press,1977),passim.;Sir Ieuan Maddock,Civil Exploitation of Defence Technology(London,NEDO,1983),pp.3-4.

Chapter Two

IDEOLOGY, STATE CONTROL & BRITISH INDUSTRIAL POLICY

2.1 CONFLICT BETWEEN LIBERAL IDEOLOGY AND STATE CONTROL IN BRITAIN.

In the previous chapter it was noted that Britain had both a centralised political system and a 'core' liberal ideological approach to markets. It was argued that the two clashed. The clash involves the legitimacy of two sets of ideas. The first set emphasises the autonomy of the state and the responsibility of Ministers to 'act' and to make decisions about industry, as about other elements of national life. In particular, Ministers are expected to 'do something' about crisis in industry. The second set of ideas emphasises the opposite. According to liberal ideology, it is industry, not the state, which is responsible for its own fate and there are clear boundaries between the two. Under one set of ideas, industry may call on government for financial aid, under the other set, government may not legitimately demand control of what industry does in return for that aid. At different points in time, both industry and government may switch from one set of ideas to the other to legitimise their actions.

The conflict between the two sets of ideas is actually structured into the British political system. On the one hand, the responsibility and autonomy of Ministers to decide affairs in the 'national interest' is emphasised, through the concept of Ministerial Responsibility. On the other, that very concept allows appeals over the heads of the bureaucracy to the Minister, which, in turn, reduces the insulation of the bureaucracy from societal constraints. At the same time, the 'core' ideology, with its emphasis on the autonomy of the company, undermines the ability of the bureaucracy to monitor companies which are the recipients of public

finance, whilst the Minister, who is notionally responsible for the policy, has little interest in assessing his own mistakes. The twin concepts of liberal ideology and Ministerial Responsibility seem to act, both to weaken the bureaucracy, and to catalyse the inauguration of new state units, in an attempt to insulate from pressure that part of the bureaucracy concerned with industry and to provide the basis for a long-term industrial strategy. But, once established, the new bureaucracies themselves become part of the tensions between the two sets of ideas and take part in the playing out between the units of the state of competition between the 'core'ideology and state control.

2.2 THE BRITISH INDUSTRIAL POLICY COMMUNITY.

Over the last ten years considerable amounts of information have become available concerning the internal workings of Britain's central government machinery. Following Richard Crossman's diaries and Hugh Heclo and Aaron Wildavsky's path-breaking analysis of the village community of Whitehall have come a variety of autobiographical accounts and academic studies of the policy making process. Almost all illustrate,[1] at least in passing, the plurality of the British policymaking process. That plurality is particularly evident in the branch of policymaking which we refer to here as 'industrial policy'.
   Writing in 1979, Brian Hogwood suggested that there existed in Britain an 'industrial policy community',made up of agencies and departments, civil servants and businessmen ,all engaged in promoting various forms of aid to industry.[2] To this list must now be added local authorities and a number of public/private sector agencies identified by Stephen Young.[3] Adding to the number of actors involved are the academics who function as part-time consultants to government, chair committees of enquiry and determine research priorities to be aided by government. Hogwood suggested that it was the organisational links and networks between these agencies which helped to determine the outcomes of industrial policy initiatives by government. The networks remain largely uncharted, but the overwhelming impression is of fragmentation of responsibility.
   The policy community concerned with information technology is large. It includes not only the Department of Industry, but also the Department of

49

Trade, the Defence Ministry, the Home Office, the Department of Employment, the Treasury, the Civil Service Department (now extinct), the Cabinet Office and the Central Policy Review Staff (now extinct) as well as the Department of Education and Science. Among quasi-autonomous government agencies it includes the Industrial Reorganisation Corporation (now extinct), the National Research and Development Corporation and the National Enterprise Board (now both within the British Technology Group), the National Economic Development Council and the Manpower Services Commission.In fact the NEDC has recently found more than twenty central government agencies and quangos involved in the sector. Among public corporations it includes British Telecom, and, in relation to public sector purchasing, other nationalised industries and local authorities. At Parliamentary level it includes the Select Committee on Science and Technology (now extinct), all-party committees such as the Computer Forum and individual MPs. In the House of Lords it includes the Select Committee on the European Communities. In the industries themselves, individual firms, companies formed into consortia to pressure government, professional institutions and telecommunications and microcomputer trade associations all participate. Specifically EEC institutions and personnel must also be added to the list.

It seems a paradox that a centralised political system should spawn so many agencies concerned with industrial policy. Yet the paradox can be explained.First the supply side of the equation may demand not only the supply of cash to industry, but also the supply of personnel, thereby involving those departments and agencies concerned with education and employment. Second, in a system which places great store on the concept of Ministerial Responsibility, the Cabinet and its attendant organs, such as the Cabinet Office,are likely to be involved. In addition, the fear of state control in industry itself and the legitimacy attached to the autonomy of the individual firm have led to attempts to woo industry into co-operation with government through the establishment of alternative agencies within the public sector. These, such as the National Enterprise Board and the Scottish Development Agency, created along both functional and geographic lines, have jurisdictions which overlap with each other and with the sponsoring Ministry, sometimes leading to competitive behaviour. It is also possible that fear of one Minister becoming too powerful limits centralisation

within the central government machinery. And, finally, one can see the fragmentation of responsibility for industrial policy as the result of liberal ideological governments, unable for ideological reasons, to term their aid to industry 'industrial policy' and thereby involving other departments, such as Defence, Employment and Environment within that aid.

Within this fragmented system, civil servants relations with industry have come under fire from industry itself. Traditionally civil servants have felt that they should keep at 'arms length'.[4] The style of communications has been formal, the civil service preferring to communicate via letters rather than the telephone.Concern for secrecy and the possibility of allegations of corruption keep informality and luncheon contacts low.Frequent promotions within the civil sevice make it difficult for companies to establish long-term relationships, or for civil servants to build up expertise over time. And relatively few civil servants have any first hand experience of industry. Writing in 1974,Neville Abraham argued that the functions of civil servants induced a conservative, no risk philosophy detrimental to their appreciation of the need for risk-taking in industry.[5] More recently the time span of civil service decisions and the amount of information required from industry have been criticised by businessmen.[6] And the plethora of agencies responsible for financial aid to industry has produced a growth industry in advice and consultancy services.

These difficulties are further exacerbated by the differences in background between civil servants and businessmen, by the lack of experience of business among civil servants and by the lack of interchange of personnel between the two sets of institutions. Within the service itself, the administrator continues to be a generalist, probably a graduate of Oxford or Cambridge, in an Arts subject. Specialists to the rank of Assistant Secretary have a separate career structure and lower status. Recently it has been acknowledged that the expertise to staff such Ministries as those of Industry and Energy is lacking.[7] Within the service there are not the specialists available. In addition, the status of the civil service has declined in recent years, with governments concentrating upon cutting its numbers, attacking its efficiency and reorganising it. Prime Ministers have created new Ministries, have merged them, split them or disbanded them.

IDEOLOGY, STATE CONTROL & BRITISH INDUSTRIAL POLICY

The difficulties which industry experiences in its relationship with the civil service are partly the product of the emphasis upon Ministerial Responsibility. The concept has a centralising influence upon departments, with decisions tending to pass upwards and with a concern for secrecy in the interests of protecting the Minister from embarrassing disclosures. The fact that, at any moment, the civil servant's decision may be overridden by the Minister, or challenged through Parliament by a disgruntled company, leads to concern for 'legality' in decisions, whilst departmental centralisation leads to delay. The system depends upon conflictual decisions being taken by the Minister, or by Cabinet, and, in that case, the civil servants may themselves become the lobby on one side, or the other, and may use, or involve, other parts of the central government machine in that lobby. In particular, one can see this process at work in the microelectronics chapter.

The pluralism within, in this case, central government, reflects the different conceptions of government's role in industry, both between individual sections of Ministries and Ministries themselves. The sponsorship role of the then Department of Trade and Industry was first described in the early 1970s, by Dr Maddock, then the Controller of Industrial Technology. He suggested that it meant "providing an avenue through which industry can approach government with its problems and also an avenue through which the government can approach industry to convey to industry the kind of things it hopes are going to happen or to discuss with industry what its views are at any particular time".[8] The concept was one of a channel of communication rather than one of leadership.

More recently, on his retirement from the civil service, the Permanent Secretary of the Department of Industry, Sir Peter Carey, revealed his ideas on the government's role in market intervention.

> The Government can never be a surrogate for the market..My experience over 35 years in Whitehall has shown me that sitting in Whitehall, not being subjected to the strains of the market place, I do not know what is best for particular firms.. What I can do of course is to collect a lot of information about particular firms...and then make a judgement about what needs to be done. But I don't claim to know best and this means that we are not in a position here to pick winners of the future..

IDEOLOGY, STATE CONTROL & BRITISH INDUSTRIAL POLICY

> The aim is to apply a spur to industry to perform better.. to erect a framework which encourages and supports good management and points directions.[9]

The ideas of sponsorship are slightly more positive in terms of leadership than those expressed in the 1970s, but reflect a prevailing liberal ideology. Yet Sir Peter criticised the Treasury in particular for its 'very deep ethos', which prevented it from understanding the problems of industry and how its policies affected industry harmfully. The Treasury was 'the bland leading the bland' in a system in which there was 'a lot of inertia' and which had a tendency to 'oversmooth running'. Equally he disagreed with those of his colleagues who believed that government could do more. Sir Peter's views have been quoted at length because they illustrate well the 'core' ideology with its emphasis on the autonomy of the company and the supremacy of markets over politics. They illustrate also the pluralism within the central government machine itself and the conflict between the liberalism, sympathetic to industry of Sir Peter, the Treasury — both liberal and upholding the autonomy of the state from industry — and other individuals within the D.of I espousing more political involvement in markets. Sir Peter's strictures on the blandness of Whitehall mirror those of Heclo and Wildavsky, who pointed out that the system suffered from lack of competition.[10]

In general, Sir Peter's ideas could be said to reflect those of industry itself. But industry is also non-unitary. Recently demands from business have been heard for a more consensual approach to industrial strategy and for a longer-term perspective.[11] Government's increasing importance as both buyer and financier and companies' own desire to stabilise their environments has led to the creation of departments within companies specifically concerned with government relations.[12] ICL may have been one of the first to establish such a department as early as the 1960s.[13] Writing at that time, J.P.Nettl saw the British business elite as being without the rugged anti-government stance of its American counterpart; as drafted into a consensus with the civil service in which the 'private' interests of business were lost as goals.[14]

Twice faced with a liberal-ideological government in the last fifteen years, the response of industry on both occasions has been to seek to

53

mitigate the harsh market mechanism for its own interests. Under the Heath Government it opposed the ending of investment grants.[15] Under the 1979 Thatcher Government it appealed for help with its fuel costs.[16] As in this latter case, many of its appeals have been made on the basis of the subsidies or protection given to its competitors in other countries. A recent book on the changing role of the big company chairman specifies that much of his time will be taken up in co-ordinating with government.[17]

The perception of this evolving interdependence between industry and government has produced a new strain of thought within the academic literature in which the policymaking process between government and industry is seen primarily as consensual. This literature echoes the comments made by Jack Hayward in the early 1970s concerning the civil service tendency to approach interest groups on equal terms and its failure to raise awkward questions in discussions.[18] The new literature emphasises the incorporation of business into government through both formal and informal mechanisms and the development of what has beeen termed 'interest corporatism'. Those who have seen aspects of this forms of corporatism in Britain have taken their evidence mainly from such fields as economic planning, agriculture and urban policy.[19] However, Wyn Grant concludes, in his 1983 work on the subject, that corporatist forms of policymaking are possible in other industrial sectors.[20]

It is clear from the evidence in the chapters on computers and telecommunications that this form of corporatism may develop between units of the state and individual companies. Interdependence between an organisation in the state sector and private companies seems to stem from a need on both sides to stable demand or supply of products. It is in the interests of major companies, even where they may wish for a free market in some products, to also have a stable demand in others. It also may be in the interests of particular sectors of the state to have captive suppliers. The obvious example is in the defence market, where some companies are almost 50% dependent on the state for their production. But, as is also evident in the computer and telecommunications industries, these neo-mercantilist arrangements are perpetually under threat from interests espousing a liberal ideology. They seem most stable in sectors where the state is autonomous — in particular in defence related work — or in those sectors which are not penetrated by

multinationals seeking to increase their market share - for instance in agriculture. In other sectors, the attack upon these corporatist arrangements may be led by other units of the state in favour of liberal ideology. Or, it may come from the dependent companies themselves, disillusioned at the political control of their markets and seeking company autonomy once more.

2.3 BRITISH INDUSTRIAL POLICY

It would be as well to emphasise at this point that industrial policy has played a relatively minor part in overall economic management in Britain. Rather, it should be noted that the major issues of economic management have concerned the balance of payments and the level of sterling (1960s), inflation (1970s), monetary targets and decreasing public expenditure (1980s). The effect of macro-economic policies can be as substantial, if not more substantial than those specifically aimed at industry.

Government aid to industry does not meet with public disapproval. On the contrary, public concern about unemployment has created the parameters within which successive governments have had to work. It is reflected in the present maze of employment related programmes, and also links with support for government aid to industry which protects jobs. Although in the past there seems to have been a trade-off between the public's perception of unemployment or inflation as the 'most urgent problem' facing the country, reported in the public opinion polls, the fact that, in general, programmes of industrial aid are received favourably, allows both parties to pursue such policies without fear of electoral disfavour.[21] Nor, despite political party labels, are MPs immune from this general concern with employment. In 1980, a poll of MPs found that, among Conservatives, one in two were in favour of increased aid to microelectronics and one in three favoured increased aid to development areas.[22]

Policies which welcome multinational corporations into Britain are backed by the lack of public knowledge or concern at their dominance of industrial sectors. A survey in 1976 found 78% of people in Britain felt positively towards multinationals, either because they speeded up modernisation or kept prices down, or were necessary to the country's economic development. In contrast to people in both France and West Germany, only a small minority of the British public (17%) were

worried that multinationals might gain a stranglehold on the economy, only 15% thought they might close down operations and only 11% were concerned about outward flows of capital. Despite attempts by Left-wing Labour politicians to bring the issue onto the political agenda the majority of the British public were unable to name any multinational.[23]

In 1979, according to government sources, 20% of British industry was foreign owned, and by 1983 there were 1500 American, 200 West German and 24 Japanese companies manufacturing in Britain.[24] Japanese investments represented a very small proportion of the total, being mainly in banking and insurance rather than manufacturing.[25] The flow has been attracted by entry to the tariff free zone of the EEC, whose regulations specificy that a foreign owned company must be treated in a similar manner to a domestic owned manufacturer. Almost inevitably, their geographic concentration in development areas and their concentration in expanding, rather than contracting, markets has increased the power of multinationals within the British domestic economy.

In general, the issue of control of foreign investment has only been raised in relation to Japan. Britain's position as an overseas investor acts as a constraint upon government action. There seems to have been a slight change in attitude among civil servants since 1968, however, when Hodges found them xenophilic towards multinationals' investment on the grounds that it increased employment, transmitted technology and increased exports.[26] IBM admitted to the Select Committee on Science and Technology that it attempted to balance imports with exports, and one official, in 1980, in evidence to the House of Lords, specifically pointed to IBM's poor export record. He suggested that one of the main reasons for supporting domestically owned companies was their better export performance.[27]

In fact it is impossible from official statistics to determine how much overseas investors in manufacturing benefit the balance of trade. Figures on exports by foreign owned companies and subsidiaries are collected, but not those on imports. We can say that in 1980 foreign controlled enterprises and UK affiliates of foreign enterprises accounted for 30% of total exports of manufactured goods. Of these almost 50% were to related enterprises overseas, but we cannot give the figures for imports from related and unrelated enterprises. In the classification covering computers, electronic components, office machinery and telecommunications, foreign controlled enterprises were responsible for

IDEOLOGY, STATE CONTROL & BRITISH INDUSTRIAL POLICY

40% of exports, with 50% of these going to related enterprises. In addition, they were responsible for a balance of trade deficit in technology payments to related enterprises (mainly in the USA) which rose from £47 million in 1974 to £110 million in 1980.[28]

The last official report on inward investment concluded that it was beneficial to the balance of trade and to regional development, but in view of intra-company trade in exports and technology, and without figures on intra-company imports, the conclusions must remain suspect.[29] Since the report pointed to the likely growth in importance to the national economy of multinationals' location in the most dynamic sectors, it seems that failure to collect statistics, or to investigate their impact on the economy more recently, can be interpreted as either a reaffirmation of liberal ideology by both parties, or the salience of employment as a domestic issue.

Since the 1960s industrial policy in Britain has been a major battleground for party ideology. The lines of confrontation have been drawn on the question of whether governments should directly intervene in industry or whether it should provide the macro-economic framework in which industry could prosper. At the ideological level, nationalisation and public ownership have occupied one end of a whole spectrum of industry related issues on which the Labour and Conservative parties have differed. The level of market competition, direct subsidies to employment, and the institutional organisation of intervention have also been the subject of party conflict.

Although publicly maintaining these ideological cleavages, the actual policy outcomes of the two parties in government show evidence of trimming to generalised public opinion. For instance, the 1964-70 Labour Government's emphasis on economic growth through technology and efficiency, rather than nationalisation, bore witness to the trend in public opinion away from support for that measure. Over a twenty year period support for nationalisation has dramatically declined, even among Labour core supporters.[30] Despite the vociferous passages on the subject in its 1974 manifesto, the Labour Government only nationalised aerospace and shipbuilding and attempted to nationalise the ports.

The Conservative Government of 1970-1974, despite its original policy of refusing aid to 'lame-duck' industries, nationalised Rolls Royce and rescued the shipbuilding industry on the Upper Clyde. The Conservative Government of 1979, despite

its ideological adherence to a 'free'market,also poured vast sums into British Leyland and British Steel.

Let us take for a moment Wyn Grant's categorisation of industrial policy into 'social market','selectively interventionist'and'socialist'. On the ideological level, the Conservative Party, at times, has espoused the social market model, whilst the Labour Party has espoused, at times, the socialist model.[31] Yet, in reality, both parties have pursued remarkably similar policies of selective intervention, in which the market mechanisms have been improved, supplemented, or cushioned, rather than left to themselves or replaced. The only major difference has been that Conservatives have intervened reluctantly,and Labour has intervened enthusiastically.

Labour Governments have not had to pass legislation to enable them to give this assistance. Following its conversion from a free market ideology, Edward Heath's Conservative government's 1972 Industry Act gave power to the Minister to intervene in any area of industry in the 'national interest'.Again,despite its espousal of a free market, the Thatcher Government has not repealed that Act.Instead it revised the relevant section to impose, as a precondition, a clause stating that the money should not be available from any other source.[32]

The Conservative style has been to give discretion to the Minister responsible. The conflict between its liberal and statist strands of ideology have been worked out by separation of the public and private sectors within its own thought. Within central government it has centralised power in the hands of the Minister and has created the conditions for 'strong' decisions made for political reasons. Espousing competition within the private market sector, and de-nationalising privately owned companies, it has yet,not only retained control over the major firms,but has abolished competition within central government and moved to establish greater control over local authorities. By abolishing, or cutting back on, the visible institutions which Labour has created to mediate between government and industry, Conservative governments have been able to maintain their ideological free market stance through a reduction in the visibility of their subsidies to industry.

Ironically,Labour governments in favour of state control have felt it necessary to establish the legitimacy of their intentions towards industry

and their respect for company autonomy by working through institutions legally differentiated from Ministers and staffed by businessmen. These institutions have also allowed Labour governments to slough off political responsibility for policies which conflicted with the interests of their Trade Union constituency. They have been used to isolate industrial policy from political pressures.[33]

Competition between the parties over institutional arrangements has allowed 'business as usual' to go on behind the scenes. The quantative evidence shows that governments of both parties have behaved with considerable similarity in their policy of aid to industry.[34] Tony Benn pointed out that, on coming to office in 1974, he found, at the Department of Industry, no less than sixteen schemes of aid in operation. They included regional development aid, investment support, general assistance, aid to aerospace, shipbuilding and tourism and government funding of research and development.[35]

There are some differences of emphases between the two parties. The Heath Government, in its efforts to combat inflation, spent over £1000 million in subsidising nationalised industries' prices. The Labour Government of 1974-79 liked to emphasise that it spent less indiscriminately and more effectively on selective assistance schemes. The Callaghan government also pointed to its employment and training subsidies. It spent almost four times as much as the Heath government on these.[36] In fact the division in Public Expenditure White Papers between regional aid and general industrial assistance has become less and less valid. It is clear that under the Callaghan Government sectoral assistance went mainly to areas with high unemployment and it is noticeable that the two schemes have been brought together under the same heading by the Thatcher Government, and downgraded in favour of employment policy.[37]

For a Conservative government, employment policy has a similar advantage to regional policy - it is not called industrial policy. It is indirect, being standard to all firms undertaking employment or training of young people. It subsidises all industry, rather than involving government and civil servants in picking out particular firms for assistance. The disadvantage with such indirect mechanisms arises from the fact that they are indiscriminate, and are therefore less likely to produce the effects for which they were intended. Whereas regional aid has tended to give finance to capital investment, rather than for jobs created, employment subsidies are said to be creating one job

IDEOLOGY, STATE CONTROL & BRITISH INDUSTRIAL POLICY

Table 2.1 Governments, Policies & Institutions.

Government	Ideology	Policies	Nationa-lisation	Instit-utions
Macmillan	Conserv.	1) Regional 2) Planning	----	NEDC
Wilson 1964-70	Labour	1) Planning 2) Rationalisation 3) Investment 4) Regional 5) Rescues 6) R&D	----	IRC DEA MinTech
Heath 1970-74	Conserv. Free Market	1) Regional 2) Investment 3) Rescues 4) R&D	Rolls Royce	DTI Abolition of IRC IDE* CCA*
Callaghan 1974-79	Labour Socialist	1) Planning 2) Investment 3) Regional 4) Rescues 5) Small business 6) R&D	Aero-space Ship-building	NEB SWPs SDA WDA
Thatcher 1979-83	Conserv. Free Market	1) Regional 2) Rescues 3) Investment 4) Small business 5) R&D 6) Defence	Privatis-ation De-nation-alisation	NEB NRDC

Table 2.1 continued....
Abbreviations
NEDC National Economic Development Council
DEA   Department of Economic Affairs 1964-70
IRC   Industrial Reorganisation Corporation 1966-70
MinTech Ministry of Technology 1964-70
DTI   Department of Trade and Industry 1970-74
IDE* Industrial Development Executive 1970-(Took over IRC functions, but internal to the civil service).
CCA* central Computer Agency 1972-81 (Became Central Computer & Telecommunications Agency 1981,internal to civil service).
NEB   National Enterprise Board 1974-81 (Became British Technology Group after a merger with the National Research & Development Corporation set up in 1948)
SDA   Scottish Development Agency 1976--
WDA   Welsh Development Agency 1976-
SWPs Sector Working Parties - established under the NEDC to plan regeneration of industry for each industrial sector.

---

for every ten subsidised.[38]

A further form of indirect aid to industry, but one which is slightly less indiscriminate than employent policy,comes under the more usual heading of urban policy. Under this heading, the Thatcher administration set up Urban Development Corporations in the London and Merseyside dock areas and has involved private sector finance in such bodies as the Financial Institutions Group to rejuvenate Merseyside. The policies are geographically defined, as is regional policy, but to more specifically defined areas.[39] Also,under this heading, many local authorities have joined with private sector sources of finance in order to fund industry in their areas to attempt to combat unemployment.

It is not known exactly how much of the money spent on regional and other assistance schemes has gone to multinational companies. But some multinationals, such as Ford, have had the whole capital cost of a factory met from public funds, and Nissan is said to have expected similar favourable treatment.Chrysler received £72 million in grants and a further £90 million in loans when it threatened to pull out of Britain with 25,000 job losses.In the electronics industry, the 1979 Labour government set aside £70 million for a micro-electronics support scheme to increase microchip

61

manufacture. Although the sum involved was reduced by the Thatcher Government to £55 million, the money set aside to finance the extension of manufacture of standard chips by the local subsidiaries of multinationals remained at the £22 million mark.

To sum up so far, both parties, despite ideological disputes, have spent money on industrial aid. Both parties have put money into declining industries. Both parties have rescued companies. The predominant style of both parties has been to place new managers into the rescued firm and then to allow them to get on with the job.[40] Little commercial monitoring takes place.[41] The IRC and the NEB are exceptions. Both bodies attempted to review company plans and the dispute between Rolls Royce and the NEB in 1979 centred around the detailed monitoring the NEB considered it should do.

Both parties have spent public money in attracting multinationals and in keeping them in Britain. Styles differ, with the Conservative party preferring indirect mechanisms of industrial aid, but, as Geoffrey Denton concluded from his analysis of industrial intervention in the period 1967- 1971:

> Without doubt the one problem above all others in provoking the growth of financial aid to industry has been unemployment. This has often been the chief justification of regional or specific industrial subsidies, even when other motives, such as regional balance, promotion of advanced technology, or improving the balance of payments have also entered into the political decision.[42]

The period from 1971 has produced no different conclusions.

At certain junctures a concern with the newer sectors of the economy has been evident in Britain. The rationale behind the Labour Government's establishment of the Industrial Reorganisation Corporation was both to rationalise industry into larger units and to provide investment funds, which it was believed were not available from the private financial market. In fact, of the total loans of £106 million, which the IRC made between 1967 and its demise in 1971, £50 million were to the declining industries of automobiles, heavy engineering, textiles and shipbuilding. A further £10 million went to aircraft manufacture. Nor was it clear that the loans it offered were on preferential terms since it was handicapped by government demands that it make a commercial return on its investment.[43]

IDEOLOGY,STATE CONTROL & BRITISH INDUSTRIAL POLICY

The NEB, established in 1975 as part of the Labour Government's new 'industrial strategy' to aid growth sectors, suffered similarly from a conflict of goals. Until relieved of responsibility for British Leyland and Rolls Royce by the Thatcher administration, the larger part of the NEB's loan facilities were taken up with subventions to the two companies. However, in comparison to the IRC a higher proportion of its funds went to funding small companies in the high technology sector. Up to the end of 1979 it had invested about £90 million in the equity of computer-related companies. In 1980 its guidelines were changed by the Thatcher Government so that it should concentrate on developments in new high technology areas and should dispose of its holdings in existing companies ' as soon as commercially practicable'. In 1982 it was amalgamated with the NRDC to become the British Technology Group, a less political animal than the NEB had become, and in 1983 it was announced that its investment functions would cease.[44]

In addition to this strand of employment related industrial policy, the British political system and the autonomy which Ministers may accrue to themselves have given rise to numbers of 'strong' decisions taken seemingly for reasons of ideology or for reasons of national chauvanism - often in the latter case because other countries are funding similar developments. Ranking in the first of these categories come the decisions by Tony Benn, as the Minister of Industry, to fund workers co-operatives in the Scottish newspaper industry, at Meriden in motorcycles and in Kirkby, in engineering.[45]

It has also been ideological considerations which have fuelled nationalisation, de-nationalisation, re-nationalisation and privatisation of public sector corporations. The Heath Government denationalised Thomas Cook, then was forced to nationalise Rolls Royce. The Callaghan Government nationalised British Aerospace and shipbuilding and attempted to nationalise the ports. Through the NEB it also took a majority shareholding in British Leyland and equity in about 60 other companies. Inter alia, the Thatcher government has sold 52% of its holding in British Aerospace, sold 49.36% of its holding in Cable and Wireless and denationalised the National Freight Corporation. Other companies, such as ICL, Ferranti, Fairey and Amersham International have been sold to institutional buyers, whilst others such as Data Recording Instruments have been sold to individual companies - often American. Privatisation plans for British Telecom were

63

announced in 1983.

Turning to those 'strong' decisions taken for reasons of national chauvanism, high technology has been an area in which governments of both parties have been willing to intervene and the two parties have not differed significantly in the projects which they have supported. The Wilson, Heath, Callaghan and Thatcher Governments have all poured money into aircraft and nuclear industries under the heading of 'industrial innovation'. Between 1978 and 1983, nuclear research alone consumed £1209 million of public funds, whilst Concorde, Rolls Royce and other aeroengine projects took another £802 million.[46]

Britain has spent a higher proportion of its Gross Domestic Product on R&D than any other Western European nation. Between 1970 and 1979 it spent over 1.2% of GDP, although in real terms the total amount was less than that spent in France and West Germany. Only the USA has consistently spent a higher proportion of its national income on R&D. In contrast to Japan and West Germany, but similarly to France and the USA, the majority of funding for industrial R&D has come from the government. In 1963 the government funded 55% of R&D expenditure in industry, a proportion which had declined to 42% by 1978.[47]

Out of this large expenditure on R&D has come a technological balance of payments in Britain's favour, reaching £36 million in 1975 and rising to £120 million in 1980. The increased balance of trade came through payments from companies unrelated to those manufacturing in Britain.[48] In turn this balance of trade has led British researchers to the conclusion that Britain's R&D is in the wrong sectors for use by Britain. Correlating Britain's R&D activity with export performance Keith Pavitt concluded that "only in aerospace and other defence related sectors does Britain do better than these (Japan, W. Germany, Switzerland, Sweden) countries".[49] British R&D expenditure has been distributed over a narrow range of industries and highly concentrated within specific large companies. In addition the proportion of total government expenditure on R&D taken by defence rose from 41% in 1970 to 55% in 1980.[50]

Although there was criticism in the late 1970s of the amount of R&D funding going to defence related work, the assumption seems to have been made that this defence expenditure would benefit civil research and commercial application. 'Spin-offs' from the American space programme were sometimes

cited as an example, although the efficacy of this form of funding was disputed by the American semiconductor companies in the late 1970s. Similar doubts were raised in a British study in 1983, which pointed out the difficulties experienced by companies in transferring technology from one product division to another and the failure, by some defence suppliers, to be concerned very much with civilian applications or exports at all.[51]

This strategy of high spending on defence R&D has been based on American experience. It contrasts with that of West Germany, where defence related expenditure fell from 18% to 12% of the total R&D budget. In Britain in absolute terms the funding of defence R&D remained steady between 1970 and 1978, whilst the funding of industrial R&D fell, from 16% to 5% of the total. In Germany, the funding of industrial R & D had increased to 7% of the total by 1978, and in France stood at 10%. Within those national allocations for industrial technology the proportions spent on electronics, includig data processing, office machinery and telecommunications varied from 38% in France, to 23% in West Germany, to 16% in Britain. Britain therefore registered the smallest proportion of R&D expenditure on industrial technology and on electronics.[52]

Although, in 1982, the Thatcher Government rectified the imbalance to some extent by an injection of a further £100 million into industrial R&D in the electronics sector, the Electronics EDC pointed out that of the £312 million spent by the government in the sector in 1978, £292 million went to defence research.[53] The effect of this concern with national prestige projects and defence within R&D spending has been to starve funds and personnel from other sectors.[54]

We shall see later that, from 1978, the Labour Government introduced government backing of information technology onto the political agenda. Partly this sudden conversion seems to have resulted from Prime Ministerial viewing of a television programme. As such it ranks with the other big political decisions on industrial policy, which the British centralised political system makes possible. The civil service contends however that it had already prepared the ground for that decision and the machinery was in place for it to take immediate effect.[55]

On the role of the Department of Industry in developing new technologies, Sir Peter Carey had this to say in 1983:

65

..what I think we can do, by looking at the market place of the future (with the help of a long-term steering group I have set up here) is to identify technologies which are going to be of great importance. Thus we are giving support in this administration to technologies, such as information technology, bio-technology, fibre optics and robotics.[56]

The question of the role of experts in these technological decisions has hardly been studied in Britain, although we know something of their impact in the nuclear field. John Jewkes points out that, where industry is concentrated, the possibility of a government receiving unbiassed advice is unlikely. A policy within government, such as that of the Thatcher administration, of cutting back on direct funding of research in universities may have similar effect. Academics may be compromised by taking research grants from industrial sources which have a stake in political outcomes. [57]

As we shall see in the telecommunications chapter, when governments are called upon to make decisions upon technology, they are amateurs in the field of professionals. Yet because of the centralised political system, major decisions on technology may be taken at Cabinet level, in its atmosphere of bargaining between departments. It seems almost inevitable that, as a consequence, 'big' decisions to back certain technologies will be taken more for the imagery they provide of forward looking government seeking to break the technological barriers of the future, rather than for the more mundane questions of their contribution to exports or import replacement.[58] Since the 1960s successive British governments have presented technology and their decisions to fund large projects as their hope of the future. Computers, System X in telecommunications, the cabling of Britain, the Fifth Generation Computer, have all been projected as solutions to British economic decline, as means by which Britain could 'take on' its competitors in the industrialised world.

Finally, defence policy in Britain has had the effect of supporting particular sectors, such as shipbuilding and electronics, and of supporting particular companies within those sectors. With the cutting back under the Thatcher Government of other public sector spending, defence expenditure has assumed increased importance as an indirect industrial policy. This importance has come from two factors. First, as a proportion of GNP, defence

spending consumed about 5% between 1973 and 1981, despite the Callaghan Government' commitment to reduce it. This proportion contrasts with an average of less than 1% for Japan, 3.4% for West Germany (without Berlin aid),4.2% for France and 3.3% for Belgium.

Second, a higher proportion of British defence expenditure goes on equipment than does that of her allies. In the period 1965-70, 16% of the defence budget went on the purchase of equipment. By 1978 this proportion had risen to 22% and by 1982 to 46%, outstripping all her industrial competitors. It is this equipment expenditure coupled with R&D which has become of increased importance to British industry as defence expenditure expanded by 25% under the Thatcher Government. Purchasing by the defence sector in 1982-3 from the home industry topped more than the £1 billion mark. As other markets have become more difficult, so companies have been drawn to the defence sector, where profits in general have been higher than in the private sector. A report from the Public Accounts Committee in 1983 pointed out that the 3.7% level of return on capital for defence work was actually much higher than the average in the private sector of about 1.2%. The result has been that those companies linked into defence markets have benefitted.

For instance, Ferranti,Racal,GEC and Plessey have done well, whilst companies linked into other areas of public expenditure reduced by the Thatcher Government, such as ICL, have done badly. By 1982, the defence market was taking 30% of electronics production, almost 40% of the shipbuilding industry's production and almost 50% of the aerospace industry's production.The electronics industry is worried by the trend. The Electronics EDC has asked that contracts take more notice of possibilities for transferring technology to the civilian sector and of export potential. Other sections of industry are also concened about the bureaucracy of the Ministry of Defence' public purchasing requirements. The issues are similar to those raised in the telecommunications chapter and demonstrate the problems of state control of markets, where those markets are subjugated entirely to the state's interests and form no part of a coherent strategy for exports.However, the defence industry draws strength from its size and from the 250 MPs whose constituencies would be affected by any cuts in defence related employment.

2.4 CONCLUSION

In this chapter it has been argued that ,in formulating an industrial policy ,Britain is handicapped by a 'core' liberal ideology, which is out of keeping with a centralised State apparatus. Others will argue that Labour governments have been interventionist in intent. That is true. But it is also true that governments of both parties work within the constraints of the prevailing culture, both among the population at large and among elites.

Prevailing support among the population has been for the protection of employment. The prevailing culture among civil servants still rests on notions of sponsorship of industry, which are concerned to leave major decisions to market forces and which respect the autonomy of the firm. Where public money is injected , business believes that companies should remain autonomous from government. Governments have acceded to this demand. The political system does not provide any constituency for monitoring of government finance. Ministers come and go and do not wish to know of their mistakes. The system of Ministerial responsibility favours short-term decisions. It favours rescues.

In this ,the workings of the political system coincide with public opinion. But because of the ideological confrontation of the parties over industrial issues, rescues are normally publicity ridden events. And if a government has publicly decided to back a particular company, then it is extremely difficult later to allow the company to crash. There comes a time ,as Martin Edmunds argues in the case of Rolls Royce , when the dependence of a company on government finance amounts to self-nationalisation.[59] Hence short-term decisions lead to long-term commitments. Company autonomy hides company dependence,as we shall see later in the case of ICL.

It was argued earlier that the most obvious mechanisms of industrial intervention for a country with a liberal ideology are those of tariff barriers and indirect mechanisms such as defence expenditure. Tariff barriers do not rely on a strong centralised bureaucracy and can be applied to a particular set of goods, or to goods from a particular country. Indirect mechanisms allow the prevailing ideology to continue, whilst the financial aid needed by industry is supplied in fulfilling another publicly pronounced policy objective. A third mechanism for a country with a 'core' liberal ideology is to use private sector financial institutions to carry out

an 'industrial policy', again allowing the ideology to be preserved in public.

Membership of the EEC rules out British government discretion on tariffs, although bilateral agreements have been reached between Britain and other countries, such as Japan. But the second set of mechanisms have been well used in Britain.The Conservative Party ,in previous years,has made good use of regional aid ,as an indirect method of financing industry. During the 1979-1983 Thatcher Government this mechanism was replaced by employment subsidies and defence expenditure. Employment subsidies, like regional policies, have the disadvantage that in being indiscriminate, they are less likely to fulfill the purpose for which they are designed, and they tend to alter the comparative advantage of all British industry, by reducing labour costs, rather than being specific to particular sectors. The Thatcher Government has also used the third mechanism to some extent by mobilising private sector institutions to manage such policies as its loan guarantee scheme for small businesses and within its urban policies of industrial renewal.

The Labour Party has tended to use less indirect mechanisms of financial aid to industry,although the Callaghan government gave various tax relief measures to industry in general. Both the IRC and the NEB attempted to monitor industrial recipients of their aid -partly no doubt because both were under instructions to make a return on capital employed. But Labour Party concern with fostering growth industries was destined to be pre-empted by its concern for unemployment. Given its trade union constituency and its reliance on the regional development areas for votes, a Labour government is a sure touch for pressure from declining firms, for multinationals which threaten to withdraw, or firms centred in development areas.

It is at this point that the economic structure of the country,in conjunction with the political system, exacerbates the problems caused by the prevailing liberal ideology and acts to the advantage of large companies. It is evident that, having established themselves in development areas, the multinationals may gain more from a Labour than Conservative government.Both multinationals and large domestic firms can become political actors .In a centralised political system where the final decision rests with the Minister,where he is likely to make a short-term decision to free himself from political embarrassment,the cards are stacked in

favour of large companies. Because the British economy is highly concentrated and highly multinationalised, any government is dependent upon the co-operation of large companies and likewise vulnerable to their pressure. In recognition of this fact multinationals have been brought together with representatives of large firms into the NEDC. They have become incorporated into the state advisory machinery, and thereby, as we shall see later, gain a structural advantage in their application of pressure.

Out of this system three sets of actors benefit. First, aid goes to large employers in response to employment pressures, be they existing or incoming firms. Second, it has gone to those large firms which have been aided before, or with which the state has become interdependent. National champion companies are obvious examples of the interdependence sometimes created between companies and state. Third, those involved in long-term technological projects have benefitted, since the long lead time of the project contrasts with the short life (average two years) of political Ministers. Defence is a sector where the second and third categories overlap, as is also telecommunications, which, traditionally, has been linked to defence.

Finally this book suggests that the incoherence of British industrial policy can be traced to the endemic tension between the 'core' ideology and strong political centralisation, exacerbated by the fragmented nature of the British State and competition and autonomy within it. British industrial policy can be seen as fluctuating between indirect policies of indiscriminate aid and 'strong' decisions taken by Ministers for political reasons. These have included Concorde, British nuclear powered reactors, and a variety of 'rescues'.

Perhaps most importantly, the necessity for governments to intervene in their domestic economy and the conflict between the concepts of state control and liberal ideology have been squared by the Thatcher Government through its support of increased defence expenditure. This expenditure seems to be distorting Britain's industrial base by its guaranteed profits and consuming scarce scientific personnel into its R&D. Yet the large expenditure on both R&D and equipment has not given the benefit of spin-offs in technology to the civilian sector, nor been particularly related to export prospects. Defence has the advantage however,

of being the area where the state is completely autonomous - where industry must do what it is told. And, because it is an indirect policy of industrial subvention, it prevents state action from undermining the 'core'ideology.

The fact that the NEDC has challenged the efficacy of defence orientated industrial policy illustrates the conficts which exist between elements within the state. Other sources of conflict have been pointed out within the state central bureaucracy, conflicts often directed towards the core ethos of the Treasury. At the elected politician level these conflicts have focussed around the extent of public ownership and the existence of those para-government agencies created by Labour governments to mediate between industry and the state. But the extent of public ownership is not necessarily related to the extent of state control (compare the state's control of the defence market with the autonomy allowed to British Leyland) and, even where the Thatcher Government has privatised companies, by keeping equity in some, it has allowed itself the mechanisms of control. The abolition of the para-government agencies, whilst reducing competition within the state, has limited, as we shall see later, the opportunities for small companies to enter into the policymaking process.The effect has been to increase the autonomy of the state from industry and to limit the flexibility of response to growth markets, which at first are likely to be fragmented. Microcomputers provide an example of this inflexibility.

As the three industry studies will illustrate, the conflict between the proponents of state control and those adhering to the 'core'ideology takes place within the plurality of organisations which make up the British state. In general, within these studies, the Treasury is shown in its concern with central government efficiency and with limitations of public expenditure,to take the side of liberal ideology and the independence of markets from the state. In this it is not always opposed by the Department of Industry, whose role in the making of industrial policy is weakened by its own conflicting objectives, by bureaucratic fragmentation and by the tension between the 'core'ideology and Ministerial Responsibility. In some cases the state is shown to be autonomous of society, imposing big decisions upon unwilling industry. In others, industry is shown challenging the weakness of the bureaucracy to appeal over their heads to the vote-maximising instincts of the elected poltiticians. And, in some

cases, bureaucracy and industry become organisationally interdependent and, in return for stable markets, industry yields control of its production to the state.

NOTES AND REFERENCES

1. See for instance:Hugh Heclo & Aaron Wildavsky,The Private Government of Public Money(London,Macmillan,1974);D.C.Pitt & B.C.Smith,Government Departments: An Organisational Perspective(London, Routledge & Kegan Paul,1981);J.J.Richardson & A.G.Jordan, Governing Under Pressure. The Policy Process in a Post Parliamentary Democracy(Oxford,Martin Robertson,1979);Hugo Young & Anne Sloman No.Minister(London,BBC 2,1982).
2. Brian Hogwood,"Analysing Industrial Policy: a Multi-Perspective Approach",Public Administration Bulletin,No.29,1979,pp.18-42.
3. Stephen Young,Privatisation,Planning and the Roles of the Public Sector(London,Croom Helm),forthcoming.
4. Hansard Society,Politics and Industry - the Great Mismatch(London,Hansard Society,1979),p.45;MORI Opinion Poll, quoted in The Economist,Vol.261,18th December 1976,p.79.
5. Neville Abraham,Big Business and Government(London,Macmillan,1974),pp.4-5.
6. Alan Lord,"A View from the Bridge",in Allies or Adversaries(London,RIPA,1981),pp.49-50.
7. On specialists see: Hugo Young & Anne Sloman,pp.32-58,104-6,The Fulton Committee,Report: The Civil Service,Cmnd 3638,Vol.1(London,HMSO, 1968);Expenditure Committee Report HC535-I(London, HMSO,1976-7).
8. Select Committee on Science and Technology, Fourth Report.Prospects for the UK Computer Industry in the 1970s,Vol.II(London,HMSO,1970-1), p.35 Hereafter Fourth Report.
9. Financial Times,5th May 1983.
10. Hugh Heclo & Aaron Wildavsky,pp.384-9.
11. Alan Lord,p.56;Geoffrey Chandler,Director General of NEDO to 1983 quoted in Financial Times, October 21st 1982.
12. Wyn Grant,"The Development of the Government Relations Function in UK Firms: A Pilot Study of UK Based Companies (Berlin, International Institute of Management,1981).
13. Interview with former employee of ICT.
14. J.P.Nettl,"Consensus or elite domination -

the case of business",Political Studies,Vol.13, February 1965,pp.27-44.

15. Wyn Grant & David Marsh,The CBI(London, Hodder & Stoughton,1977),p.164.

16. Sunday Times,12th December 1982.

17. C.Graeme Roe,The Changing Role of the Chief Executive(Stroud,Glos.,G.M.Jerrold,1977), pp.59-63.

18. Jack Hayward,"The politics of planning in Britain and France",Comparative Politics,Vol.7,1974-5,p.288.

19. On 'corporatism'see for instance: A.Cawson, "Pluralism,Corporatism and the Role of the State", Government and Opposition,Vol.13,1978,pp.187-199;Trevor Smith,The Politics of the Corporate Economy(Oxford,Martin Robertson,1979);Philippe C.Schmitter & Gerhard Lehmbruch eds.,Towards Corporatist Intermediation(London,Sage ,1979); Gerhard Lehmbruch & P.C.Schmitter eds., Patterns of Corporatist Policymaking(London,Sage,1982).

20. Wyn Grant,"Studying Business Interest Assocations: Does Neo-Corporatism Tell Us Anything We Didn't Know Already?",Paper to Annual PSA Conference,Newcastle,1983.

21. See for instance: Gallup Political Index Nos.138-149(London,Gallup Polls,1970-71) for the most urgent problem facing the Heath Government.

22. P.Kellner,"Thatcherism:What MPs really think",New Statesman,Vol.99,24th October 1980,p.5.

23. Georges Peninou,M.Holthus,D.Kebschull, J.Attali,Who's Afraid of the Multinationals. A Survey of Opinion on Multi-national Corporations (Farnborough,Saxon House,1978);Labour Party, International Big Business.Labour's Policy on Multinationals(London,Labour Party,1977).

24. Trade and Industry,Vol.37,19th October 1979,p.100.

25. British Business,11th-17th March 1983,p.423.

26. Michael Hodges, Multinational Corporations and National Governments:A Case-Study of the UK's Experience(Farnborough,Saxon House,1974),pp.121-2.

27. Fourth Report,Vol.I,para.72;Reay Atkinson,Under Secretary for Information Technology,in evidence to House of Lords,New Information Technologies,Q.39.

28. Business Monitor MA4,(London,HMSO,1980).

29. M.Steuer et al.,The Impact of Foreign Investment on the UK(London,HMSO,1973).

30. Mark Abrams & R.Rose,Must Labour Lose (London,Penguin,1960),p.35.

31. Wyn Grant,Political Economy of Industrial

Policy,pp.12-22.
32. Industry Act 1980,Sect.17.
33. Douglas Mitchell, "Intervention,Control and Accountability:the NEB",Public Administration Bulletin,No.38,1982,pp.40-65;Jill Hills,"The Industrial Reorganisation Corporation: the Case of the AEI/GEC and English Electric Mergers",Public Administration,Vol.59,1981,pp.63-84.
34. Government support for industry and employment (at 1977 survey prices) totalled £2,257m in 1972-3;£3,209m/1973-4;£3,035m/1975-6; £2603m/1976-7;£2,396m/1977-8. In cash terms aid totalled £2,233m/1977-8;£3,036m/1978-9;£2881m/1979-80;£4,011m/1980-81;£5,319/1981-2;£5,854m/1982-3. See: Government Expenditure Plans 1977-78 to 1981-2, Cmndn 7049-II (1978);1983-84 to 1985-86, Cmnd 8789-II(1983).
35. Tony Benn,Arguments for Socialism(London, Penguin,1980),pp.54-5.
36. Labour Party,Industry and the Regions (London,Labour Party,1979),pp.1-15.
37. See: 'Regional & General Industrial Support',Cmnd 8789-II.
38. Ian Hargreaves,"The Dilemmas of Job Subsidies",Financial Times,4th August 1982.
39. Stephen Young, forthcoming.More than 100 local enterprise agencies have also been set up since government gave tax relief for contributions. See: The Guardian,April 8th 1983.
40. Wyn Grant, p.128.
41. Brian Hogwood,"Monitoring of Government Involvement in Industry: the Case of Shipbuilding", Public Administration,Vol.54,1976,pp.409-24. Sixth report from the Public Expenditure Committee, Public Money in the Private Sector,(London,HMSO, 1972),Chap.4.
42. Geoffrey Denton,"Financial Assistance to Industry",in W.M.Corden & G.Fels eds., Public Assistance to Industry.Protection and Subsidies in Britain and Germany(London,Macmillan,1976),p.161.
43. Industrial Reorganisation Corporation,Cmnd 2889 (London,HMSO,1966),para.7;Geoffrey Denton, p.133.
44.Financial Times,30th June 1982;Sunday Times,27th February 1983.
45. These were the decisions notorious for the fact that Sir Peter Carey entered a formal note of dissent from the decision and this action was leaked.
46.Cmnd 8789-II(London,HMSO,1983).
47.Government financing of R&D 1970-79(Brussels,Official Publication Office of the

European Communities,1979),pp.55-6;R.Arrundale,"R&D Expenditure and Employment",Economic Trends, No.309,July 1979,pp.100-122;J.R.Bowles,"Central Government Expenditure on R&D"Economic Trends,No.346,August 1982,pp.82-85;J.R.Bowles, "R&D Expenditure and Employment in the Seventies" Economic Trends,No.334,August 1981,pp.94-9.

48. Business Monitor MA4,1980.

49. Keith Pavitt,"Technology in British Industry: a Suitable Case for Treatment",in Charles Carter,pp.88-115;Christopher Freeman,"Technical innovation and British Trade performance",in F.Blackaby ed., De-Industrialisation,pp.56-73.

50. Sir Ieuan Maddock, "Science,Technology and Society",Proceedings of the Royal Society (Mathematics & Physical Sciences),Vol.345,1975, pp.295-326;Economic Trends,No.346,August 1982, p.96.

51. Sir Ieuan Maddock,Civil Exploitation.., passim.

52. EEC,Government Financing of R&D,pp.59, 168-73.

53. Electronics EDC,p.13.

54. Geoffrey Chandler in The Guardian,25th April 1983.

55. Interviews.

56. Financial Times,5th May 1983;Sixth Report from the Expenditure Committee,Vol.III,Q. 2533,2544.

57. On the independence of technical advice see: John Jewkes,"Government and High Technology" in G.Boyle,D.Elliot & R.Roy,The Politics of Technology (London,Longman,1977),pp.88-97;Roger Williams, "Accountability in Britain's nuclear programme"in Bruce L.Smith and D.C.Hague,The Dilemma of Accountability in Modern Government. Independence versus Control.(London,Macmillan,1971).

58. See for instance ,Kenneth Baker,in The Guardian,27th May 1983,"For the first time in our industrial history companies which compete vigorously in the market place are pooling their basic research. No other country in Europe has done this, but it's the only way we can stay in the race."

59. Martin Edmunds,"Self-nationalisation",in D.C.Hague,W.J.M.Mackenzie,A.Barker,Public Policy and Private Interests. The Institutions of Compromise.(London,Macmillan,1975).

Chapter Three

MARKETS: TELECOMMUNICATIONS, COMPUTERS AND MICRO-ELECTRONICS

3.1 INTRODUCTION

It was argued in Chapter One that government policies differ according to the structure of domestic markets. But domestic markets, themselves, are affected by the international structure of markets. This chapter, therefore, discusses international and British market structures in the industries of telecommunications, computing and microelectronics. In addition, technology itself, and access to technology, affects the actions of both companies and governments. Each of the three industries is an industry in which technological push plays a direct part in growth. The chapter therefore reviews the historical and technological development of each of the industries.

Today the three traditionally separate industries are converging technologically into what is called the 'information technology' sector. Technological changes in components, from valves to transistors, to microchips, have both reduced the size of computers, and increased their power. Computing techniques have evolved from those of the card-fed large stand alone models of the 1950s and early 1960s, through on-line processing with terminals linked to a central computer, to a distributed communications network. Within telecommunications, the advent of computer controlled telephone exchanges has introduced a similar evolution in design. Communications networks, incorporating interactive word processors, microcomputers and document transmission through facsimile, now link the markets of data processing and telecommunications. The traditional legal separation of voice and data transmission becomes increasingly difficult to maintain as the technologies converge, and as satellites provide

fast transmission of both mediums in addition to the transmission of radio and television.

In each of the traditional industries Britain originally led other European countries in exports. Yet, in each, the present market situation is one in which British manufacturers hold a minority or declining share of both domestic and world markets. This decline takes place at a time when market forecasts predict a continuing growth in the demand for information technology products. This chapter explores the structure of information technology markets, both domestic and international, the historical development of the markets in Britain and some of the technological features specific to the industries concerned.

3.2 TELECOMMUNICATIONS

3.21 The evolution and structure of the telecommunications market.

Of the three industries — telecommunications, computers and microelectronics — that of telecommunications is the oldest. It also differs from the other two in being mainly a public rather than a private market. In 1978, of a world market of $34 billion, $24 billion was spent by either state-owned Post and Telecommunications administrations (PTTs), government departments or government regulated utility companies. More than 50% of this $24 billion was spent by 20 PTTs and 80% was spent by North American, Japanese and European networks. Outside this PTT market, the remaining $10 billion went to supplying private telephone exchanges, inter office-networks, defence and railway networks and systems for banks.[1] Market forecasts for telecommunications products suggest a worldwide expenditure on telecommunications of $640 billion over the next decade.[2] In particular this demand is expected to come from Asia, from oil rich developing countries and from China.

Telecommunications differs from data processing in its technical requirements. Whereas, in general, a computer from one manufacturer needs only to be compatible with smaller or earlier models, telecommunications equipment has to be constructed to be compatible with the existing network. It therefore has to meet the specifications of local administrations. Even in the private market for small business telephone exchanges, national administrations tend to demand certain specifications to be met before allowing the private equipment to be

connected to the national network. In turn these technological requirements and local idiosyncracies have produced an international and national structure specific to the industry.

The telephone system can be divided into transmission equipment (cables,telephones etc.) and switching equipment (exchanges). Until the late 1970s and the introduction of optical fibres and satellite transmission, it was mainly in the field of switching that technology competed for markets. With the development of microchips these switching systems evolved from the manual operation of the early twentieth century to those of computer control of the 1980s.

The telephone was developed by Alexander Graham Bell in the USA. At first exchanges were manually operated. Then, in 1889, an automatic switch was developed by a Kansas undertaker called Strowger. The Strowger switch employs an arm called a wiper, which when a call is made hunts up and down a rack of contacts until it finds a free contact. Each contact is physically seized by the arm. The process, which is known as step by step, is bulky,slow and noisy. In addition, since mechanical parts wear out quickly,the system requires a great deal of maintenance and is heavy on manpower costs. Set against its high maintenance costs are its low initial capital costs. In the early twentieth century, it was thought cheaper and more reliable than the alternatives available, and the British Post Office (now British Telecom) decided to opt for the Strowger switch.

The alternative technology,called cross-bar, was developed in Sweden.Cross-bar is also an electro-mechanical switch. It was patented in 1915 and was at first mainly used in Sweden and Norway. Although it was less noisy and cheaper to maintain than Strowger, it was also more costly to produce. But cross-bar gained in popularity as labour costs became a growing proportion of PTT costs. By 1945 a variant of the Swedish cross-bar switch was being used in the USA and the market for cross-bar grew into the 1960s.[3]

Countries such as Japan, which modernised its telephone system after the second world war, did so on the basis of the cross-bar system. In fact cross-bar proved to be more compatible than Strowger with the first steps in computerisation in the early 1970s. But, in Britain, cross-bar was rejected by the British Post Office for inclusion in the public network until the late 1960s. In contrast to the rest of the world,Britain developed an alternative

intermediate technology based on reed relays, whilst it continued to install Strowger equipment. The intermediate system adopted by the Post Office, known as TXE2 and TXE4, although often referred to, for public relations purposes, as 'electronic' and based on electronic principles, in fact utilised hard-wired solid state circuitry. Circuits could be changed, but only by rewiring the system.

The intermediate technology of cross-bar and reed relays was followed by fully electronic telephone exchanges. These electronic, computer controlled exchanges allowed the easier transmission of speech and data and resulted in an increase in data networks, both public and private. The first computer controlled exchange was installed in 1960 in the USA and the decision to manufacture in bulk was taken in 1965. In Canada the first prototypes went into service in 1969, in Japan in 1970, in Sweden in 1972, in Germany in 1973, in Holland in 1972 and in France in 1970. In Japan, volume production of these exchanges started in 1974.[4]

But in Britain, for reasons which will be discussed later, the PTT and the manufacturers were slow off the mark in moving towards an electronic exchange, with the result that development work did not begin until 1977. In 1979, 90% of all British exchange connections were made by Strowger equipment, much of it over 30 years old. These figures compare with 26% in the USA and 19% in Japan. Only amongst the industrialised countries did West Germany use a similar proportion of the old switching equipment.[5]

Technically this old equipment resulted in slow transmission, which became of increased importance as data communications increased. Although some digital transmission took place within the network, at each end the digital signals had to be translated into analogue form, itself unsuitable for any but simple data communications. With growing pressure for a better public data communications service, the Post Office response was to introduce an experimental packet-switching system in 1977 which it extended in 1980. However, experts continued to criticise the data communications features of the British network.[6] The advent of the 'integrated office' in which machinery in one location needs to be able to communicate with others in different geographical locations, increased pressure on the British system. On the transmission side, the arrival of satellites, and, in particular, the decision by the American goverment to liberalise the private monopoly over transmission of AT&T, led

INTERNATIONAL & DOMESTIC MARKETS

to further pressure for similar de-restriction to take place in Britain.[7]

In 1980, in America, a consortium launched a small business satellite (Satellite Business Systems) to provide fast data communications and access to other value-added services such as facsimile. SBS was originally developed for the large business user and for data links, although, because the build-up of data traffic has been slower than expected, it has tended to take telephone traffic rather than data traffic.[8] For the large user in Britain, satellite transmission provides the possibility of access to services which would not be provided until the 1990s by terrestial means. For the British PTT, land-based electronic exchanges, plus optical fibre links instead of cables, may eventually provide the cheapest fast form of data transmission, but meanwhile the PTT has been forced into the satellite transmission market to compete with a private consortium named Mercury.

By 1983 therefore, the technological shape of the British publicly controlled telecommunications network was in the melting pot. On the one hand the PTT was attempting to modernise its network through the installation of System X into its trunk exchanges, overlaying it onto an out-of-date electro-mechanical system with analogue transmission. On the other, it was involved in satellite transmission in competition with a private consortium. From the point of view of exports, however, the new technology of System X has not yet paid off. At the time of writing it had landed only one small order in China.

3.22 The international structure of the industry.
Three quarters of the world's market in telecommunications was shared in 1978 by a dozen companies, as Table 3.1 demonstrates. The largest of these companies, Western Electric, supplied 24% of the market, followed by ITT, another American company, with 13%, Siemens of West Germany with 9% and General Telephone and Electronics of America and L.M.Ericsson of Sweden with 5% each. In fact the market was more concentrated than the table indicates. Western Electric was the manufacturing arm of AT&T of America and supplied mainly the American domestic market. Since the deregulation of telecommunications in the USA, Western Electric has been released onto the international market, a factor which will increase international competition.

Figures given by Nicholas Jequier, for 1975, in

INTERNATIONAL & DOMESTIC MARKETS

Table 3.2 reflect the degree of multinationality among the major telecommunications manufacturers. The firms ranged from the truly multinational, ITT (USA), Ericsson (Sweden), and Philips (Holland), to the purely national firms such as Western Electric (USA) and United Telecommunications (USA). Jequier pointed out the wide variation of companies in the telecommunications business, ' ranging from the ex-multinational in the process of re-establishment', such as Siemens of Germany, to the aspiring multi-nationals such as Northern Telecommunications of Canada or Nippon Electric and Fujitsu of Japan. Companies also varied between the pure exporters, such as the Japanese Hitachi and Oki Electric and the Italian STET (Societa Finanziara Telefonica), to the newly multinational, such as GTE of America.

Table 3.1 Market Shares of World Telecommunications Equipment 1978 %

WESTERN ELECTRIC	24
ITT (US)	15
SIEMENS (W.GERMANY)	9
GTE (US)	5
L.M.ERICSSSON	5
NORTHERN TELECOM (CANADA)	4
NIPPON ELECTRIC (JAPAN)	4
PHILIPS (HOLLAND)	3
CIT, THOMPSON & OTHER FRENCH COMPANIES	4
PLESSEY & GEC (BRITAIN)	3
TOTAL	76

Source: The Economist 28.10.78

With the exception of Western Electric, Nippon Electric and Ericssons, a relatively low proportion of total sales accrued to the major manufacturers from the sale of telecommunications equipment. But the development of firms into multinationals has in the past been necessary for expansion in the telecommunications market.

Jequier's data also showed that companies in small countries with small home markets, such as Ericsson and Philips, have had to become multinational in order to grow. In particular, because the Swedish PTT manufactures its

81

Table 3.2 Share of Total Sales in Telecommunications Equipment Made by the Main Manufacturing Firms Outside Their Country of Origin.(1)%

ITT	USA	95
ERICSSON	SWEDEN	82
PHILIPS	HOLLAND	65
SIEMENS	W.GERMANY	38
GTE	USA	30
GEC	BRITAIN	30
THOMSON-BRANDT	FRANCE	30
PLESSEY	BRITAIN	30
AEG-TELEFUNKEN	W.GERMANY	20
NIPPON ELECTRIC	JAPAN	17
NORTHERN TELECOM	CANADA	14
CGE	FRANCE	13
FUJITSU	JAPAN	10
OKI ELECTRIC	JAPAN	10
CONTINENTAL TEL.	USA	5
RCA	USA	5
HITACHI	JAPAN	5
STET	ITALY	5
WESTERN ELECTRIC	USA	0
UNITED TELECOMMS	USA	0

(1)Figures based on direct exports from the home country and the sales of the companies'foreign manufacturing subsidiaries and affiliates.

Key to abbreviations
ITT International Telephone and Telegraph
AEG Allgenzeine Elektrizitagesell schaft
GEC General Electric Co.
GTE General Telephone and Electrics
STET Societa Finaziara Telefonica
RCA Radio Corporation of America

Source: N.Jequier,"Telecommunications" in <u>Transfer of Technology by Multinational Corporations Vol.II(Paris,OECD,1975),p.210.</u>

own equipment, Ericsson has had no home market on which to rely. But the figures also reflect the historical point in time when a company first entered the market. The companies which created the telecommunications industry, such as AT&T (which sold its foreign subsidiaries to ITT in 1925), Siemens (which had its overseas subsidiaries

confiscated during the Second World War) and Ericsson, all expanded overseas in the pre-war period through the creation of local manufacturing units. That expansion continued for ITT and Ericsson after the war. [9]

Despite this tendency to become multinational, political control of domestic markets, and the protection thereby afforded domestic manufacturers, has allowed companies to exist which are predominantly concerned with supplying the domestic market. Traditionally, companies in Britain, France and Japan have tended to manufacture predominantly for the domestic market and to export equipment designed for that market,but in 1982 Plessey took over Stromberg-Carlson, a major American manufacturer of exchanges.

The traditional way into a foreign telecommunications market has been through the acquisition of a local manufacturer. The proportion of domestic markets taken by overseas owned local manufacturers in 1973 varied from more than 95% in the case of Belgium, Spain and Portugal, to more than 50% in France,Switzerland and Italy, to 25% in West Germany and Britain,to 10% in Sweden and less than 1% in the USA and Japan. Since 1973 the proportion of the French market taken by overseas - owned subsidiaries has declined as a result of the French desire to have domestic control over its home market. In the 1970s one ITT subsidiary and a Philips subsidiary were taken over by French interests backed by the French government. More recently the Socialist government of President Mitterand followed with the nationalisation of the one remaining ITT subsidiary. That position contrasts starkly with Britain where the proportion of the market taken by foreign manufacturers has increased.

3.23 Structure of the British Market.
As can be seen from Figure 3.1 British experience is in direct contrast to that of France. There are now more multinationals in the British market than was the case in the 1950s, when only Standard Telephone Cables, a subsidiary of ITT, was present in the public exchange market.

STC gained access to the public exchange market before the second world war. It has sought to appear British in character,but its linkage with ITT has caused dissension between the two major British manufacturers, GEC and Plessey, and the PTT. The issue has been how far the company should have access to British technology developed in

conjunction with the PTT. In addition, although 23% of its sales were in exports in 1980, the firm did not compete with ITT (Europe). During the 1970s the Callaghan Labour Government attempted unsuccessfully to merge it with Plessey. In 1979 ITT sold 15% of its shares to British interests, following this with the sale of a further 10% in the Spring of 1982, and a further 40% in October 1982. A few weeks later it was announced that STC would withdraw from manufacture of System X. At the time the stock market interpreted the announcement as being detrimental to STC, but later it seemed that the decision probably reflected the weak export potential of System X compared to ITT's electronic exchange.

Figure 3.1 Major Telecommunications Manufacturers in the UK market.

1950s	1970s	1980s
AEI — GEC — MARCONI —	GEC	GEC
PLESSEY	PLESSEY	PLESSEY
ERICSSON (SWEDEN) withdrew 1957	ERICSSON (re-entry)	ERICSSON
	PYE-TMC (HOLLAND-UK)	PYE-TMC
STC (USA)	STC	STC
THORN	THORN-GTE (UK-US)	—
	IBM	IBM
		FERRANTI-GTE (UK-US)
		MITEL (CANADA)

INTERNATIONAL & DOMESTIC MARKETS

Whilst ITT control of STC was established by a takeover in 1924, later foreign entrants to the British market have tended to gain access through minority stakes in British companies. The second overseas controlled firm to gain access to the public exchange market in the 1970s was Pye-TMC. Philips of Holland originally took a minority stake in the company, then later took a controlling interest. The PTT decision to allow Pye-TMC to take part in research and development for the new electronic exchange, System X, provoked a storm of protest from British owned manufacturers. In March 1982, British Telecom ordered its first public exchange from Pye-TMC.

Ericsson of Sweden was present in the British market before the second world war. It withdrew in 1947, selling off its shares in its British subsidiary on the grounds that its factory was employed in making outdated Strowger equipment. At that time it entered an agreement to stay out of the market for 20 years. Then in 1973, it gained acceptance for both its private electronic exchange, and for a public international exchange. In the same year it entered an agreement with Thorn. Its systems are now marketed by Thorn Ericsson. It has not yet been allowed entry into the public exchange market.

Further overseas incursion into the public exchange market took place in 1981 with the signing of an agreement between the PTT and Mitel of Canada. Mitel supplies electronic components to British Telecom, GEC and Plessey for the System X exchange. A more recent entrant to telecommunications is Ferranti. It has entered a technological agreement with GTE of America for the manufacture of telecommunications equipment. In March 1982 the PTT also ordered a public exchange from IBM.

It is however in the private exchange market that the major incursions of overseas firms have taken place. As Table 3.3 demonstrates, by 1974 foreign companies with private exchanges to sell had gradually displaced British companies in the domestic market. IBM, which was first allowed entry by the British PTT in 1969, to enable it to test one of its own private exchanges at its Havant headquarters, subsequently took over 30% of the British market. Both its and Ericsson's inroads into this market can be traced to the electronic technology of their exchanges, in advance of that offered by British firms. Mitel's PABx is now sold by British Telecom and International Computer Ltd. Mitel has also signed an agreement with IBM to link

85

INTERNATIONAL & DOMESTIC MARKETS

its PABx with IBM's office equipment to form an integrated package. The two British manufacturers, GEC and Plessey, who market small PABx, both do so under licence from Northern Telecomm(Canada) and Rohm (US) respectively. It is probable, in view of these factors, that the proportion of the British market taken by overseas suppliers is much higher than the 25% estimated by Jequier.

Moves towards concentration have taken place over the last twenty years, with first the takeover of AEI by GEC, then its merger with English Electric and its takeover of Marconi. These moves may in fact have created conditions favourable to the establishment of such overseas suppliers as Philips. The redundancies created among telecommunications personnel released them for alternative employment.

3.24 Telecommunications Markets

Figures for the 1950s show that Sweden and the USA, with 0.4 and 0.3 telephones per capita had almost three times the number of telephones per capita of the UK. Similar data for the 1970s show also that other countries had expanded their telephone network at a faster pace than Britain. Britain, which in 1956 ranked sixth in the world in its per capita telephone coverage, by 1979 with 0.4 telephones per capita, had dropped to tenth, only just ahead of France.[10]

Table 3.3 UK Market Share of Major Manufactures in Private Telephone Exchanges (PABX).

	1966	1974	
PLESSEY	22	11	
TELEPHONE RENTAL	29	8	electro
RELIANCE GEC	25	7	mechanical
ITT/STC (USA)	24	30	Mainly
ERICSSON (Sweden)	-	23	electronic
PYE-TMC (UK/USA)	-	3	technology
IBM (USA)	-	17	

Abbreviations:
STC Standard Telephone Cables
TMC Telephone Manufacturing Co.

Source: Financial Times 30.12.75

INTERNATIONAL & DOMESTIC MARKETS

After the OPEC oil price rise of 1973, OPEC countries began to place large orders for telephone equipment. There has been a commensurate attempt by Western industrialised countries to capture these markets as well as those in the NICs and China. In this world market, equipment has to be internationally compatible, resulting in two international committees to arrange that compatibility - the International Consultative Committee for Radio and the International Consultative Committee for Telephone and Telegraph (CCITT) of the United Nations - but there is no overall international standardisation of equipment or systems. National eccentricities mean that equipment made for one market is not immediately marketable in another. For instance, technology designed for the British market is not immediately marketable in France.

In turn the national administration's power to lay down specifications has had two effects. First, if the specifications set are of a higher standard than those demanded by other administrations, or if the technology specified is so idiosyncratic that other nations are unlikely to buy it, then the effect is to impede exports. Although it is possible for manufacturers to produce equipment specifically for sale abroad, if a home market does not exist for that equipment, then it is more difficult to reduce unit costs through volume production. The telecommunications industry is one where manufacturers have, not only to work in close conjunction with the PTT in the development of new technology, but also where they tend to be dependent on the government administration, as well as on market decisions.

Recognising this interdependence, governments of the industrialised West have increasingly become involved in arrangements with companies to increase telecommunications exports. In particular, the French and Japanese governments have involved themselves in this way, followed more recently by the British. And as telecommunications markets have become more important to the balance of payments of industrialised countries, so political factors have been crucial in gaining market advantage for national companies. On the basis that the first large-scale order is likely to determine subsequent orders, competition has particularly centred on those first orders.

Increasingly the most important factors in whether newly developing countries buy a particular system is not so much the technology as the financial package accruing to the purchase.

Preferential loans made by governments are now an intrinsic part of large-scale purchases, and those countries, such as Japan and France, where governments have been aware that the first technology bought tends to produce after-sales, have benefitted from the backing of such packages. In this respect British firms have not only been handicapped by having no electronic system to export, but have suffered from Britain's poor economic performance.

In 1979 British companies exported $1.2 billion of telecommunications equipment, compared to the $3.1 billion of Japan, $2.4 billion of America, $2.0 billion of West Germany and $1.0 billion of France. But whereas Japanese exports in the period 1970 to 1979 increased by 25%, French exports increased by 23%, Dutch and Belgian exports increased by 20% and West German, Italian and Swedish increased by about 18%, those of Britain increased by only 16%. As mentioned in Chapter One, annual import/export ratios of telecommunications equipment for Britain show a decline from 1965 to 1974 from a ratio of 2.98 in 1965 to a ratio of 0.91 in 1974. Figures for the late 1970s indicate some recovery from the trough of the early 1970s. By 1979 the ratio had increased to 1.32, but a considerable proportion of British telecommunications exports are of electro-mechanical Strowger equipment for replacements and spares. If this old technology is ignored, the export/import ratio reduces to 1.19 in 1979, 1.07 in 1980, and to below parity in 1981.[11]

Export/import ratios are not easy to interpret. They reflect technological competitiveness, PTT policy and the activities of multinationals within the domestic economy. For instance, in Belgium where multinational subsidiaries take 95% of the small domestic market, increased imports may reflect transfers between multinational subsidiaries. Similarly, multinational subsidiaries are likely to account for much of the increase in export share of Italy.

Of those countries with domestic telecommunications manufacturers, Britain and France both lost ground in exports to the Japanese and West Germans. But whilst France maintained a balance between imports and exports to 1975, liberalisation of the private telecommunications market on the part of the British PTT may well have affected the rate of imports of equipment from 1972 onwards. Of equal importance, however, has been British manufacturers' declining technological base. As markets have changed to cross-bar and electronic technology,

INTERNATIONAL & DOMESTIC MARKETS

British manufacturers have been unable to compete. At the same time the expanding domestic market has taken increased proportions of total production. In the following chapters we explain how it is that Britain, which led the rest of Europe in telecommunications exports in the immediate post-war period, is now in the position of importing such a large proportion of her domestic needs.

3.3 COMPUTERS

3.31 Features of the Computer Market.
Within the general heading of 'computers' there are in fact three types of merchandise to be sold - the mainframe computer itself, the peripherals such as print-out machines and teletypes, and the software which forms the instructions for using the machines. The computer market is not a unified entity. It consists of several specialised markets each needing computers of different sizes or different potential. The office sector market originally needed large mainframe computers capable of performing simple calculations on large quantities of data. But, as computers have become tools of modern management, so the demand for mini and microcomputers has increased. The industrial sector needs computers to drive automated tools. The banking sector requires numbers of interlinking small computers to connect branches with the large central computer. The scientific sector requires computers to process small amounts of data but able to carry out complicated calculations to a high degree of accuracy. The personal computer market is expected to produce a demand for microcomputers providing access for the user to a variety of information services, and linking with communications systems. Computers have also become part of other technological sectors, for instance, telephone exchanges. But it has been in the 'data processing' or office sector that, until recently, major mainframe computer manufacturers have concentrated. And it has been predominantly in the sale of hardware that governments, through national computer companies, have competed.

The importance and domination of national governments' policy by mainframe manufacturers came about for several reasons. At first the hardware of the computer itself was the most expensive item in a computer installation, representing about 60% of the expense of an installation, although that proportion has since dropped rapidly. Because of the non-stand-

ardisation of peripherals and software, a consumer who installed a computer from one manufacturer, found it easier to replace that computer with one of the same make. To switch to another manufacturer involved the expense of changing both peripherals and software. The first sale to a customer became the sale of primary importance, and those companies which were first in the field gained market dominance. Market share became a function, not so much of technological superiority, but of the time at which a company entered the market.

Competition took place between manufacturers firstly on market share, and then, secondly, on technological innovation. Customer base and customer loyalty being of primary importance, computer hardware manufacturers found that they had to provide efficient and adequate servicing and back-up facilities for customers. But technological innovation was also important to compete with the market leaders and retain customers.

It has become usual for the life of a computer to be estimated at five years, with new generations of machines featuring major technological advances. The first generation (pre-1960) used valves as components; the second generation used discrete transistors (1960-65); the third generation introduced in about 1966 were fully electronic and used solid state technology. The fourth generation, introduced after 1971, featured no new components, but had expanded input/output capabilities and increased processing speeds.[1]

Each generation of machines has involved huge costs in research and development. Government funding has been of primary importance. Without that funding R&D has had to be met from internal profits generated from the existing customer base. In this respect also, those firms which have been longest in the market, have benefitted from, what Hu and Jequier term, the 'experience curve'. This curve refers to the phenomenon whereby the costs of installations of computers are reduced by virtue of the number of units installed. Companies which have already installed large numbers of computers have lower costs per unit installed, not only by virtue of size, but also because they have the experience of thousands of installations behind them. Hu estimates that the 'experience curve' begins to operate only when a firm holds ten per cent of world market share. Smaller firms therefore face the double handicap of higher production costs and high installation costs, whilst attempting to maintain expenditure on R&D.[2]

INTERNATIONAL & DOMESTIC MARKETS

In addition, the smaller firm suffers from cash-flow problems, which result from a tendency on the part of customers to rent machines. At first, when computers were status symbols, the trend was for users to buy a computer installation outright. But then, as computers became regarded as no more than office machinery, customers increasingly rented rather than bought installations. Rentals are geared by manufacturers to recuperation of their production costs over three years, whereas the rental life of a machine is between five and seven years. But, because it has become the norm to market a new 'generation' of machines every five years, customers tend to bunch their orders into the first years of a 'generation' and hold off in the last two years of its life. Computer manufacturers therefore face the maximum outflow of funds at the introduction of a new 'generation'. These problems of cash-flow have led to the failure of some manufacturers such as ICL, discussed in Chapter 5. They have also led in some countries, notably Japan and France, to government intervention to provide the necessary finance for a rental base.

3.32 Technological and historical development.
The computer was originally developed during the second world war by the cryptographic division of the Ministry of Defence. Specialist computers developed with the aid of American resources were used for code-breaking and for ballistic calculations, but the development of a computer suitable for general work was delayed until after the war. In 1948 Manchester University produced its Mark 1 computer and in 1949 Cambridge University produced EDSAC,which was then about one year ahead of the Americans. A British government contract was given to the firm of Ferranti to produce a commercial version of the Mark 1. That machine is claimed to have been the first commercially available computer, marginally ahead of the American Univac.

IBM first entered the computing field using patents from the Manchester Mark 1. But with the introduction of the transistor in the 1950s in the USA,British computer manufacturers began to fall behind the technological innovation of the American. Britain's answer to IBM was the Ferranti' Atlas, claimed on its introduction in 1962 to be the most powerful computer in the world. However, its applications tended to be limited to scientific work.

91

Meanwhile, IBM had seen the possibilities of the computer for office work. Its expansion in the field rested on its existing customer base for office equipment, its aggressive salesmanship, its reputation for service to customers and its R&D capability. The history of the last twenty years in the computer industry, therefore, has been one of other computer manufacturers seeking, first to catch up with IBM in market share, second, to ensure that IBM was not allowed the field to itself in technological innovation, and, third, to diversify into fields where they were not in such direct conflict with the American giant.

De facto, IBM has determined standards in the computer industry. A major question, to be met by all smaller manufacturers, has been whether to make their machines compatible with IBM machines. Originally many companies attempted to make their machines different from IBM's. But competition has led to the development of IBM-compatible machines and peripherals, such as those of Amdahl(US-Japan) and Itel (US), which have competed with IBM on price alone. IBM has rejoined to that competition by refusal to service customers using non-IBM peripherals. In turn this action has led to anti-trust suits against IBM.

Diversification away from direct competition with IBM has led smaller firms to concentrate on such sectors as mini, micro and small business computers, the leasing of old computers and preparation of specialised software. But in the 1970s, as the market for large computers slowed down, so IBM diversified into the minicomputer market. It followed, in the 1980s, with entry into the personal computer market. Smaller manufacturers find themselves once again in competition with IBM.

3.33 International Structure of the Industry.
As Table 3.4 demonstrates, the world computer market was dominated by American manufacturers from the early 1960s. IBM entered the computer market in 1953 and by 1956 took 75% of the American market. In 1967, IBM and the other American manufacturers, Honeywell, Control Data Corporation (CDC), Burroughs, RCA, Sperry Rand and National Cash Register were responsible for 80% of total world ouput. In terms of world export shares, the USA took 75%, West Germany took 12%, France took 8%, Britain took 5% and Japan took less than 1%.[4]

But these figures on output and exports underrate the true influence of American companies on the

European market. The early 1960s were years when they opened up manufacturing facilities, and entered licensing agreements with European companies. By 1967, IBM had manufacturing outlets in four West European countries, and was followed by Honeywell and General Electric.[5] Hence production in the West European countries was partly that of American companies.

A truer picture of the amount of total production taken by American firms is given by Table 3.5 which covers the whole of Europe. Britain had the lowest proportion of its manufacturing output produced by American firms. West Germany was almost wholly dependent on American companies, not only because of IBM's local manufacture, but because of technological agreements between Siemens and RCA and between AEG-Telefunken and General Electric. In France, in addition to IBM's local manufacture, Bull-GE had a licensing agreement with General Electric and Compagnie Europeene d'Automatique had an agreement with SDS(Xerox).[6]

During the 1970s IBM retained its dominance of the world market, taking 71% in 1974. With increasing demand for mini and micro computers and the entry of other manufacturers into those markets, IBM's share of the total European market was estimated to have decreased to 40% in 1980. But in the mainframe data-processing sector it remains a clear market leader still with over 50% of the West European market.

The minicomputer market started out more evenly spread between firms than that of mainframes. The major companies in the market were, however, all American. They included Data Equipment Corporation, Hewlett Packard, Data General, General Automation, Honeywell, Texas Instrument and IBM. In 1976, Digital Equipment Corporation (DEC), was reported to take 40%, with Hewlett Packard following up with 17% and other American companies, including IBM taking a further 29 per cent. But the Western European market seems to have been less dominated by American suppliers than was the mainframe market. Locksley quotes figures to show that American manufacturers took approximately 50% in 1975 with the other 50% shared with European suppliers.[6] By 1981 the position had changed once more as minicomputers gave way to microcomputers and small business systems. The giant IBM emerged once more as the market leader in this fastest growing sector of the market.

INTERNATIONAL & DOMESTIC MARKETS

Table 3.4 World Market share in 1965 (US)
%

IBM	65.3
SPERRY RAND	12.1
CONTROL DATA	5.4
HONEYWELL	3.8
BURROUGHS	3.5
GENERAL ELECTRIC	3.4
RADIO CORPORATION OF AMERICA	2.9
NATIONAL CASH REGISTER	2.9
PHILCO	0.7

Source: G.W.Brock, The US Computer Industry (Cambridge,Mass.,Ballinger,1975), p. 16.

Table 3.5 Computers Installed by US Firms or Subsidiaries, and Computers Manufactured by European Firms Under Licence as a % of Total Computer Installations.

Belgium-Luxembourg	63.4
Netherlands	55.0
France	50.9
Germany	75.5
Italy	79.4
UK	20.5
US	99.8

Source: Gaps in Technology (Paris,OECD, 1969), p. 41

3.34 The Structure of the British Industry
In the 1950s the structure of the British domestic mainframe computer industry was highly fragmented. Seven companies competed for what was a small domestic market. But then, between 1958 and 1966, a series of mergers took place . Powers Samas and British Tabulating Machines joined forces in 1958 to form International Computers and Tabulators (ICT), which then took over the computer interests of Electrical Musical Industries (EMI)in 1962, and,a year later,those of Ferranti. Lyons Leo, which had developed computers out of its tea shop interests, merged with English Electric, which then took over the computer side of Marconi. In 1967,with government backing, it also took over the failing Elliott

INTERNATIONAL & DOMESTIC MARKETS

Automation which had specialised in computers for industrial automation.(Figure 3.2)Finally, in 1968, again with government backing, ICT merged with English Electric to form International Computers Limited (ICL).
But, as Jequier has pointed out,if a market is expanding,rationalisation is not necessarily a good policy.[7] Locksley notes:

> If the growth rate is 20 per cent per year, turnover will double in four years. So if two firms of equal size merge this is equivalent to the size that one firm alone could achieve alone in four years. The faster the growth rate the smaller the advantage. However,the problems of mergers,particularly with non-compatible technologies and product lines, often slows the rate of growth so that over time the newly merged firm loses its relative position.For example if the new firm grows at 10% whilst the market continues at 20%,the advantage of larger size will disappear in eight years.[8]

These disadvantages hit the British computer industry. By 1963 ICT was selling ten different computers, often incompatible with each other, where it should have been selling three sizes of compatible computers.
ICT chose to concentrate research and development on producing a British technology for the 1970s. By designing technology which was incompatible with IBM, ICT deliberately chose to meet IBM head-on in competition. In contrast English Electric bought in an American design for its third generation of computers from Radio Corporation of America. Both ICT and English Electric in the 1960s were dependent on American technology, which in turn limited their export of computers. At one stage, ICT imported Univac computers and sold them under its own name.The fragmentation of computer development and the subsequent necessary rationalisations, coupled with the licensing of American technology, had an obvious impact on both the import and export of computers. One of the few markets not dominated by IBM, and therefore open to British manufacturers, was that of Eastern Europe. But the ability to export to that market depended, not only on negotiations through CONCOM, the international committee dealing with exports to the Communist bloc, but also on the absence of American technology within the machines themselves.ICT may have been pushed along the road to developing a British technology because

INTERNATIONAL & DOMESTIC MARKETS

Figure 3.2 Concentration in the British Mainframe Computer Industry.

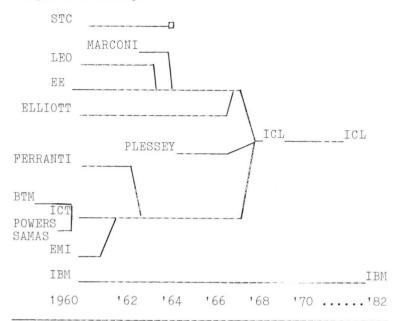

Abbreviations:
STC: Standard Telephone & Cables
LEO: Lyons Electronic Office
EE: English Electric
ICL: International Computers Ltd.
EMI: Electrical & Musical Instruments
IBM: International Business Machines
ICT: International Computers & Tabulators

Source: N.Jequier,"Computers",in Raymond Vernon ed., Big Business and the State(London,Macmillan,1974) p.215.

of the importance of these markets, which paid cash for its machines rather than rented them.

From a position where in 1963 British industry exported £ 3 million worth of computers and imports were negligible, the import/export ratio deteriorated in 1964. In that year, compared to £6.5 million worth of exports, Britain imported £12.5 million. The export/import ratio remained below 0.5 for the rest of the 1960s. And as Table 3.6 indicates the majority of that import penetration came from American manufacturers.

Table 3.6 US and UK Controlled Computers in the UK as % of Total Computer Installations.

Country of Control	1959	'60	'61	'62	'63	'64	'65	'66
UK	100	96	85	64	55	52	47	46
US	-	4	15	37	45	47	51	52
Others	-	-	-	-	-	0.2	2	2

Source: Gaps in Technology (Paris, OECD, 1969) p.42.

By the mid 1970s major American computer mainframe manufacturers had subsidiaries in Britain. These included IBM, Honeywell, Univac, Burroughs, Control Data Corporation and NCR. In total, they accounted for 60% of the British market, and employed about 38,000 people, in comparison to ICL's employment of 29 thousand. IBM, Honeywell and Univac had factories operating in Scotland, but the rest were mainly centred in the South and South East. Of them all IBM was the only one with research facilities in Britain.[11]

Table 3.7 provides a comparison of American, European and Japanese computer companies in 1978. It demonstrates their inequality in terms of size. This inequality allowed IBM to spend more on research and development than ICL gained in turnover. The table also shows that ICL, the part French owned Honeywell and German owned Nixdorf (a mini-computer manufacturer) were the only European companies to have 100% of their turnover in data processing. This factor, which was to prove a handicap to ICL, is discussed in Chapter Five.

3.35 The British Domestic Market.
In the mid 1970s Britain was the only European country in which IBM did not take more than 50% of the domestic market. Even so, products from American manufacturers accounted for over 60% of the British market. By 1978 imports of equipment accounted for almost 90% of home demand.[12]

The continued increase in the balance of payments deficit in computers can be traced to the number of multinationals operating from the country and their importation of parts and peripherals. The peripherals industry has been particularly weak. As early as 1964 it was already evident that this was the case. The export/import ratio[13] of peripheral equipment in that year was 0.1. By 1966 the

97

INTERNATIONAL & DOMESTIC MARKETS

Table 3.7 Top Firms in the Data Processing Industry in 1978.

	COUNTRY	DP REVENUES $million	DP REVENUES AS % TOTAL REVENUE
IBM	US	17072	81
BURROUGHS	US	2107	87
NCR	US	1932	74
CONTROL DATA	US	1867	68
HITACHI	JAPAN	1830	17
SPERRY/UNIVAC	US	1807	48
TOSHIBA	JAPAN	1633	22
DEC	US	1437	100
HONEYWELL	US	1294	37
FUJITSU	JAPAN	1248	71
CII-HB	FRANCE	1061	100
ICL	UK	1019	100
OLIVETTI	ITALY	789	42
SIEMENS AG	GERMANY	703	5
NIPPON ELEC.	JAPAN	672	21
PHILIPS NV	NETHERLANDS	602	4
NIXDORF	GERMANY	554	100
OKI ELEC.	JAPAN	200	35
MITSUBISHI	JAPAN	190	5

Source: G.Locksley, p.96.

British peripherals industry had almost disappeared. With the exception of ICL's major supplier, Data Recording Instruments, the market was highly fragmented. ICL itself also imported peripherals from the 1970s.

The impact of multinationals on the British balance of trade in computers is noted by Locksley for 1977.[14] By 1980, with an increase in their activities, the impact of their imports of parts and peripherals was even more pronounced.[15] Estimates suggest that 80% of the data terminals used in the EEC are imported, and that 50% of them are supplied by IBM.[16]

Nor has the position of British manufacturers in the markets of mini and microcomputers been much better than that of mainframes. In 1977, in comparison to their 35% share of the mainframe market, in the markets of minicomputers and small business computers British companies took 32% and 30% respectively, a proportion which had reduced to about 25% by 1982.[17] In comparison to the maturing

mainframe market, which now has a growth of 5% per annum, the mini and micro sections of the market are expected to grow at more than 20 % per annum. Hence British manufacturers are becoming less well represented in the fastest growing market sector.

The software market is provided by both mainframe manufacturers and the Computer Services Industry(CSI).The CSI market includes bureaux,which hire out time on computers to small companies, and consultancies, which provide programmes and equipment for specific applications. The software services industry in Britain still constitutes a growth sector. From a highly fragmented industry, concentration took place during the late 1960s. By 1976, although 60% of the companies were small, 29 provided 46% of the industry's turnover.Of these companies two, Dataskil and Basic were subsidiaries of ICL.[18] Several of the largest companies are American owned, whilst others have been for capital to the USA. The industry's turnover more than doubled between 1971 and 1978, whilst numbers employed by the industry increased from 15000 to 23000. The industry is also a net earner of foreign business. Out of total billings of £330 million in 1978, £20 million came from overseas clients.[19] Market forecasts predicted a growth of 400% in the demand for the industry's services between 1980 and 1984.[20]

This section has outlined the domination of both the mainframe market and later the mini and micro computer markets by American companies. Only in the software sector is the British market predominantly served by British companies. Hence, in framing a policy for the industry, one of the major concerns of government is likely to be the presence of multinationals in the sectors concerned.

3.4 MICROELECTRONICS

3.41 Historical Development of Integrated Microcircuits.

The major components for the first generation of computers and other electrical goods,such as radios, were valves. Then the transistor was developed at AT&T's research laboratories in 1948. As the transistor became cheaper to produce than valves, so it took over the market for electrical components. Transistors developed into the staple product of the semi-conductor industry.

It is worthwhile considering for a moment what followed in the transistor industry. Experience there has been repeated in the case of micro-

circuits. Although the transistor was invented, developed and patented in the USA, within ten years that country's technological advantage had been eroded by the transfer of technology elsewhere. In particular, by the end of the 1960s Japan was exploiting the transistor for consumer electrical goods, such as the cheap transistor radio. By 1972, Japan exported 45% of its production in those goods, produced 51% of total world output of transistors, and held a 40% share of the world market in electronic goods.[1]

This cycle of initial advantage, gained through technological innovation, then lost to countries with lower wage costs, or higher productivity, is one which is recurrent. As new technological know-how spreads, so the race becomes one of adapting and lowering the new technology's cost to that of the previous technology. At a certain point, in cost terms, the cost advantages of the new technology are enough for manufacturers to find it acceptable. Then a mass market develops.

Japan's successful exploitation of the transistor depended, first, on its importation and adaptation of foreign technology, second, on its low labour costs, and, third, on its capital investment. Meanwhile, forced to compete on price alone, American manufacturers established production in cheap labour areas, such as Taiwan. Similar considerations took the Japanese into overseas investment in Korea from 1968 onwards.[2]

With the technological innovation of the integrated circuit, a similar product cycle began. But, unlike the transistor, which remained of a similar construction throughout its lifetime, the microintegrated circuit has progressed technologically. It no longer replaces transistors alone, but also replaces the wiring which controls them. A microprocessor is programmable like a computer. But, whereas a computer is programmed through the software instructions fed into it, a microprocessor has the software instructions written into the circuit design.

Microchips may be memory chips designed to store data, or logic chips, designed to drive a computer, or microprocessors. Each has a different function and a different market. In addition, microchips may be standard chips, designed for a wide range of potential users, or 'specialised' chips, designed for a particular market, such as telecommunications equipment, or 'custom built' chips, designed for one firm's special needs. Further, with new discoveries in fundamental

materials research, the microchips themselves may utilise different materials or technologies.

British electronics history has it that the microchip was invented in 1952 by W.A.Dummer at the Royal Radar Etablishment.[3] Finding no backers for the invention its originator took it to the USA. American history has it that the integrated circuit was first developed by Robert Noyce in the USA, utilising a new material called silicon.[4]

At first the yield of usable chips from each production batch was as little as 25%, and with heavy R&D costs, prices remained uncompetitive with the transistor until the late 1960s. During this time the American industry was supported by the Space programme, but, as that programme was cut back, so the European market gained in importance. By the mid 1970s, with the development, first of the microprocessor and the medium scale integrated circuit (6K RAM), and then of large scale circuits (16K RAM), demand, particularly from computer manufacturers, took off. The 64K RAM was announced in 1978, and came into commercial production in 1980.

The Japanese have now achieved technological parity with the Americans. In 1974 American estimates placed the Japanese technological capability two years behind the American - a technological gap which American firms such as IBM expected to keep as a result of their refusal to licence their microchip technology to Japanese firms.[5] But then Fujitsu announced the successful development of the 64K microchip at the same time as IBM and Texas Instruments. In 1981 a Japanese manufacturer announced the first production sample of 256K RAMs, whereas three of the major American manufacturers had failed to produce a viable 64K RAM.[6] The issue of the failing technological leadership of the United States has given rise once more to the involvement of the military in supporting American manufacturers. In addition, in response to the Japanese threat, in 1981 American companies began to explore the possibility of forming a research cartel. The move has been brought about by the huge R&D costs in the industry, said to be as high as 13% of turnover, low prices of Japanese chips and the failure of companies to raise capital from the financial market. Fifteen of the major semi-conductor companies are said to be involved in the project.[7]

3.42 The International Structure of the Market

The major production of microcircuits until the 1980s took place in the USA. Until the late 1970s American companies were responsible for 80% of the world market. But, by 1978 this proportion had decreased to 60%, as the Japanese challenged them in both the American and European markets.[8]

Within the American industry itself, considerable concentration has taken place. Traditionally new microchip companies arose as individual entrepreneurs left established firms to set up on their own. With the increase in capital costs involved in microchip manufacture these independent manufacturers have suffered considerable cash-flow problems. One survey, in the late 1970s suggested that microchip manufacturers were actually

Table 3.8 Acquisitions in the US Semiconductor Industry

Year	Acquisition	Buyer	Price Paid $ million
1975	Signetics	Philips(Holland)	49
1976	MOS Technology	Commodore Internat	1
	Litronix	Siemens(W.Germany)	16
	AMD (20%)	Siemens	27
	Solid State	VDO(W.Germany)	5
	Intersil(24%)	Northern Telecom (Canada)	11
1978	Electronic Arrays	NEC(Japan)	9
	Spectronics	Honeywell	3
	Synertek	Honeywell	24
	American Microsystems(25%)	Bosch(W.Germany)	14
1979	Mostek	United Technologies	349
	Microwave Semicond.	Siemens	25
	Fairchild	Schlumberger(France)	397
	Unitrode (14%)	Schlumberger	10

Abbreviations:
    AMD   Advanced Micro Devices

Source: Business Week 3.12.79

spending 102% of their profits on R&D, although only 5.8% of sales.[9] The low price of Japanese chips was forcing American manufacturers to underprice their own products. This in turn meant that they did not have the yield on capital necessary to raise external

finance and were ripe for takeovers.

In addition, as microchip components have become essential to other industries, such as aeroplanes, consumer durables and automobiles, so a process of vertical integration has taken place. Periods of falling value in the American dollar have helped to make this process one of international integration, as Table 3.8 indicates. Coupled with the fact that major computer manufacturers tend to produce their own chips for in-house use, the result of this process of concentration was to produce a situation where, in 1979, 30% of the world production of microchips was for in-house use rather than for the open market.

In the 1980s, of the major American producers of microcircuits, National Semiconductor, Texas Instruments, Motorola, General Instruments and ITT all have plants in Europe. The Japanese company, Nippon Electric (NEC) operates from plants in Scotland and Ireland, and Hitachi manufactures in West Germany.

In total in Europe there are about twelve domestically owned manufacturers of microcircuits. These include two subsidiaries of Philips of Holland (English Mullard and French RTC), Thomson-CSF(France), Siemens(W. Germany), AEG-Telefunken (W. Germany), Valvo(W. Germany), EFCIS (France) and the three British firms, Ferranti, GEC and Plessey. On the whole these companies have concentrated upon producing chips for specific applications and have not entered the market of standard chips. In general, Europe has been dependent upon supplies of chips from America and upon supplies generated by American multinationals in Europe. In 1970 50% of the European market was taken by Texas Instruments, ITT and Motorola.[10] By 1979 the position had worsened. European product manufacturers used $1.6 billion of chips, but European chip manufacturers' sales were less than $500 million.[11]

Once again, as in the mainframe computer market, these figures underestimate the extent of influence of American multinationals upon the European market. Licensing agreements between European owned firms, and joint ventures with American firms, increase European dependence on American technology. In Germany, AEG-Telefunken has a licensing agreement with Mostek(US) and Siemens has an agreement with Intel(US). In Italy SGS, owned by Olivetti, has an agreement with Zilog, a subsidiary of Exxon (US). In France, there are joint ventures between Matra and Harris(US), between St. Gobain Pont a Mousson and National Semiconductor, and between

Thomson-CSF and Motorola. In Britain, GEC formulated an agreement with Fairchild (US) but that failed when Fairchild was taken over by French Schlumberger. It then signed an agreement with Mitel(Canada).So also did Plessey. In Britain, the jointly owned US-UK company,Inmos, also relies on American technology. [12]

To compound this trend, in 1980, European and American manufacturers joined together in an organisation called Stack, whose objective is 'to enhance large-scale integrated (LSI) and VSLI circuit development outside Japan'. Through this organisation companies may exchange know-how. Those participating companies included GEC(UK), Racal(UK), Nixdorf(W.Germany), Siemens (W.Germany), ICL(UK), Control Data (US),Plessey (UK),British Telecom (UK). By using a similar form of research cartel to that which has been used by Japanese companies,backed by MITI, the intention of the organisation is to challenge Japanese technology. Hence both European and American firms are meeting the Japanese challenge by research cartelisation.[13]

Finally,such firms as GEC and Siemens have been active in taking over small semiconductor companies in the USA. In 1981 Siemens owned five American semiconductor companies. GEC took over Circuit Technology (US)in 1980.[14] The intention in these takeovers is to transfer technology from America back to the home country at a relatively cheap cost.

3.43 The Structure of the British Industry.

In 1966 in Britain there were four British manufacturers interested in the manufacture of integrated circuits - Ferranti,Marconi,Elliot Automation and Texas Instruments. Of these, Elliot had a licensing agreement with Fairchild (USA) and Texas Instruments was American owned. At £ 4.5 million the market was small and American manufacturers claimed 80% of it.[15]

Responding to this import threat, in 1966 the Labour Government imposed a 30% tariff on imported circuits. The tariff had the effect of increasing the numbers of American multinationals establishing manufacture in Britain. In the late 1960s Fairchild, ITT and Philips of Holland, through its subsidiary Mullard, developed production lines in Britain. Except for Ferranti, which claimed a 10% share of the market, British companies had a paltry proportion of the market. [16]

Between 1968 and 1972 the output of integrated circuits in Britain increased from £ 2.6 million to

£18.9 million or by a ratio of 1:7. As the factories of the American multinationals came on stream, so the export/import ratio improved from 0.34 in 1968 to 0.49 in 1972.[17] Although British companies exported their special chips to Japan and the USA, the standard chip market in Britain and Europe continued to be dominated by American imports.

In 1978 came the first hints of a worldwide shortage, particularly of memory chips, and recognition in Europe of the dangers of dependence upon an imported American supply. There followed intervention by the British government to increase domestic manufacture. By 1980, IBM, ITT, National Semiconductor, Texas Instruments, Motorola, and General Instruments had subsidiaries in Britain, as also did Philips of Holland. Of the American multinationals, four had plants in Scotland as also did NEC of Japan. Mitel (Canada) has also set up manufacture of telecommunications' chips in Wales.

The four British companies which manufacture microcircuits are Plessey, GEC, Racal and Ferranti. Each is primarily concerned with special chips — Plessey and GEC most recently for the telecommunications market ;Racal and Ferranti for the defence market. For each company, microchip production is not a major source of revenue. In fact Plessey considered withdrawing from the market altogether in 1978.[18]

By 1981, following the increased activity of multinationals based in Britain, the export/import ratio improved to 0.6.[19] But the price for this improvement in the balance of payments is that in a world market which is estimated to grow from the 1979 figure of $10.5 billion to $21.5 billion in 1984, Britain is highly dependent upon American technology.

3.5 CONCLUSION

In each of the three markets which have been discussed the international market is dominated by American multinationals. In each the British market has been penetrated by these multinational companies. But the proportion of the domestic market accounted for by American companies varies from 25% in telecommunications public sector market, to 60% in the computing mainframe and minicomputer markets, to 80% in the computer peripherals and microcircuit markets. Dependence on American technology is even higher than these figures suggest.

It was pointed out in Chapter One that

dependence on foreign technology and multinationals raises certain problems for the host country. Besides the problem that multinationals tend to increase imports, in general the technology produced locally tends to be second-best.Microcircuits on sale in Europe are estimated to be two years behind those on sale in the USA. In addition, R&D facilities may be kept in the home country of the multinational,thus reducing the efficacy of technological transfer. It was noticeable that within one month of claiming the arrival of the 64K RAM in the USA,ITT closed down a factory in Britain manufacturing out of date technology.
For British governments the dominance of multinational companies within the computing and microcircuit markets has created parameters to action in support of domestically owned manufacturers. As the reader will see in the following chapters, the predisposition of British governments to welcome inward investment has increased the vulnerability of the British economy to international factors.

NOTES AND REFERENCES

TELECOMMUNICATIONS
    1. The Economist,Vol.280,22nd August 1981, Survey,p.7.
    2. The Economist,Vol.269,28th October 1978, pp.82-3
    3. C.Harlow,Innovation and Productivity under Nationalisation The First Thirty Years.(London,Allen & Unwin,1977),pp.101-102.
    4. P.Lucas,"Progress of Electronic Switching Throughout the World" reproduced in Communication and Electronique (SOCOTEL), No.44,January 1974.
    5. D.Moralee,"British telecommunications and the Information Age",Electronics and Power,Vol.25,June 1979,p.433.
    6. I.Barron & R.Curnow,The Future with Microelectronics (London,Frances Pinter,1979), pp.170-171.
    7. Financial Times,14th October 1981.
    8. Private communication from business consultant.
    9. Artur Attman & W.Olsson, L.M.Ericsson 100 years Rescue Reconstruction Worldwide Enterprise 1932-36. Vol.II,(Stockholm,C.Jacopaeus,1976),passim.
    10. The Economist,Vol.280,22nd August 1981, Survey,p.4

INTERNATIONAL & DOMESTIC MARKETS

    11. Figures compiled from PQ363,Business Monitor(London,HMSO,various years).

COMPUTERS
    1. Gareth Locksley,A Study of the Evolution of Concentration in the UK Data Processing Industry with Some International Comparisons(Brussels, European Commission,1981),pp.15-28.
    2. Nicholas Jequier,"Computers"in R.Vernon ed., Big Business and the State(London,Macmillan, 1974),p.213.
    3. Simon Lavington,Early British Computers(Manchester,Manchester University Press,1980),pp.83-4.
    4. The Economist,Vol.219,11th June 1966,p.1209.
    5. Gareth Locksley,p.19.
    6. Ibid.p.27.
    7. Nicholas Jequier,p.212.
    8. Gareth Locksley,p.39.
    9. The Economist,Vol.216,31st July 1965,p.461; Vol.218,26th February 1966,p.824;Vol.237,10th October 1970,p.84.
    10. Figures compiled from Electronics(London, HMSO,1970,1971,1972).
    11. Gareth Locksley,pp.73-83,106.
    12. Ibid.,p.108.
    13. Collated from figures given by the Board of Trade: Official Report,Vol.747,col.179-180.
    14. Gareth Locksley,pp.107-8.
    15. Computing,18th October 1980.
    16. Computer Weekly,18th September 1980.
    17. Financial Times,8th June 1982.
    18. The Times,4th May,11th May 1976.
    19. Computer Services Association,Report on the UK Computing Services Industry (London,Computer Services Association,1976),pp.3/5 - 3/7;Information Technology Sector Working Party,Policy for the UK Information Technology Sector,(London,NEDO,1982), pp.14-16.
    20. Financial Times,17th December 1981.

MICROELECTRONICS
    1. UTM,International Manufacturing and the Role of Technology(Tunbridge Wells,UTM,1977),p.101.
    2. Electronics,Vol.51,5thJanuary 1978,pp.144-5.
    3. The Economist,Vol.218,19th March 1966,p.1147, Vol.224,9th September 1967,pp.898-9.
    4. The Economist,Vol.265,16th April 1977, pp.101-2.
    5. US International Trade Commission,Competitive Factors Influencing World Trade in Integrated Circuits(Washington D.C.,US Government Printing

INTERNATIONAL & DOMESTIC MARKETS

Office,1979),p.14.
6. Semiconductor Industry Association, The International Microelectronic Challenge. The American Response by the Industry, the Universities and the Government(Washington D.C. Semiconductor Industry Association,1980),p.19.
7. Financial Times,2nd March 1982.
8. Ibid.,28th July 1982.
9. Data from Standard & Poor, quoted in Electronics,Vol.50,17th January 1980,p.83.
10. BIPE study,October 1970 quoted in evidence: Select Committee on Science and Technology,Fourth Report: Prospects for the UK Computer Industry in the 1970s,Vol.III,p.33.
11. Financial Times,8th September 1981.
12. Gareth Locksley,pp.25-6
13. Computer Weekly,12th February 1982.
14. US Trade Commission,pp.36-40.
15. The Economist,Vol.224,2nd September 1967, p.807.
16. Ibid.,Vol.217,27th November 1965,p.979; Vol.221,15th October 1966,p.291.
17. Calculated from Electronics, various years.
18. The Economist,Vol.269,14th October 1978,p.132.
19. Trade and Industry,14th September 1979,p.546.

Chapter Four

TELECOMMUNICATIONS

4.1 INTRODUCTION

Until recently, strategy towards the telecommunications market on the part of Western industrialised nations has been remarkably similar. The importance of communications to defence requirements provided the rationale for a strategy, which limited imports and gave public preference to domestic manufacturers. The need for telecommunications equipment to be compatible with the existing network has brought about an interdependence between manufacturers, PTT's and governments, comparable probably only to the defence industry itself. Britain is not alone in this respect. For instance, John Zysman comments on the dependence of French electronics manufacturers upon government.[1] But Britain stands alone in one respect. The continuing tension between liberal market ideology, central government control and the exigencies of the technology have led to fluctuations in British government strategy towards the market. Strategy has varied from promoting corporatism to promoting competition.

Because of the particular features of the market, the telecommunications manufacturing industry in Britain has been dependent upon PTT ordering for its home market. It has also been dependent upon Post Office (later British Telecom) approval for any equipment to be attached to the telephone network. The industry has been affected, therefore, by the capital investment and technological decisions taken by the PTT. In turn, those technological decisions, themselves, have been dependent upon the Government's relations with the PTT. They have depended upon the amount of capital investment allowed by governments, and upon other political demands made of the organisation. Because equipment has a life of twenty to thirty years,

109

decisions, made in the 1950s, still affected the telecommunications industry and the national telecommunications network in the late 1970s. To appreciate the impact of government intervention, it is therefore necessary to go back beyond 1964, and to consider the technological and financial decisions made in the post war years. Similarly, because the organisation of the Post Office as an institution has had an impact, both upon its financial resources and its relationship with manufacturing suppliers, the present organisation of British Telecom needs to be looked at in historical perspective.

Throughout the period, ideological predispositions on the value of public control, or competition, have affected both the structure of the Post Office and the legal definition of its monopoly. Conservative governments have tended to favour increased competition between the manufacturing suppliers to the Post Office, and to favour a limited monopoly on telephone equipment. On the other hand, Labour Governments have favoured a monopoly, which would include equipment not yet invented, but have espoused the Conservative doctrine of 'more competition' to cajole reluctant manufacturers to increased performance.

Without exception, all governments, of whatever ideological predisposition, have intervened in almost every facet of the telecommunications market. There seems hardly an element of the telecommunications network, administration or manufacture which has not become their concern. From the structure of the manufacturing industry, to general investment control, to forward planning, to decisions on technology itself, all have been the subject of political debate and political intervention.

Reasons for that political awareness can be found, from the 1950s onwards, in the embarrassment of a telephone service which failed to meet the expectations of its users. This embarrassment was compounded, from the 1960s, by the realisation that exports in a crucial, advanced technology, industry had diminished, and could not be revived without a new public telephone exchange. Although developed for the home market, this exchange had to be technologically competitive with products from foreign manufacturers. Crucially, this realisation led to government pressure on the Post Office, both to act outside its legal responsibilities, and to take on board its responsibility for the development of a technology which could be exported.

The organisational structure of the Post

Office, its legal responsibilities, its financial control by government, its relationship with its manufacturing suppliers, and its technological decisions, are all interdependent. But, in attempting to clarify political intervention, this chapter is organised around three main areas. First it discusses governmental decisions and political debate on the structure and organisation of the Post Office. Then it focusses on intervention in the cartel arrangement between suppliers and Post Office.Finally it looks at the politics of technological decisions taken by the Post Office,and at intervention in the industry's structure.

4.2 POST OFFICE ORGANISATION AND ITS MONOPOLY: TOWARDS A FREE MARKET.

The way in which the Post Office has been organised over this century has had a crucial impact on the funding of telecommunications, and on the manufacturing industry. In addition, its monopoly has affected both the structure of the domestic market, and the technology developed. This section, therefore,reviews developments in both organisation and monopoly.
  Already possessing a monopoly of postal mail, in 1911 the Post Office acquired a monopoly of telegraph and telephone facilities. In contrast to other public utilities, it was organised as a government department,staffed by civil servants and subject to absolute Treasury control,until the late 1930s. All expenditure had to be approved by the Treasury. Appropriation Accounts had to be submitted to and voted on by Parliament each year. Bureaucratic procedure dominated the organisation, with decisions on minor investment passing upwards to the Postmaster General, a political appointment.
  During these inter-war years, the problems caused by the Post Office' status as a civil service department, and its lack of financial autonomy, became increasingly obvious. They were debated in Parliament during the 1920s and 1930s,but the consensus remained that both posts and telecommunications were public services, and,as such,should be publicly accountable through a Minister.[2]
  The issue revolved around the capital requirements of the telephone service. The manual exchanges of the late nineteenth and early twentieth century were slow and high in labour costs. But, to replace them with the automated exchange equipment of the Strowger variety, and to expand the network,

demanded heavy capital investment. Since all surpluses passed to the Treasury, and investment had to be contained within the annual Appropriation Vote, the possibility of long-term planning on the part of the telephone administration in the Post Office was minimal.

The first external inquiry into the Post Office during this pre-war period suggested that, to allow more financial freedom, the Post Office should be allowed to pay over a fixed sum of £10 million plus 50% of any surplus each year to the Treasury. The recommendation was put into practice. But, the new arrangements had only just come into effect, when war broke out. The Treasury resumed full control again.[3]

In common with other sectors of manufacturing industry, during the war, telecommunications companies diverted production to defence needs.[4] Installations were rationed both during and after the war and the Post Office was directed to fulfill only essential demand.[5] Partly as a result, and partly due to unsatisfied demand for telephones left over from pre-war days, by 1950, over half a million people were waiting for a telephone connection. At the same time, one in three exchanges were working to full capacity.

The Post Office was already caught in a dilemma which remained with it for thirty years - how to plan long-term capital investment when that investment was subject to Treasury control and used as a tool for manipulation of macroeconomic demand. The problem was particularly acute during the period from 1951 to 1964, when the stop-go economic policies of the Conservative government precluded high capital investment. In fact, during this period Post Office capital expenditure, the majority of it on the telecommunications network, fell by 7%.[6]

To meet the explosion in residential demand for telephone connections, political pressure came from Parliament for an increased, more efficient, expanded network. A feature of the 1950s and 1960s was the regular spate of weekly questions in Parliament to the Postmaster General on when telephones would be provided in 'X' town. Yet residential connections were uneconomic. Residential consumers under-used the telephone. They made, on average, one local call per day and one trunk call per week. As a result, although residential connections consumed large amounts of capital, they generated little revenue. Political pressure was therefore at variance with commercial sense.[7]

By the end of the 1950s, although the waiting

TELECOMMUNICATIONS

list had been somewht reduced, antiquated equipment, some of it more than thirty years old, was still in use. Maintenance costs were high and breakdowns common. The, then, Director General of the Post Office, later commented:

> enough money was certainly not put into the system, in retrospect to maintain the standard of quality, or indeed to replace the equipment which was getting to the end of its useful life.[8]

For the manufacturers, whilst the Post Office's forward planning took place on an annual basis, it was impossible to plan production of equipment. Dependent on Post Office buying for their home market in public exchange equipment, the manufacturers annually anticipated cuts in Post Office investment to meet other economic demands. With manufacturing facilities taking from twenty to forty-five months to establish in full production, the manufacturers lived in a constantly uncertain environment. As a previous assistant to the Postmaster General commented in 1961:

> beginning with a new budget every year it (the Post Office) had to indulge in a bit of guesswork, rather than calculation, and since the guesswork depended partly on Cabinet policy, and partly on complacency of the House of Commons, it was more than ever hazardous.[9]

In 1955, with a Conservative government moving towards the concept of 'planning ' of the economy, and after considerable pressure from the Post Office, the previous post-war arrangements on Post Office finance were re-introduced. Although the Post Office had still to present Appropriation Accounts to Parliament, the new arrangment allowed it to keep surpluses of about £5 million.[10] The then Postmaster General, Charles Hill, considered that he had won a 'resounding victory' over the Treasury.[11] But the manufacturers were not so impressed. They pointed to the first year of the new financial arrangements, in which the government cut £5.5 million from Post office investment.

By 1959, pressure for expansion of the telephone service had become sufficiently acute politically for the Conservative Party to include an item in its manifesto, promising the Post Office more investment autonomy. Following the Conservative victory in 1959, a a White Paper on Nationalised

113

Industries grouped the Post office with other utilities to be treated as a commercial undertaking rather than as a public service.[12]

The Post Office Act of 1961 gave the Post Office a degree of financial independence. The Act established a Post Office fund into which the service paid its revenue and out of which it made payments. It substituted an Annual Report to Parliament for the Appropriation Accounts. Treasury control became limited to pay, grading and conditions of staff, foreign exchange controls and investment control.

In fact the Act made little difference to investment, which was still under Treasury control. Although the Act allowed the Post Office to borrow £ 80 million pounds in the first instance, new borrowing needed both Treasury and Parliamentary approval. Neither was the Post Office free to set its own tariffs. These had to be laid before Parliament, which could veto them.

There were two side effects from the legislation. For the first time in 1962, with the publication of annual accounts, both politicians and public were able to differentiate between the loss-making postal side and the profit making potential of telecommunications. Secondly, the Annual Accounts were subject to the scrutiny of the Auditor General, and to that of the Public Accounts Committee. This new public scrutiny opened up to political debate the relationship between the Post Office and its suppliers.

With release from the very detailed control of the Treasury, the Post Office telecommunications administration decided to devote long-term investment to the upgrading of the existing network and, in particular, to the automisation of trunk exchanges. At the same time a down grading took place in the importance attached to the extension of the network to new residential subscribers.[13] Economically the policy may have been necessary given the restrictions on investment imposed by the Chancellor, Lord Thorneycroft, in 1962 and 1963.

The internal generation of revenue became of increased importance in 1963, with the publication of a White Paper by the Conservative Government setting a target of 8% return on capital invested for the Post Office. The 8% referred to overall performance for the two sides of the Post Office taken together. It was telecommunications profit which balanced the less profitable postal side and allowed the Post Office to meet its financial target in subsequent years.[14] The figure of 8% seems to

have been arrived at by the Treasury, by 'rule of thumb' and the Treasury later admitted that it had given no thought to what the Post Office needed in terms of capital investment, or what returns were needed to finance expansion.[15]

The early 1960s witnessed a sudden burgeoning of informed comment on the Post Office's internal organisation. The establishment of national planning machinery - the NEDC - in 1961, gave a public forum for what had previously been internal debate. The Post Office Engineering Union submitted a memorandum to the NEDC pointing out the failures of the reforms of 1961. Frustration at the capital restrictions imposed by Lord Thorneycroft in 1962 and 1963, was exacerbated by the failure of the Post Office management, either to plan in a long-term manner, or to give priority to the expansion of the telephone network.[16]

From 1961, the publication of figures showing the disparity of performance between telecommunications and the postal service, coupled with the necessity of meeting a target return on capital, almost inevitably led to a division of opinion between the Post Office Engineering Union and the Union of Post Office Workers. The POEU took the stance that the two sides of the organisation should be split, a view later endorsed by the management of the Post Office. On the other hand, fearing redundancies if made to go it alone, the UPOW maintained that the two services should remain under the same umbrella.[17]

The expansion of telecommunications fitted in neatly with the overall philosophy of the 1964 Labour Government, with its stress on the 'white heat of technological revolution'. At its first Annual Conference after the change of government, the POEU took the opportunity to lobby Tony Benn, the new Postmaster General, on the need to expand the network, and on the necessity of public corporation status for the Post Office. It is obvious that Tony Benn paid close attention to their demands for an expansionist approach to telecommunications.[18]

The new philosophy, embodied in the National Plan of 1965, envisaged a major increase in telecommunications investment. Overall the Plan foresaw an increase in growth in the national economy of 25%. It forecast growth in telecommunications at an annual rate of 11% with investment rising from £168 million in 1964 to £336 million pounds in 1970.[19] Tony Benn claimed to be the first postmaster General to have enough capital at his disposal.[20] There was

little doubt of the priority accorded telecommunications by the Labour government. In 1965 its capital investment escaped unscathed from the round of public expenditure cuts brought about by the balance of payments problem.

However, by this time, the provision of capital investment was not a complete palliative to the Post Office's problems. In addition to the half million people on the waiting list at the end of the 1950s, from the early 1960s, the Post Office was faced with demand for residential connections then growing at 12% per year.[21] The Post Office continually underestimated demand in its market forecasts. Yet, even had it been accurate, its relationship with its suppliers was such that it would have had difficulty in obtaining the equipment necessary to meet the demand. Once the Labour Government had released capital investment, the supply side of the equation became crucial.

Inured as they were to investment plans being cut by governments for macro-economic reasons, telecommunications manufacturers were reluctant to suddenly increase production. Speaking to the Telephone Engineering Manufacturers Association, Tony Benn underlined the problem:

> ...you, who are manufacturers and would gladly have expanded your production years ago if the orders had been forthcoming, now find immense demands made upon you at relatively short notice.. To meet the growth the Post Office needs over the next four years more than 350,000,000 pounds worth of exchange equipment. This was three times what the Post Office bought in the previous four years.. and you as manufacturers have undertaken to more than double your current output of Strowger equipment within four years.[22]

Despite these undertakings by the manufacturers, it was clear that there would be a shortfall in the supply of public exchanges for the following two or three years.

With the growth in public dissatisfaction with the telephone service, the House of Commons Select Committee on Nationalised Industries altered its terms of reference in 1965 to enable it to investigate the Post Office. In the same year, following warnings in the National Plan that the target growth for telecommunications could not be met without improvement in the relationship between suppliers and the Post Office, and without better

long-term planning strategies, the Government established an Economic Development Committee, to bring together government, manufacturers and trade unions to 'plan' telecommunications.[23]

The 1966 General Election intervened in the midst of this investigative activity. Tony Benn took over from Frank Cousins at the Ministry of Technology, and Edward Short became Postmaster General. By this time, for a Labour Government committed to new technology, the telephone service had become an acute political embarrassment. Both MPs and Ministers were kept busy answering correspondence complaining about the waiting time for telephones. Possibly in anticipation of the Select Committee Report, possibly in response to the report of a management consultancy, called in by Tony Benn, possibly in response to pressure from the POEU, or possibily because organisational reform was the only feasible action open to the government in a situation where it had no control over the supply of telephones, in 1966, Edward Short announced that the Post Office was to become a public corporation.[24] At the same time the Post Office announced plans for accelerated expansion of the network. Manufacturers were called upon once more to revise output upward.

Within a year of the announcement of Public Corporation status, the Labour Government cut £140 million from telecommunications capital investment. Once more, therefore, Post Office planning was subject to use as a macro-economic tool. At the same time the Government introduced a much increased deposit for the installation of residential telephones.[25] The increase made economic sense, in so far as residential connections took a large amount of capital investment, but, it can be seen as a political move to dampen down the embarrassingly high demand for residential telephones. In fact demand slowed down for only a short period and by 1972 the waiting list for telephones stood over 200,000.

Because of pressure on legislative time, the Post Office Bill did not come before Parliament until 1968. The Bill passed in 1969 amid considerable inter-party agreement and congratulation, Disagreement arose only over three items in the Bill. The Conservatives wished to see telecommunications and posts split into two corporations, wanted the Post Office to receive only a monopoly limited to the existing services it provided, and wished to see that monopoly legally vested in the Minister rather than the Corporation.[26]

Combatting this criticism the government produced weak arguments. It pointed to the savings accrued from joint research and development and to the recommendation of the Select Committee that there should be one corporation.[27] Probably the government's reason for pushing ahead with one rather than two corporations was more closely related to the strength of the Union of Post Office Workers within the Labour Party. That Union had 200,000 members, in contrast to the POEU's membership of 50,000 members. Their size reflected their respective strength in the policy-making of the Labour Party, the leader of the UPOW also being a member of the Party's National Executive.

Although it became clear during the Bill's passage that some Conservative members wished to see the Post Office split, so that the profit making telecommunications service could be sold to private industry, the major ideological clash between the two parties arose over the provisions of the Post Office monopoly. The Conservatives argued that the legal monopoly granted to the Post Office should be limited either by a definition of 'telecommunications', which excluded any but existing services, or should be limited by vesting the monopoly in the Minister rather than in the Corporation. They claimed that this would allow greater flexibility in the future, when new uses for the telephone network might develop.

In contrast, the Labour Government took the view that the monopoly should be as all embracing as possible.[28] Government also contended that to place the legal responsibility for the monopoly in the hands of the Minister, would allow him, or her, to break it without recourse to Parliament.[29] Throughout the debate there ran an undercurrent of concern that a future Conservative Government might decide to 'privatise' the telecommunications functions of the Post Office. Hence, the 1969 Act gave the new Corporation:

> the exclusive privilege of running systems for the conveyance through the agency of electric, magnetic, electro-magnetic, electro-chemical or electro-mechanical energy of
> a) speech, music and other sounds
> b) visual images
> c) signals serving for the impartation (whether as between persons and persons, things and things or persons and things) of any matter otherwise than in the form of sound or visual images and

d) signals serving for the actuation of control of machinery or apparatus.[30]

The Post Office retained a monopoly of transmission, except for those instances where the transmission occurred solely on an individual's or company's premises or between offices of the same company. Therefore, for instance, no company could lease time on its private communications network to other companies. No company which hired lines from the Post Office could sub-let those lines, possibly at a cheaper rate than that charged on the public network. The Post Office also retained the right to manufacture, install and maintain 'anything required for the purposes of its business'.[31]

It, therefore, retained a monopoly on the maintenance of private telephone exchanges attached to the public network, thereby protecting the jobs of Post Office engineers. The provisions of the Act meant that the Post Office could specify what kinds of exchanges (PABx) could be installed, if they were to be attached to the network, and in the case of data transmission, what kind of modems could be installed. The Act, therefore, vested in the Post Office an almost total monopoly of both transmission and equipment specification.

The Post Office Bill had been on the statute book for only six months when the Conservative Government of Edward Heath was elected. Ideologically committed to the disengagement of government from industry, and in favour of 'competition', it seemed at first that the new government might breach the Post Office monopoly and might allow the maintenance of equipment by private companies. The NEDC Committee was abandoned. But the new Minister of Posts and Telecommunications (the new title of the Postmaster General), Christopher Chataway, remained unconvinced and eventually it was decided that the the monopoly should remain unchanged.[32]

However, within a year of taking office, as part of its anti-inflationary strategy, the new government insisted that the Post Office should not raise its tariffs. Yet, as the Post Office commented in its Annual Report of 1970:

> average return on the rental of a telephone put into an office or a home was less than the rate of interest on money borrowed for capital investment.[33]

Further intervention in Post Office affairs came with the sacking of Lord Hall, the Chairman of the

Post Office. Such a dismissal was unprecedented.[34] The very possibility of public dismissal could not have eased the relationship between the Chairmen of the nationalised industries and the government.

In fact the early 1970s witnessed a gradual deterioration in the relations between nationalised industries and government, culminating in a report from the National Economic Development Office. Commenting specifically on Post Office relations with the Department of Industry, NEDO said that, there was:

> no clear and agreed understanding ..about those matters in which it may be appropriate for Government to intervene and those executive managerial matters in which it is not appropriate.[35]

NEDO also commented that:

> The Post Office Act gave no clear and specific guidance on the definition and extent of public service obligations. The board sets its own business aims and objectives. Ministers and civil servants in the Department of Industry have not wished to contribute to this process but are not necessarily in agreement with the consequences of the board's interpretation of its role.[36]

This rather oblique statement referred to a row which had developed between the Post Office and its suppliers in 1974. The row concerned the technology which the Post Office was prepared to buy during the 1970s, and whether that technology held out any prospect of being competitive overseas. The legal duties imposed on the Post Office by the 1969 Act were to:

> exercise its powers as to meet the social, industrial and commercial needs of the British Islands..and,in particular, to provide throughout those Islands... such telephone services as satisfy all reasonable demands for them.[37]

The duties did not mention responsibility for exports. Yet, because the Post Office was the monopoly buyer on the home market, the technology demanded by the Post Office affected the equipment available for export.

There seems to have been some concern at the Department of Industry about the Post Office's

commitment to exports. Reflecting this uncertainty, a Review Committee was set up under the Chairmanship of Professor Charles Carter, an economist, to consider whether any changes in the organisation and its use of assets would enable the Post Office to function better.[38]

In the time between the establishment of the Post Office Corporation and the Carter Committee's deliberations, within the organisation itself, the two services of telecommunications and mail had become increasingly separated. By 1975, both Post Office management and engineering opinion had crystallised into a desire to see the two services split into two corporations. Only the UPOW held out against the idea. The Carter Committee recommended that the Post Office be split into two corporations, but, possibly reacting once more to UPOW pressure, the Labour Government did nothing.[39]

The Committee also recommended the ending of the Post Office monopoly on the maintenance and installation of apparatus to be attached to the telephone lines. After a visit to the USA where, from 1969, American subscribers had had the option of connecting their own apparatus to the network, the Committee were of the opinion that no damage to the American network had occurred. They recommended an experimental trial of such limited liberalisation.[40]

In this they were also acceding to the views of the British telecommunications manufacturers. The manufacturers claimed that they operated at a disadvantage to foreign competitors, because the Post Office insisted on specifications for equipment of 'battleship' standards. These specifications made equipment costly and uncompetitive in export markets.[41]

The manufacturers' position had become particularly acute after 1969. Until that date, the two British manufacturers, and STC, operated in a market in which they were the only suppliers of Post Office approved private exchanges of over 20 lines. From 1969 the picture changed. In that year the Post Office allowed the Greater London Council to install an exchange manufactured by Ericsson of Sweden. The manufacturers cried 'foul'.[42] They argued that Ericsson's order had been £70,000 cheaper than that of Reliance (a GEC subsidiary), because Reliance had designed to Post Office specifications.[43] The firms realised that once the principle of allowing private maintenance on one exchange had been admitted, it would be difficult for the Post office to refuse other installations. In this they were

correct. By 1974 Ericsson had 20% of the market in private exchanges.[44]

The entry of Ericsson into the British market was followed by IBM. At first, when IBM announced that it had a new private exchange geared to both 'voice and data switching', the reaction of British telephone men was that no computer company could design equipment to meet the cost and quality specifications necessary for telecommunications equipment.[45] But IBM's product was technologically ahead of anything British manufacturers could offer and had considerable customer appeal. By mid 1969, the Post Office was allowing IBM to test one of its switchboards in Britain at its Havant headquarters. Gently IBM eased into the market and by 1981 had become the market leader in British private exchanges.[46]

Therefore, despite its monopoly position, the Post Office had proved pliable under pressure from customers wishing to install advanced equipment. Given the de facto entry of foreign firms, and the liberalisation of the monopoly in their favour, it is hardly surprising that the British manufacturers campaigned for legal liberalisation, which would free them from Post Office specifications.

In 1979 the arguments over the telecommunications monopoly surfaced publicly, once more. The Conservative manifesto committed the party to the sale of profitable parts of the nationalised sector. It seemed that telecommunications might be a prime target for such 'hiving off'. However the Telecommunications Bill did not include provision for the sale of the telecommunications network to private hands, but rather put into effect some of the proposals first debated during the passage of the 1969 Act. The Bill split the Post Office into two corporations, British Telecom becoming responsible for telecommunications. The Act also broke the monopoly on equipment to be connected to the network and proposed the ending of the Post Office monopoly on the maintenance of equipment. In addition, following a report on the likely effects of ending its monopoly over transmission and value-added services, by an economist, Professor Beesley, these were also liberalised.[47]

Just as, in 1969, the Conservatives argued that the legal monopoly should be vested in the Minister, so the 1980 Bill gave that power to him. The Minister was enabled to decide whether the British Telecom authority should be allowed to provide any particular service, or whether it should be provided by private industry.[48]

TELECOMMUNICATIONS

In 1981 the Minister used his power to issue licences for transmission of telephone and data to a consortium, Mercury,led by Cable and Wireless, which intended to transmit via satellite. British Telecom were however able to delay agreement on the land lines to be used by the new consortium for long enough to enable it to also reach agreement on satellite transmission with Satellite Business Systems in the USA. The agreement effectively contained the new opposition to the British, less profitable market,and gave IBM an opening into Europe. It is noticeable that IBM was active in lobbying Parliament for the liberalisation of tele-communications, through a new pressure group,the Telecommunications Council.[49]

The new legislation gave the British manufacturers a breathing space of two years in which to revamp their products to meet the competition of a free market. Under the legislation, any equipment, which meets certain safety standards, will be allowed to be attached to the network. In the interim period, British Telecom was initially given the responsibility for testing equipment to safety standards. But, possibly because it used the mechanism to delay approval,this function is being taken over by the British Standards Institute. Meanwhile, British Telecom has become more like a private company with commercially-orientated product divisions.It has begun to commercialise its R&D, to manufacture up-graded products to meet the expected demand,and has formed a new subsidiary, British Telecom Enterprises to market them.[50]

Government intervention has not ended at that point. With concern for the public sector borrowing requirement predominating in macro-economic policy, British Telecom 's borrowing was curtailed in 1980. Eventually, the need for massive investment funds has led to the proposal to privatise the organisation,announced in 1982 and scheduled for 1984.[51]

4.3 CARTEL VERSUS COMPETITION   THE RELATIONSHIP BETWEEN THE POST OFFICE AND ITS SUPPLIERS

Historically the relationship between telecommunic-ations manufacturers and the Post Office has been a close one. The formal organisation of their symbiotic relations began in the 1920s and contin-ued to the 1960s when it was broken by government intervention. Their closeness was fostered by the

particular necessity for all new equipment to be compatible with that already installed. Thus standardisation became of paramount importance.

Prior to 1924, the manufacturers competed in design of equipment. Then, deciding that lack of standardisation involved wastage of resources, in 1924, the Post Office signed seven bulk supply agreements. These agreements covered almost all the equipment used in the telephone service.[52] From the manufacturers' point of view, the agreements allowed planning on the basis of a steady share of the Post Office's purchase of equipment. The agreements ran for five years at a time, with prices renogiatable after two and a half years. Under the original agreement, the Post Office was disbarred from purchasing equipment from any manufacturer who was not a party to the agreement.[53] In effect the agreements meant that no new manufacturer could enter into competition for Post Office orders.

In the switching field of telecommunications, that is in the field of telephone exchanges, once the Strowger system had been adopted as standard in 1920, the Post Office licensed five manufacturers for its production. The five were the General Electric Company (GEC), Associated Electrical Industries (AEI), Automatic Telephone Engineering (ATE), Ericssons (no relation of the present Ericsson (Swedish) company) and Standard Telephone Cables. The five formed what came to be known as 'The Ring'.[54]

The manufacturers formed a Bulk Contracts Committee serviced by a permanent secretariat responsible for sharing out work on an equal value basis.[55] The Post office in conjunction with the manufacturers formed a Joint Technical Committee (BTTC) to standardise the introduction of new parts. No equipment other than that approved by the committee might be connected to the network.[56]

The procedure for the introduction of new technology was therefore cumbersome. Any small change had to be agreed by all the manufacturers. The Post Office was to acknowledge later that, although the system had its advantages in standardisation and simplified maintenance, it also 'hindered designers taking full advantage of technological advance'.[57] Because the Post Office set the price of standard components at the level of cost plus a fixed percentage, and since costs included R&D, virtually 100% of the companies' research costs were covered.[58]

As the need for the Post Office to have assured supplies of equipment diminished, so the bulk supply

agreements ended.[59] That for bulk transmission equipment ended in 1946, that for telephone cords in 1952, that for batteries in 1956 and that for cable and loading coils in 1963.[60] Especially prior to the publication of Annual Accounts, the system left room for clientelism. Several of the agreements terminated following public discussion and controversy, the most contentious being the Apparatus Agreement. The Post Office tried unsuccessfully to end this agreement in 1964, when it discovered that it could purchase supplies from outside the agreement at 25% lower cost. The manufacturers refused on the grounds that 'termination was not in the best interests of the development of telecommunications equipment or of close association on research and development'. The row simmered on with the POEU entering the fray, claiming that the agreements had not led to increased exports from a stable home market.[61] In 1964, Tony Benn pledged himself to do away with the agreement on apparatus, but held his fire on that for exchange equipment.[62]

The real bone of contention between manufacturers and government were the delays on equipment delivery. The freeing of Post Office finance from the restrictions of votes in the House of Commons, coupled with increased demand from the Post Office, had left the manufacturers floundering to satisfy the home market. The expansionist policy undertaken by the Labour Government exacerbated the problem because the demand from the Post Office was for Strowger equipment. The manufacturers knew that Strowger would be obsolescent within ten years. They were being called on to make massive capital investment in capacity, which they knew would be closed in a relatively short period.

The Chairman of TEMA explained the problem to the Select Committee on Nationalised Industries. First his members had had to satisfy themselves that the orders would be forthcoming over a sufficient number of years, and that the Treasury intended to back the expansion. Understandably, after years of one year financing and cutbacks in investment, in the 'national interest', manufacturers were cynical about Post Office forward estimates of investment. Then, having satisfied themselves on this score, manufacturers had to negotiate the phasing of demand with the Post Office. The original plan, which was unacceptable to the manufacturers, involved a very high expansion in the first few years and then a very sharp cutback. The manufacturers insisted on slower expansion and contraction. Once this had been

agreed, the manufacturers began to establish new plant in areas of high unemployment - Northern Ireland, the North East and Scotland The whole process took time.[63]

Meanwhile, the increased demand for residential telephones continued to place the Labour Government in an embarrassing position. Edward Short plaintively moaned at the manufacturers:

> I know it is a Minister's function to take the blame, but every day I spend alot of my time writing forty or fifty or sixty letters to people up and down the country telling them that we are sorry that the telephone we promised them in 1968 will not come along till 1969 now... I get the blame, but you lot are the culprits and you really must do something about this ... about these delivery dates.[64]

In the same speech Short announced that the first task of the newly appointed Industrial Reorganisation Corporation would be to carry out a survey of the industry, in order to help improve its competence, productivity and organisation. From later remarks it seems that the two major reasons for the IRC intervention were the lack of equipment supply, coupled with political fears about the viability of a number of small manufacturers in the face of European competition.[65] Like his Conservative predecessor, Short was concerned at the lack of exports of telecommunications equipment:

> Your European competitors will want to do business ....and expect to do business with the British Post Office..Whether or not they succeed will depend entirely on you...I hope that your relations with the Post Office... our procurement policy, will help you to exploit the huge market of a United Europe.[66]

Like his predecessors, Short wielded the stick of possible competition in the home market against the reluctant suppliers.

But the dilemma for the manufacturers was not solved by the cajoling of successive Postmaster Generals, nor could it be solved by competition in the home market. The problem arose from the technological requirements of the Post Office, which demanded Strowger equipment already obsolete in export markets. The Brookings Institution, reviewing Britain's economic prospects, clarified the manufacturers dilemma. It said, it would be:

a serious mistake to induce a major enlargement of domestic capacity to produce conventional equipment, since net yearly demand for this equipment will probably decline later in the 1970's. If suppliers expand optimally for their own long-run growth, they would fall short of Post Office requirements for the next ten years. If, instead they expand rapidly enough to meet Post Office needs, they will forego chances to develop more advanced products as well as create seriously excessive capacity in narrow and obsolescent production lines.[67]

Brookings found the dilemma of lack of supply further intensified by the Post Office's determination that its exchange equipment design was so distinctive that it had to be supplied from domestic manufacturers and could not be bought from abroad. The Post Office, therefore, tied itself to 'suppliers who prefer to minimise overexpansion in just those lines it requires'.[68] Brookings suggested that the way out of the dilemma was for the Post Office to buy equipment on the international market, which would then free domestic manufacturers to reinforce efforts to expand exports. It also suggested that the Post Office could make the 'system design more competitive internationally', could expand its research activities, and should consider ' acquiring one of the stronger supplying firms for production and experimentation'.[69]

The Post Office rejected all these options, preferring instead to limit procurement to domestic manufacturers. As Sir John Hall, the Director General of the Post Office, explained to the Public Accounts Committee, the problem was to find the incentive for the British suppliers to provide the equipment.[70] That incentive might have been large short-term profits in the knowledge that capital costs would have to be written off over a short period of time. However, the Post Office rejected that option also.

The row which had been simmering since 1963 over the pricing of the bulk purchasing agreements came to a head in 1967. The Post Office demanded a reduction in prices for the second half of the agreements 1965-8. It argued that manufacturing output had increased threefold in the period and that therefore production runs allowed savings on overheads. The manufacturers disagreed. Since one of the manufacturers had changed its method of costing,

so that comparable data with preceding periods was not available, the Post Office found itself arguing the toss on limited costing data.[71] Nor was the Post Office's hand strengthened by the fact that it could not apply to any firm outside the ring for the manufacture and installation of complete systems. No firm outside the ring had that capability. The Public Accounts Committee reported that there should be 'more competitive arrangements'.[72]

To sum up, for the Post Office, the problem was that its own specifications and concern for standardisation limited its suppliers, yet public control of its finance precluded it from paying enough to make it worthwhile for them to supply the equipment. For the manufacturers, the problem was to balance supply of the obsolescent equipment, demanded by the Post Office, with the development of more technologically feasible equipment for future markets in Britain and overseas. For the government, the problem of unfulfilled demand in telephones provided a political embarrassment, whilst the decline in exports caused economic concern. Since the Post Office was unwilling to expand its own manufacturing facilities to provide the equipment needed, the only mechanism left for the government to use in order to increase supply was the introduction of more competition in the home market. But this neither met the problem, nor could be used as a whip to cajole the manufacturers until the Bulk Supply Agreements ended their contractual term in 1968. The situation illustrates nicely the problems which arise when governments expect industry to pursue the 'national interest' at the expense of its own.

The reader may ask why the Labour Government did not nationalise one of the manufacturers. The possibility of a public take-over of one (probably STC) was considered by the Post Office and was raised by the Public Accounts Committee. It is probable that the answer lies in the lack of ideological commitment to nationalisation in the Labour Government of 1964-70, its emphasis being on socialism through economic growth and technological advance. It placed heavy emphasis on the role of the IRC in reshaping British industry, and until the 1970 Industry Act relied on the IRC for its direct intervention in industry. In the first year of its life, 1966-7, when it produced its survey of telecommunications industry, the IRC was concerned to 'work with' industry.[73] Although its report was never published, from later comments, it seems that the IRC favoured competitive tendering for public

sector contracts.[74] Perhaps, not surprisingly, there are hints that the IRC found the manufacturers less than helpful.
  The two bulk supply agreements were not renewed Instead, in 1969, the Government shifted to inducing competition between manufacturers. The Post Office, now a public corporation, stood to 'gain greater efficiency, better prices and better performance' according to its new Chairman. Yet, there was some ambivalence over the new arrangement.

> Demands of the 70's will only be met by some form of closer tie which the new status of the Post Office and its powers under the 1969 Act would help make possible,[75]

said the Chairman.
  As the Post Office relinquished its cartel arrangement with the manufacturers, so it also relinquished its power to place research with a particular manufacturer. The result was several new technologically different systems all emerged from the manufacturers concurrently. The integration of these new systems into the network gave rise to 'complicated design problems and consequent delays in production'.[76] Rather than easing the problems of supply, the new competitive era compounded them. Each new technology, or redesigned part of previously standard equipment, demanded increased training of Post Office Engineers on maintenance and increased documentation. Until 1970 no costing of the hidden consequences of competition had been done.
  To meet the problem, a new form of manufacturer/ Post Office co-operation emerged. Called the Advisory Group on Telecommunications Systems Definitions (AGTSD), the Post Office and representatives of the three manufacturers sat on the Committee, which was specifically responsible for advising the Post Office on 'definitions and specifications for the telecommunications system and subsystems of the mid 1970s and beyond'. For its first task it undertook the analysis of the costs of introducing new designs to the network.[77]
  The group analysed the likely costs to the Post Office following from the introduction of specific parts, sub-systems or whole systems in the network. They found that even a minor variation on one form of exchange, with orders of £10 million would give rise to excess costs to the Post Office in documentation, training, planning, procurement and maintenance, of between £1.3 million and £6 million.

They concluded that excess costs incurred by the introduction of new systems, or major variants of existing systems, were 'unlikely to be offset unless the new design is purchased in some large quantity'. For instance, £100 million of a major variant of an exchange would be needed to offset excess costs, even if the new system showed a 10% advantage in price, operating savings or added capability.[78]

Thus the stage was set for an end to the competitive technology era of the manufacturers/Post Office relationship. The need to integrate new technology into the existing network, and the exigencies of its maintenance, demanded a closer relationship between manufacturer and buyer. A way was found, therefore, for manufacturers and Post Office once more to co-operate on R&D of a new system. But that co-operation came about only after extensive wrangling on the part of the manufacturers, each of whom wanted to see its own system, developed during the competitive era, adopted as the standard system with which to replace Strowger. Technology and politics interwove in a complicated argument which reached to Cabinet level.

4.4 POLITICS AND PUBLIC EXCHANGE TECHNOLOGY

At this point it is necessary to go back in time to explain how it came about that the Post Office was still ordering equipment in the 1960s and 1970s, which was technologically obsolescent by the 1950s. The story starts after the Second World War. Up to the 1950s, equipment was all of the Strowger electro-mechanical variety, standardised through the BTTC. Then, with the increase in demand, a more advanced technology, one which was faster and required less maintenance, was needed in telephone exchanges.

One possibility was to use electronic exchanges to replace Strowger, but to continue to use Strowger until the electronic exchanges were ready. During the war, some Post Office staff, including Teddy Flowers, later to become Chief Engineer of the Post Office, had been involved with the development of the electronic computer, "Colossus", which had been used in German code cracking and was to provide the beginnings of the post-war computer industry. This computer used valves as electronic switches. Writing in 1948 Flowers said:

.. even before the recent war there was a

movement in the direction of replacing heavily worked mechanical switches by electronic switches.. and during the war this process was accelerated, notably in the direction of fully electronic computers which reached giant proportions. This work greatly advanced the knowledge and practical experience of electronic switching devices one of the results of which was an increased confidence in the ability of electronic switching apparatus to compete with electro-mechanical apparatus in cost and reliability.

Since the war, attention has been given by telephone engineers to the possibility of partially or fully electronic telephone exchanges and it is not inconceivable that the systems of the future will be fully electronic.[79]

Already by 1948, there was considerable optimism that electronic exchanges were just around the corner. If electronic exchanges could be introduced within a short period, then it made economic sense to keep using Strowger until the electronic equipment was in production.

A second possibility was to use the existing intermediate technology of cross-bar, whilst developing the electronic exchange. A working party, set up by the Post Office in 1947, to study whether existing equipment was capable of meeting an extension in subscriber dialling, visited both Sweden and the USA. They returned very enthusiastic about cross-bar's potential. But the drawback to cross-bar was that it was expensive to produce. at a time when the Post Office was subject to annual funding by Parliament and when capital had to be devoted towards renovating the existing system.[80]

In 1950, Flowers was promoted to Staff Engineer in the Research branch. It was said about his promotion:

> he has built up and is directing a team whose present efforts may well lead to remarkable changes and improvements in the practice of the art.[81]

It seems that, by 1950, a decision had already been taken within the Chief Engineer's office, based on the economic competitiveness of cross-bar. That decision was to aim for fully electronic exchanges and, meanwhile, to continue to use Strowger.[82] How much the decision rested on the reputation of Flowers himself is difficult to determine, but there

is no doubt that, after the secret success of Colossus, his reputation was considerable.

In 1951, a small experimental prototype electronic exchange was built. But it was another five years before the manufacturers agreed to pool research effort with the Post Office. It seems tht the delay came from the manufacturing side, possibly because the industry still had captive markets for Strowger equipment in the Commonwealth. (In 1956, 40% of telecommunications output was exported.) A further difficulty in the drafting of the agreement seems to have been the manufacturers' reluctance to enter into a similar form of government by committee as that of the BTTDC, with its over-standardisation and bureaucracy.[83] Since the Post Office, at this time, was a government department, negotiations took place between civil servants and the manufacturers. In 1956 they eventually agreed to set up a Joint Electronic Research Committee (JERC).

Under the JERC, the Post Office provided the Chairman of a Joint Executive Board, which directed and co-ordinated efforts and resources and a project manager for each project. Development in each of the manufacturing fields was allocated to individual manufacturers. Each manufacturer had its own design teams and each was bound by the agreement to divulge full information on new developments to the others. However, formal production was left as a matter for individual manufacturing responsibility.[84]

The first main project was an electronic exchange at Highgate Wood. This was put into service in December 1962. By then some engineers were expressing disappointment that the system had taken so long to develop. But an element of national chauvinism seems to have crept into the decision to pursue the electronic exchange. What was important said the Postmaster General, in 1960," was that we (Britain) should stride out ahead of other countries with this development".[85]

Even before the Highgate Wood exchange went into service, it was clear that it would not be economically viable. Under the JERC the Post Office continued to explore alternatives and, in 1960, decided to concentrate research on three specific systems, none of which was cross-bar. A further decision followed in 1963 that the future system should be based on reed relays, semi-electronic devices the use of which had been developed by AEI, STC and ATE(later taken over by Plessey).

By 1966, with residential demand surging, it became obvious that the large reed relay exchange, being developed by AEI and STC would not be ready in

time, although the first small reed relay exchange, developed by GEC and Plessey, was cut into service in 1968. Faced with a crisis of supply, the Post Office decided to introduce cross-bar systems as a temporary expedient. There were two such systems available but only one of British technology - that developed by Plessey for export. The other was the Pentaconta system of ITT to which STC had access. The Post Office opted for both.[86]

By 1968, GEC had obtained a licence to manufacture the Plessey system. In turn that meant that AEI was the only major manufacturer to be concentrating solely upon reed relay technology for large exchanges. It was at this point in time that the Labour Government's Industrial Reorganisation Corporation intervened in the industry.

In 1968 there were four and a half telecommunications manufacturers - GEC, AEI, STC, Plessey and Pye-TMC. In addition, Marconi undertook some telecommunications work. In terms of domestic market share, GEC took 23%, AEI took 13%, Plessey had 41% and STC had 21%. STC was American owned and Pye-TMC was owned by Philips of Holland. It was not a particular secret that the Post Office would have preferred fewer manufacturers of larger size.[87]

However, the IRC intervention seems to have come about by accident, rather than design, and as a result of rationalisation in the heavy electrical industry, then facing overcapacity for domestic demand. Following an approach made to it by the IRC in March 1967, in September of that year GEC made a takeover bid for AEI. AEI fought the takeover with plans for rationalisation. Among those plans was a merger of its telecommunications business with that of STC. Had AEI successfully defended itself against the GEC bid, then day to day management of the combined STC/AEI telecommunications company would probably have passed to STC. STC's potential control of 34% of the domestic market held the risk that it would not have exported equipment in competition against ITT. Part of the reason for the IRC intervention may have been this threat to British interests. Government spokesmen were later to allege:

> it was largely in pursuit of rationalisation in the telecommunications industry that the IRC gave its support to the GEC bid for AEI.[88]

In supporting the rationalisation the Labour Government argued that the country could not afford to waste scarce research and development talent. In

133

retrospect it seems strange that the Government was arguing on the one hand for co-operative research, while, on the other it was also intent on breaking the Bulk Purchasing Agreement on switching equipment which made the co-operative research possible.

As for AEI itself, it had a full telecommunications order book, but had lost £4 million in 1966-7 on that part of the company. The losses were said to stem from its development of reed relay technology for large exchanges, which was, of course the technology chosen by the Post Office for future British systems.[89] There were two aspects to AEI's research. On the one hand in conjunction with STC it was developing systems for the domestic market. On the other it had developed an exchange, REX18, specifically for export markets, which had reached the production stage .

There was talk at the time of GEC 'being desperate to get its hands on AEI's research'. It was said that Arnold Weinstock, the managing director of GEC, had pared GEC's own research to the bone and was therefore desperate to get his hands on somebody else's. The talk probably originated from knowledge that the Bulk Supply Agreement and, with it, the joint research arrangements, were due to end in 1968. But the talk proved wide of the mark.[90]

GEC sacked the telecommunications research staff of AEI based at Blackheath and Harlow, and closed the AEI research laboratories at Manchester and Rugby. Some of the AEI staff moved to Marconi. In addition, GEC scrapped the REX telephone exchange.

It seems the Post Office were as surprised as anyone at the GEC decision to scrap reed relay technology. But it should be remembered that GEC had just bought into the Plessey cross-bar system, and the Post Office had agreed in 1966 that it would buy that system as a temporary stop-gap. By scrapping reed rely research, GEC thereby ensured that demand for its crossbar system would be prolonged. Meanwhile, the costs and responsibility for developing the reed relay large exchange fell onto STC with its small resrach staff. The core of the AEI research team was finally broken up, in 1968, when GEC merged with English Electric which had already taken over Marconi.[91]

The first proving models of reed relay exchanges were introduced in Leighton Buzzard in 1966 and in Central London in 1968, but proved too expensive for wide application.[92] Following the demise of AEI, it took until 1971 for development to reach a stage where the Post Office could place orders for the equipment. The initial contract for

20 exchanges given to STC seems to have been kept quiet by the Post Office for several months after its signature.[93] In view of the row which followed it may have been hoping to present GEC and Plessey with a fait accompli.

In the subsequent two years, GEC and Plessey kept up a running battle with the Post Office. They argued that the future of the British system should be based on cross bar with the additional features of Stored Program Control (SPC), a form of computer control. Versions of cross-bar with SPC had already been adopted for future systems in the USA and Japan. GEC and Plessey argued that the reed relay technology being pursued by the Post Office would retard the development of SPC. They also argued that the technology had no export market.[94]

The Post Office was due to make its final decision on future ordering at the end of 1972. GEC lobbied hard and up to Prime Ministerial level, with the result that the Cabinet was called on to make a decision on whether the future technology of the British telecommunications system should be reed relays or cross bar.[95] One can imagine the glazed faces as Christopher Chataway explained the advantages of reed relays. The Cabinet's decision is unknown, but subsequent events suggest that it wanted the Post Office to attach more weight to the export potential of the technology it ordered. It is also probable that the Cabinet, through the Department of Employment, considered the employment implications of a switch from electro-mechanical systems to electronic. Strowger and cross-bar, electro-mechanical systems, employed a predominantly male labour force, whilst electronic components, such as reed relays, employed mainly female labour. Certainly, employment factors were emphasised by both GEC and Plessey. In particular, they stressed that their factories 'for the most part' were in development areas.[96]

Soon after that Cabinet meeting a Ministerial reshuffle took Christopher Chataway, who had largely been sympathetic to the Post Office, to the Department of Industry. His place was taken by Sir John Eden, considered by the Press to be a weak Minister. Towards the Autumn of 1972, it became evident that the new Minister was limbering up in preparation for a politial decision on the future ordering of the Post Office. A senior team of an economist, statistician and a merchant banker were said to be advising the Minister. Their self-proclaimed task was analogous to that of a Merchant Bank, with the Minister of Posts in the role of

investor. This emphasis on City methods invoked some criticism. Commentators questioned the wisdom of using methods which were notoriously bad at assessing the risk of high technology projects and notoriously bad at supporting them.[97]

In the event, possibly reacting to the threat that its whole investment programme might be shot down by the Ministry, the Post Office Board came up with a compromise solution. It would continue to order TXE4 exchanges and to continue its pursuit of reed relay technology, but the amount of crossbar it would order would be increased. The Post Office decision seems to have gone to the Minister at the end of January 1973. Two weeks later, after the Minister had refused to make the plans public, the Post Office made its own public announcement.[98]

The plan itself foresaw a total expenditure of £540 million on modernisation of the telephone system. Of this sum, £100 million was to be spent on TXE4, £90 million was to go to small reed relay exchanges, and an unspecified amount was to be spent on Strowger replacement. The plan also increased the amount to be spent on cross-bar, from £30 million in 1971 to £44 million and, in total, from £45 million originally planned to £350 million pounds.[99]

It was not surprising that the three manufacturers pronounced themselves satisfied with the proposals. However, it was not until April 1973, after scrutiny by an inter-departmental committee from the departments of Trade, Employment and the Treasury, that the Minister approved the plan. He announced that the Post Office was to collaborate with its suppliers to minimise local employment problems, and that a joint committee of the Post Office and the industry was to be set up on exports. The remit of the committee was to ensure that ' export considerations were born fully in mind in the further development of exchanges for domestic use'. For the first time, the Post Office was to be pushed into consideration of the effect of its technological requirements on equipment sales abroad, and had to take into account matters which were legally outside its responsibility for the domestic network.[100]

Within a short time it became apparent that the compromise Post Office plan was a good deal more favourable to GEC and Plessey than had at first been realised. In June 1973, <u>New Scientist</u> reported Plessey executives talking about the new plan as a 'licence to print money'. At GEC, Sir Arnold Weinstock was said to have been pressing his general

managers either to get similar returns out of other government work, or to drop it altogether. The compromise proposals gave ' an enormous boost in return on the capital invested by the two companies in cross-bar'. Although the evidence was there in 1972, it took until 1973 for the suspicion to manifest itself publicly that return on capital, not employment, nor exports, had been the motivating force behind the companies' public pressure on the Post Office and government.[101]

Despite this success there were still some obvious problems for GEC and Plessey. In the long-run the Post Office was still intent upon the introduction of the reed-relay based TXE4 exchanges. If these could not be supplied in sufficient numbers by 1980, when the Post Office plan envisaged a run down in cross-bar orders, then overseas suppliers might be enabled to enter the market. Both Ericsson and Philips had electronic exchanges installed overseas by 1973. The problem for both GEC and Plessey, given the huge cross-bar orders, was whether they had the time to develop reed relay exchanges. It was reported that few people in the industry or the Post Office believed that they had.[102]

Almost in answer to this criticism, GEC announced an agreement with STC for a period of ten years. The agreement covered collaboration in ' the design, development and engineering of equipment for public telecommunications switching systems'. It covered co-operation in R&D but not in manufacture and gave GEC access to STC's R&D reed relay technology. Plessey's reaction to its isolation was to state that discussion between the industry and the Post Office on collaborative development had been going on for some time and that it was confident that these talks would lead to a ' new national policy' of which it would be part.[103]

The 'new national policy', referred to by Plessey, involved collaboration between the Post Office and the manufacturers on a new electronic exchange to be introduced in the 1980s. This new exchange, code named System X, was to be fully computer controlled and digital. The concept of the new exchange arose from the joint AGSD committee, set up in 1971. But it was not until 1974 that the Post Office placed the first development contract for System X with GEC.

Signing of the contract was held up for more than nine months because of yet one more confrontation between the Post Office and its three suppliers. The quarrel, equally as public as that over TXE4, concerned the entry of Pye-TMC, owned by

Philips, into the group of Post Office approved manufacturers. The story went like this.

Following its establishment as a public corporation and given the delay on supplies of public exchanges, in 1969, the Post Office had trawled for new suppliers. Pye-TMC had expressed interest, hoping originally to sell to the Post Office,the PRX system manufactured by Philips and adopted in Holland. When the Post Office turned that system down, Pye agreed to accept the position of supplier of Strowger equipment, on the basis that it would gain an 'entry ticket' into the production of the TXE4 exchange and that of the new System X. The Post Office is said to have accepted Pye's position as a supplier on this basis, but the other manufacturers seem not to have been informed. Following the Post Office decision to pursue TXE4, in 1973,Pye laid claim to a share in the know-how, and a share in production of both TXE4 and System X. But GEC,Plessey and STC all refused to supply Pye with know-how, even on a commercial basis, and fought against its admission as a full member of the group. They objected to both its nationality (although STC was American owned) and to its lack of qualifications for electronic telecommunications work. Against them, Pye argued that it had its parent company's expertise to draw on.[104]

In January 1974, the four companies met to sort out the problem, but no solution emerged. The three established suppliers lobbied Department of Industry officials,who were said to be sympathetic.[105] Finally, a change of government in February 1974, and Tony Benn's return to the Department of Industry, may have tipped the scales against Pye's entry. The compromise solution worked out allowed Pye to enter production of TXE4 only after the other three manufacturers had gone fully into production. Pye would share in the production of System X, but also only after the three other suppliers had established a lead.[106]

It is possible to understand the panic of both GEC and Plessey. Having fought to gain cross-bar orders, both had been slow to adapt premises and production methods to the TXE4 exchanges. The first thirty five of those exchange orders went to STC, and the first TXE4 orders to GEC or Plessey were not placed until November 1974. Therefore, when Pye was negotiating for entry, neither Plessey, nor GEC, had received TXE4 orders. And, despite the Post Office compromise plan of 1973, it had also become clear that the Post Office was pressing ahead with the ordering of the large reed relay exchanges as fast

as STC could adapt its manufacturing to accommodate them. STC had responded quickly with the result that the Post Office had upped its orders for TXE4 in 1973 and again in 1974, at the expense of cross-bar. To have allowed a fourth supplier into the market in 1974 might very well have cut the GEC and Plessey share considerably.

GEC was awarded a £100,000 contract for the development of the central processor (computer) of System X in November 1974. (Plessey, which had been given a defence contract for a similar processor was later to claim that failure to use its processor delayed System X.) But the new relationship between suppliers and the Post Office was not fully established until 1975. Delays were later put down to difficulties in combining the principles of the joint development of System X, followed by independent manufacture, with the interests of individual companies. Delay was also caused in the necessary clearing of the new contractual agreement with the Monopolies Commission.[107]

Frustrated at the delay, Plessey first signed a marketing agreement with Bell Northern of Canada, and then entered an agreement with the French firm CIT-Alcatel, whose electronic exchange "Felicity" was to be complete ready for ordering in 1976. Even after the contractual relationship between the Post Office, Pye and the three supplies had been established, further delays occurred. The task of overall project definition did not begin until the Spring of 1976, and substantive development work did not start until one year later.[108]

In 1977 the Carter Committee found cause for concern in both the progress and organisation of the System X project. It pointed out that the three manufacturers were not natural partners, that GEC and Plessey were suspicious of STC, because of its American connections, and that GEC and Plessey's interests would be served better in the short term by an expansion of cross-bar orders. Each manufacturer was concerned that the system might be too expensive, or too late, for export markets, where it would be in competition with the second generation of fully electronic systems from foreign competitors. In addition, the manufacturers were aware that the timing of System X, although crucial for exports, was not particularly crucial for the Post Office, which by 1977 had placed no firm orders for the system. The Committee considered it to be hardly surprising that, given these uncertainties, the manufacturers were double-banking by entering into licensing agreements with foreign companies to

manufacture foreign designed exchanges.[109]

The Committee found cause for worry also in the actual organisation of the project. Although the Post Office was supposed to be leading the project, in fact decisions were reached essentially by consensus between equal partners. In effect the project was being managed by committee, a reminder that organisational forms tend to reoccur - the System X committee was not unlike that of the JERC or the BTTDC. The Committee felt that the management of the project was weak, and that decisionmaking within the Post Office, organised along functional lines, tended to be slow and cumbersome. Specifications had a tendency to become rigid and overelaborate. The Committee recommended that the management and specification of the project should be split ito two departments and one person given overall responsibility in each. They also recommended that the Post Office should give more emphasis to the project.[110]

The Carter Committee saw the major problem in the management of the project. It was not qualified to consider whether the technology was adequate for the needs of the 1980s. In 1976 the Department of Industry became worried whether the technology, itself, was of the right kind. Certainly the Post Office was most secretive about the system on the grounds of the 'national interest' and it may be that D notices operated at that time.[111] Some concern was expressed at the influence of defence requirements on the complexity and cost of the project. The POEU, now with worker directors on the Post Office Board, pressed for information on progress.[112]

These various pressures, coupled with concern on the part of the government's chief scientist, resulted in the appointment of a committee by the Department of Industry, headed by an academic within the telecommunications field, to conduct a technical audit of System X. The committee was internal and private. Its function can be seen as much to provide information to the Department, starved of that information by the Post Office, as in actually evaluating the technology. It seems unlikely that the Department could have overruled the Post Office in its choice of technology, but the enquiry served to offload the department's responsibility.[113]

The enquiry seems to have found that the System X technology was adequate for the task, but, some doubts about its export viability was reflected in a request, in 1977, to the National Enterprise Board to investigate possible export markets. A joint study by an outside consultant was commissioned and,

following on from that study came the establishment of British Telecommunications Services, a joint organisation of manufacturers and the Post Office to market the system.[114]

The management of the project was not easy for the Post Office. GEC was responsible for development of the central processor. Plessey was responsible for the switches. STC was responsible for the provision of the management systems for the system. Each was pursuing the development work in different locations. As a result the top executives of the Post Office and the companies were ' constantly gasping for information from those at the sharp end'.[115] The participants were also historically weak in software - none of them were major computer manufacturers - and a high turnover of software engineers helped little.

The management of the project seems to have improved following the appointment of Peter Benton as the Managing Director of Post Office telecommunications. He is said to have galvanised all the participants into action.[116] In the event, the 1979 deadline for a working prototype for the International Geneva Conference of telecommunications systems engineers was met.

But, once the technology became public, it also generated a great deal of criticism from the computer community. Despite the advice, in the early 1970s, from one government computer adviser, that a computer manufacturer should be involved in the project, no government action had been taken on the proposal. The computer community argued that the technology with its large central processors was out of date and elephantine and reflected lack of computer expertise on the part of the manufacturers. Others saw the whole system as being too expensive for export markets.[117]

In 1980 British Telecom began installing the first showpiece system ahead of schedule. Both civil servants and British Telecom Services talked of a possible market for the system of £10 billion worldwide, the majority in lesser developed countries. The political importance attached to the export potential of System X stretches across the two major parties. For the first time Ministers were to be seen promoting British telecommunications exports at the Geneva Conference. But System X has yet to prove itself in terms of exports, reflected in the fact that in 1982 the government agreed to subsidise the export marketing of GEC and Plessey, whilst STC withdrew from the manufacture of the system in return for assured orders of the reed

TELECOMMUNICATIONS

relay exchanges.British Telecom was to speed up the digitalisation of trunk exchanges with System X,and,under accelerated modernisation plans intends to spend £2 billion by the end of the 1980s. British Telecom Services has been disbanded.[118]

4.5 CONCLUSION

This industry study demonstrates the propensity of British governments over a long period to starve telecommunications of the finance necessary for its development. Basically telecommunications was used as a revenue source by the Treasury until the 1960s. Even after the Post Office Act of 1961 and the demand that it should make a return on capital, telecommunications profits were used as cross-subsidies for the postal services.

When times have been hard, capital investment in nationalised industries has been hit. In general,telecommunications has been no exception. The public corporation, with its formal 'arms length' relationship with government, but practical confusion over the extent of political control, is a prime example of the conflict engendered by belief in company autonomy on the one hand, and the centralised political system on the other. Governments have felt justified in demanding a return on capital employed, whilst themselves controlling prices, or restricting investment, or restricting borrowing.

Since pre-war days, the pendulum has swung to and fro between those who argue that telecommunications is a service, to those who argue that it is a business, with government unable to make up its mind on the matter. Nor does an ideological predisposition towards a free market on the part of government seem to ease the conflict of objectives.The Heath Government controlled tariffs; the Thatcher Government passed an Act which put British Telecom into competition with other suppliers, but then reserved the right for the Minister to decide if the organisation might provide a service or not. Similarly,in its privatisation plans, made public at the time of writing, the government will continue to retain 51% of the shares of British Telecom, thereby giving it the option of political control. That political control will also be apparent in the licence which the Minister intends to issue to British Telecom, which will insist on service provision to distant rural areas.[119] Party competition over whether the Post

TELECOMMUNICATIONS

Office should be split into one or two corporations and over the privatisation of British Telecom has hidden the extent of political control. Formal changes in organisation have made little difference to that control.

Nor has this conflict between competition and a free market on the one hand and political centralisation on the other been limited to the Post Office's relationship with the government. It has reached to the organisation's relationship with its suppliers. Governments of both parties have set out from the view that the relationship between Post Office and suppliers has been 'too cosy'. The Labour Government of the 1960s expected the manufacturers to increase production of outdated Strowger equipment, despite the fact that it was against their interests to do so. Then, seemingly frustrated at the failure of his attempts to improve the telephone service, Tony Benn instituted the era of competitive technology, with the intention that market competition should stimulate supply. That era produced enormously increased costs for the Post Office. But under that Labour Government, neither civil service nor the IRC seem to have been aware of the exigencies of a national telecommunications network. The Thatcher Government originally insisted that the public exchange market would be opened to competition. Yet it was after talks between government, British Telecom and the manufacturers that STC withdrew from manufacture of System X. The decision was presented as an opportunity for 'British industry to benefit'. As under the previous 'ring', suppliers are guaranteed orders, but now, instead of five manufacturers only two are involved. The wheel has turned full circle since the 1960s.

The accidental intervention of the IRC in the industry illustrates the dangers attached to the use of semi-autonomous agencies by government to act as its intermediaries with industry. That the IRC did not consult the Post Office on the likely effects of the GEC/AEI merger, and that no conditions were imposed upon GEC in return for IRC backing, led to considerable extra costs and delays in the modernisation of the telephone network. Clearly no one had given due weight to the interest GEC had in divesting itself of development work on the large reed relay exchange. The IRC intervention, with its support for 'proven management' in the form of Arnold Weinstock, also illustrates the importance attached to the autonomy of the firm, even where, as in this case, government backing was crucial to GEC's takeover bid.

TELECOMMUNICATIONS

GEC's subsequent behaviour and that of Plessey, in lobbying as far as the Prime Minister for cross-bar technology, demonstrates the power in the British political system which accrues to large companies. Crucially, the argument both companies used was employment related. Their supposed concern for exports proved to be the chimera it always was. In fact, Plessey, whose cross-bar system GEC had licensed into, had always been vague about the amount of its exports of that technology. Whilst the two companies made large profits on their cross-bar orders, the modernisation of the network was further delayed by the need to integrate three different systems - Strowger,TXE4 and cross-bar.

That the Cabinet could take decisions on technology, and the Minister could insist later that the Post Office acted outside its legal status to take account of exports,demonstrates the extent to which political control can reach.GEC and Plessey's success on that occasion, and their success later in their confrontation with Pye-TMC, demonstrate the difficulty of establishing bureaucratic control within the prevailing political system. The companies were always able to appeal over the heads of the Post Office to its political masters, and could expect those Ministers to make decisions with short-term interests in mind.

The Post Office and British Telecom have been criticised for lack of leadership in the System X project, but, to a large extent, leadership is commensurate with authority. The organisation's own poor relationship with governments, and the perpetual possibility of company appeals over its head, left it without the political backing necessary to establish that authority. Without that political backing the relationship between Post Office and manufacturers degenerated into dependency and exploitation on the part of the manufacturers and resentment on the part of the Post Office. The manufacturers argued that they needed a home market for technology to export, the Post Office argued it was responsible only for the home market and not for exports.With technology which could not be translated into exports, the manufacturers settled for gaining as much as they could out of supplying the Post Office and British Telecom. The manufacturers blamed the Post Office for lack of exports, the Post Office blamed the manufacturers and the POEU blamed both, but mainly the manufacturers.The cycle is currently repeating itself with System X technology.

The technical specifications of System X were

TELECOMMUNICATIONS

set by manufacturers and the Post Office, with it seems some intervention from government. One does not know, but one may speculate, that defence interests had a hand in drawing up those specifications, that the commercial applicability of the technology was affected by considerations of the 'national interest'. If that is the case, then technology was subject once more to political control.

It is possible to argue that the whole history of telecommunications technology in Britain would have been rewritten, if the Post Office had not been so underfunded in the immediate post-war period. Without the financial strictures upon it in the 1950s, the decision to opt for electronic exchanges in preference to cross-bar, might not have been taken. Without that decision to keep Stowger operational until electronic exchanges came into service, the great majority of the history of the telecommunications technology detailed here would not have taken place. The three manufacturers would have produced cross-bar exchanges and with the later addition of SPC, a gradual evolution to fully computer controlled digital exchanges would have occurred. Britain would then have been in the same position as Japan, or Sweden.

One of the problems highlighted by the study is the tendency for British researchers to go for the 'best' rather than the adequate technology for the job. Electronic exchanges were to put Britain ahead of the world, but were too costly to run. The Post Office was accused by the manufacturers in the 1960s of demanding specifications to 'battleship standards'. System X is castigated for its over-elaborate technology, for doing more than is needed and for needing technical changes for export markets.

The system was not without its critics during the years of its development, but these were effectively silenced by the secrecy with which its development was surrounded. Academics were advised that to publicise criticism would be to 'rock the boat' and against the national interest. And the autonomy of the Post Office allowed it to keep the technological development of the system away from the eyes of the Department of Industry.[120]

For its expertise on telecommunications, the civil service relied and still relies on external advisers and internal committees chaired by external academics, or on British Telecom itself. But several academics during the period covered here were in posts funded by the Post Office, or relied on

research money from that organisation, and a conflict of interest was bound to arise. External advice is not necessarily advice without constraint. Given the dearth of specialists within the civil service, the actual wielding of political control over the industry has lacked the technical, cost, or market consciousness necessary for effective intervention.

Hence, even in liberalisation of the market, the British government has not effectively exerted control over British Telecom. Lack of understanding of the importance of that organisation's control over the land links between satellite ground stations and consumers, led to a failure to write in relevant clauses in the 1981 Act. It would be hardly surprising to find some disillusion with liberalisation within the Department of Industry.

NOTES AND REFERENCES

1. John Zysman,"French electronics policy: the Costs of Technological Independence", in S.J.Warnecke & E.N.Suleiman, *Industrial Policies in Western Europe*(New York, Praeger, 1975), pp.227-245.
2. See Viscount Wolmer MP, *Post Office Reform its Importance and its Practicability*(London, Ivor Nicholson and Watson, 1932) on this period in the Post Office' history.
3. *Report of the Committee of Inquiry on the Post Office*, Cmnd 4149, (London, HMSO, 1932)
4. *Official Report*, Vol.432, col.925; Vol.449, col.976-7, Vol.450, col. 1258-1260.
5. Post Office Press Release, quoted in E.J.Potter, *History of Exchange Switching System Development in the UK*(M.Sc in Telecommunications, Project Report, University of Essex, 1975, unpublished).
6. *TEMA Annual Report 1958-9*, p.11
7. Select Committee on Nationalised Industries, *First Report on the Post Office*, Vol.II, (London, HMSO, 1967), Appendix 35, para.5-6.
8. Ibid., Minutes of evidence, Sub-committee B, Q.66.
9. *TEMA Annual Report 1960-61*, p.28.
10. *Report on Post Office Development and Finance*, Cmnd.9576, (London, HMSO, 1955).
11. *TEMA Annual Report 1956-7*, p.13.
12. *Financial and Economic Obligations of the Nationalised Industries*, Cmnd.1337(London, HMSO, 1961).
13. Select Committee on Nationalised Industries, Vol.1, p.104.
14. *The Inland Telephone Service in an*

TELECOMMUNICATIONS

Expanding Economy,Cmnd.2211,(London,HMSO,1963).
   15. Select Committee on Nationalised Industries,Vol.II,Q.128,212-3.
   16. Douglas Pitt,The Telecommunications Function in the British Post Office(Farnborough, Saxon House,1980),p.148.
   17. Ibid.,pp.150-1.
   18. Ibid.,p.144.
   19. The National Plan,Cmnd.2764 (London,HMSO,1965),p.157.
   20. TEMA Annual Report 1965-66 p.25.
   21. Ibid.,p.32.
   22. Ibid.,p.25.
   23. Douglas Pitt,pp.142-3.
   24. The Economist,Vol.220,6th August 1966, p.576.
   25. Post Office Telecommunications Journal, Vol.20,Spring 1968,p.1.
   26. Official Report,Vol.773,Cols.49-154.
   27. Douglas Pitt,p.152.
   28. The Economist,Vol.232,9th August 1969, Survey,p.viii.
   29. For a synopsis of the issues, see: Douglas Pitt,p.154.
   30. Post Office Act 1969,Section 24(1).
   31. Ibid.,Chapter 48,Section 7.
   32. Interviews.
   33. Post Office Report and Accounts 1970-1, p.3.
   34. The Economist,Vol.237,5th December 1970,p.80.
   35. NEDO,A Study of UK Nationalised Industries: Their Role in the Economy and Control in the Future(London,HMSO,1976),p.57.
   36. Ibid.,p.24.
   37. Post Office Act 1969,Section 9(1).
   38. Report of the Post Office Review Committee,Cmnd.6850,(London,HMSO,1977).
   39. Ibid.,p.20.
   40. Ibid.,pp.106-109,129-130.
   41. On the perfectionist standards of the Post Office see Select Committee on Nationalised Industries,Vol.II,Q.348.
   42. Financial Times,28th April 1972.
   43. The Times,15th & 19th February 1969.
   44. Financial Times,30th December 1979.
   45. The Economist,Vol.232,9th August 1969, survey,p.xiii.
   46. Financial Times,30th December 1975, 26th March 1980.
   47. Liberalisation of the Use of the British Telecommunications Network,Beesley Report,(London,

HMSO,1981).
48. British Telecommunications Act 1981, Section 6.
49. Computer Weekly,4th December 1980.
50. Sunday Times,30th October 1981.
51. Financial Times,21st May 1982, July 24th 1982.
52. Select Committee on Nationalised Industries,Vol.II,Appendix 55,para.17.
53. Ibid.,Q.299-318.
54. Ibid.,Q.304.
55. R.W.Palmer & W.L.Brimmer,"The BTTDC",Post Office Electrical Engineering Journal, Vol.41, 1948-9,p.193.
56. Select Committee on Nationalised Industries, Q.299-318.
57. Ibid.,Appendix 53,para.15.
58. Ibid.,Appendix 80,Section 4.
59. Ibid.,Appendix 55,para.18.
60. TEMA Annual Report 1962-3,p.18.
61. Committee on Public Accounts,Fifth Report (London,HMSO,1967),paras.148-9.
62. TEMA Annual Report 1966-7,p.26.
63. Select Committee on Nationalised Industries, Vol.II,Q.351.
64. TEMA Annual Report 1966-7,p.23.
65. Sunday Times,7th May 1978.
66. TEMA Annual Report 1966-7,p.26.
67. Richard Caves,Britain's Economic Prospects (Washington D.C.,Brookings,1968),p.404.
68. Ibid.
69. Ibid.
70. Committee on Public Accounts,Q.482.
71. Ibid.,Q.459.
72. Ibid.,para.155.
73. IRC,First Annual Report (London,HMSO,1968), p.5.
74. The Economist,Vol.227,13th April 1968, p.60;Post Office Telecommunications Journal,Vol.20, 1968,p.1
75. TEMA Annual Report 1969-70,p.21.
76. Ibid.,p.12.
77. AGSD Report No.1.(London,Post Office,1970)p.i.
78. Ibid.,p.12.
79. POEEJ,Vol.43,July 1950,p.51.
80. POEEJ,Vol.41,July 1948,p.113.
81. POEEJ,Vol.43,July 1950,p.156.
82. POEEJ,Vol.41,July 1948,p.147.
83. C.Harlowe,p.116.
84. Select Committee on Nationalised Industries, Appendix 53,para.16.
85. TEMA Annual Report 1959-60,p.16.

TELECOMMUNICATIONS

86. M.T.Hills,"A Comparison of the Switching Systems Development Process in the UK and Japan." Telecommunications Group Report,No.116,(Essex, Essex University,1977,roneo).
87. Sir William Ryland,STC Communications Lecture,17th May 1976,roneo.
88. Official Report,Vol.759,col.396.
89. Jill Hills,"The Industrial Reorganisation Corporation:The Case of the AEI/GEC and English Electric Mergers",Public Administration,Vol.59, Spring 1981,pp.77-78.
90. The Economist,Vol.225,8th October 1967, p.447.
91. Personal communications,Financial Times, 8th May 1978;Sunday Times,7th August 1978.
92. The Economist,Vol.232,9th August 1969, survey,p.xii.
93. The Economist,Vol.242,5th February 1972, p.75.
94. The Times,25th February 1972.
95. Sunday Times,14th January 1973.
96. TEMA Annual Report 1971-2,p.20.
97. Financial Times,8th February 1973;The Guardian,26th September 1972.
98. Financial Times,12th February 1973.
99. Ibid.
100. The Guardian,19th April 1973.
101. New Scientist,Vol.58,7th June 1973,p.617.
102. Ibid.; The Times,29th June 1973.
103. Financial Times,26th March 1973.
104. Computing,17th January 1974,Financial Times,11th & 12th January 1974.
105. The Times,17th January 1974.
106. The Times,17th January 1975.
107. Electronics & Power,Vol.25,August 1979, pp.544-551.
108. Financial Times,26th March 1973.
109. Report of the Post Office Review Committee, pp.129-130.
110. Ibid.,pp.128-9.
111. Computer Talk,25th October 1978.
112. Personal communications.
113. Interviews.
114. Electronics & Power,Vol.25,August 1979, pp.544-551.
115. Sunday Times,7th May 1978.
116. Financial Times, 9th May 1978, Computer Weekly,18th September 1980.
117. Electronics and Power,Vol.25,June 1979, pp.433-4,437-8;The Economist,Vol.279,27th June 1981;Vol.280,22nd August 1981,survey,p.10.
118. Financial Times,5th October 1982.

TELECOMMUNICATIONS

119. *Financial Times*, 14th July 1982.
120. *Personal* communications. Dr M.T.Hills, then Reader in Telecommunications at Essex University, a post funded by the Post Office for its first ten years, wrote a letter to *The Times* in 1977 drawing attention to the cost & complexity of System X. The letter was unacknowledged & unpublished. Two offers to give evidence to the Carter Committee were also ignored. During this period he was the author's husband.

Chapter Five

COMPUTERS

5.1 INTRODUCTION

The argument presented in Chapter One was that Britain lacked the bureaucratic-industrial relationships which have characterised such countries as France and Japan. Instead British policy is characterised on the one hand by "strong" political decisions and on the other by weak leadership from the bureaucracy. A strong political component in terms of a centralised bureaucracy leads to political intervention at the level of the firm, but the 'core' liberal ideology leads to weak institutional arrangements mediating between the bureaucracy and industry and the retention of the autonomy of the firm. Despite this autonomy, where companies are primarily geared to meeting the demands of the public sector, a form of dependence may ensue. That dependence may suit both the bureaucracy and the manufacturer, but in turn may lead to lack of adjustment on the part of industry to the marketplace. In other words, dependency on central government can lead to rigidity in product design because the company gears its production to its major buyer.

In the telecommunications public exchange market, described in Chapter Four, the answer of the government was to break the client relationship by instituting competition between companies. In turn this action led to increased costs to the major buyer itself - the public sector. This section on data processing documents a similar dilemma - how far can government support a company without turning it into a public institution?

The markets in technologically based industries, such as computers, are those most likely to change rapidly as technological innovation alters products. One might therefore expect that any policy

of intervention in these product markets would need to be flexible, both anticipating and responding to changes in the markets. As the problems and the markets of the expanding industries change, so one might expect government policy to change. However, as we shall see in this section on the computer industry the British government's intervention in the computer market has not been flexible.

Although the strong growth forecasts for the minicomputer market, for the peripherals market, and for the software market, might lead one to expect that the government would have pursued a policy of supporting UK firms in these markets, government policy, first made in 1966, continued to have the same focus through to 1981. The major goal of the policy has been the support of one manufacturer – ICL. The features of this support are to be found in public procurement of its products, support for rationalisation of manufacturers, support for research and development and, most recently, a bailing out operation.

At times other goals have been added or subtracted. In the 1960s, for instance, the Government attempted to increase the usage of computers through financial incentives, and in the 1980s a programme to develop their use in schools began. But, in general, with the exception of these programmes and some financial help to smaller companies from the National Enterprise Board, the focus of computer policy has rested on ICL.

Where policy changes have come about it has been through political pressure either from within departments of Whitehall or from external sources, such as Parliament. The weakness of that position is that companies must turn into political animals. The history of the computer industry suggests that flexibility of industrial policy results only from pressure brought from outside the particular part of the bureaucracy involved in dependency relations. Where growth industries have declined under imports, those political pressures are unlikely to be available. Only the introduction of competitive bureaucracies then alters industrial policy towards those sectors.

At no time has there been any attempt by the British government to deny access to foreign technology to British companies or to control the penetration of foreign capital into the computer industry in the country. The intention has been therefore to build a British computer industry within a free market of technology, and within a liberal market policy towards multinational

penetration of the British market.

5.2 IMPORTS AND R&D

No British 'computer policy' existed as such until 1964, although before that date the National Research Development Corporation (set up in 1948 to help innovations reach production) funded one or two computer related projects. The political rationale for intervention in the computer market had been laid out, however, in 1963,when Harold Wilson himself identified import substitution as one of the prime targets for an industrial and technological policy. The new Ministry of Technology,established by Harold Wilson,in 1964, was given the responsibility for 'sponsorship' of the computer industry, although what 'sponsorship' meant was not defined exactly.[1]

Since much of the 1964 Labour Government's manifesto was concerned with bringing Britain into the twentieth century, once the problem had been identified. the increasing penetration of imports in the computer field was easily placed on the political agenda. In fact no separate statistics on the import of computers existed until 1964,when the Electronics EDC prevailed on the Customs and Excise Department to collect them.

In January 1965,George Brown, then head of the Department of Economic Affairs,drew attention to those figures, in off-the-cuff remarks to the Press. The remarks produced an immediate defensive statement from the Treasury. It intended to order forty two computers for installation by 1970, it said, suggesting that it already perceived some obligation upon itself to support the British computer industry with orders of equipment. The same remarks also provoked an analysis in the Board of Trade Journal by International Computers and Tabulators (ICT) detailing the reasons why British computers lagged behind those of the USA.[2]

A similar theme was taken up in 1965 by the Electronics Committee of the NEDC. That committee identified a balance of trade deficit with the USA in electronic goods. It also pointed out that Britain had an export/import ratio for electronic goods of approximately half that of either the USA or West Germany. In discussing the heavy imports of computing equipment from America, which took over 50% of the domestic market, the committee made the point that imports were often caused by 'lack of

suitable British machines' and by the 'greater reliability' of American machines. In particular it mentioned problems with British software.

In themselves, of course, these kind of public statements detailing the superiority of American computers, justified their import penetration, and removed from government the option of raising tariffs against them. Even within the then current atmosphere, where technology was a politically sensitive subject, it is evident that both the Labour Government and NEDO were content to begin a 'computer policy' within the framework of increasing internationalisation of technology and investment. The NEDO report actually welcomed import penetration. It saw that penetration as the adjunct of an increased specialisation in international markets, from which it was assumed that Britain would benefit.

It is also interesting that no mention was made in the report of the fact that much of the increased imports of computing equipment could be traced to the sale by British companies of American computers on licence. In particular, at this juncture, ICT was selling Univac (US) computers under its own label. Nor was any mention made in the report that English Electric manufactured computers under a licensing agreement with RCA of America.

The report made clear, however, as did previous statements by Harold Wilson, that the Labour Government was aware of the competitive advantage derived by American manufacturers from the heavy support of defence R&D by the American government.[3] In turn the American pattern of heavy R&D expenditure seems to have influenced the methods of support for the industry adopted by the Labour Government. Yet that is not surprising. In view of the pre-eminent position of the USA in technology, a British government, basing its ideology on modernisation through technology, was likely to take the American spending pattern as its model. It is equally clear that the government was unaware of the importance of customer-base to the computer industry.

The Labour Government tended to be taken up with technological excellence. In opposition, in 1963, Harold Wilson had spoken of the need for technological breakthroughs ' where a breakthrough could mean supremacy for Britain', and called for 'development contracts' between government and industry to gain the breakthroughs.[4] The idea of these contracts came from American experience in the defence industry and were to become part of a coded language in favour of more government intervention

in industry. The idea of this kind of contract between central government and industry was not new. It was mentioned in a report of the Advisory Council on Scientific Policy in 1953, as a means whereby government could increase innovation in industry. But, in view of the direct links the contracts involved between central departments and industry, the mechanism was considered suitable only for research on raw materials, such as fuel. It was felt that other research contracts were better carried out through industry research associations, which were in more direct contact with industry than were government departments.[5] The importance of government departments as large, if not monopoly, buyers of other equipment was not recognised. Nor were the institutional differences between British and American government methods of funding research searchingly examined.

Whereas American research funding went through federal spending programmes directly to be carried out in the companies themselves, in Britain centrally funded research tended to be done in the public sector itself, and to concentrate on 'pure' rather than 'applied'research. The one government institution which sought industrial co-operation in the development of inventions into production models was the NRDC, whose borrowing powers the incoming Labour Government increased. At the same time its terms of reference, were revised to allow it to support long-term research.[6] It was to the NRDC that the Labour Government turned for the administration of its first research grant to ICT.

The grant of £5 million and an allocation of £1 million to universities and research associations for the development of computing techniques was announced by the new Minister of Technology in March 1965. A further sum of £10 million was earmarked to bring university computing facilities up to date.[7] There had been a considerable build up in the press for the new 'computer policy', but the reality was greeted with disappointment. The Economist called it 'Mr Cousins' mouse' and complained that the amount was not only 'chicken feed', but that the industry needed custom not more research.[8] Although the stated intention of the new policy was to provoke:

> a rapid increase in the use of computers and computer techniques in industry and commerce

and to provide ' a flourishing computer industry', the actual finance provided went mainly on research.[9]

155

5.3 PUBLIC PROCUREMENT

However, the 1965 policy produced a new central government institution - the Computer Advisory Unit. The Unit's job was to conduct an 'objective survey' of computers then available, and to advise government departments on their suitability for various applications. Frank Cousins made it clear that the Unit would be 'objective' in its assessment, meaning presumably that it would not favour one particular manufacturer. He also indicated that the individual Departments in central government would continue to remain responsible for the purchase of computers and that non-British owned firms would not be excluded. In reality, the Unit proved to be the mechanism for the beginnings of a public sector preference towards domestic manufacturers. [10]

By the end of Labour's first year in office, the outlines of a British policy towards the computer industry could be discerned. First came a strong link with one company, ICT, which itself was arguing for rationalisation of the industry. Second came public sector preference for domestic manufacturers, and third was R&D support.

Following the establishment of the Computer Advisory Unit in the Ministry of Technology, an informal Buy British policy began to develop in the Ministry. That the policy did not reach out to all government departments was evident from the figures released in May 1966, which showed that of 23 computers on order by government departments nine were for machines from American manufacturers, of which six were from IBM. Some of these were updates for existing machines, and others had been on order since 1964. [11]

By 1966 the policy of preference towards ICL had been formalised. Its impact on IBM's share of government orders was considerable. From taking 32% of the central government market in 1966, IBM's share of government orders had dropped to 13% by 1968, and a 30% share of orders from public corporations in 1966, had dropped to 2% by 1968. Only amongst local authorities did IBM still hold the substantial share of 25% of the market by 1966. [12]

The new policy coincided with a change of personnel at the Ministry of Technology, where Tony Benn took over from Frank Cousins. In July 1966, Benn made the first public statement on the public sector preference policy. He stated that:

purchases of computers will be made from

British firms whenever reasonably possible. Each case is however to be considered on its merits, price being only one of the many factors which will have to be taken into account. No directive has been given to other public authorities but they have been invited to take into account the desirability of supporting British industry. Machines made in Britain by subsidiaries of foreign firms are regarded in this context as British.[13]

At first glance it seemed that the policy was aimed at reducing imports - the industry to be preferred was that manufacturing locally. But the statement was also made with EFTA regulations in mind. Those regulations entitled foreign owned subsidiaries manufacturing in Britain to be regarded as 'British'. As it transpired, the definition of 'British' was to centre, not on manufacture in the UK, nor on British ownership, but on the mainframe product of one company - ICT. For a time, therefore, there occurred an ironic situation. The British government bought primarily ICT machines which had a large proportion of American made components, and which were manufactured under licence from the USA, in preference to computers made by subsidiaries of American firms 90% of whose components were British made.[14]

It can be assumed, however, that standardisation on the products of one or two manufacturers was in the interests of both the Ministry of Technology and the Treasury. For the Ministry of Technology it carried into practice its sponsorship of the British industry discreetly enough for major American manufacturers to feel their investment in Britain was worthwhile. No real attempt seems to have been made to control the local authority market until the latter 1970s, and IBM was still able to find contracts there.[15] In the 1960s, the public sector represented more than 30% of the total market in mainframe computers. Without some access to that market, American multinationals might well have felt that their investment could not pay off. By the 1970s the private computer market had grown considerably.

From the Treasury point of view it made economic sense to standardise central government purchases. It had the advantage of cutting training costs and making software interchangeable. It is noticeable that both the French and West German governments pursued similar policies - the French by standardising software and the Germans by buying

mainly from Siemens.

From 1968, after ICT merged with English Electric computers to form ICL, the preference policy seems to have tightened further. By 1968,ICL was taking 51% of the central government market,56% of the local authority market and 60% of the public corporation market.[16] More than 40% of ICL's turnover came from the public sector.

The policy of standardisation did not reach as far as the weapons systems of the Ministry of Defence. Despite the large sums of money invested in defence R & D, little found its way into the British data processing industry. In the interests of economy, the Minister preferred to use existing commercially available machines in its weapons systems, rather than pay for the development of new machines. It also had rigid specifications, which the machines it used had to meet. In 1971, on the 'standard' list of suitable machines were Ferranti and Marconi computers. The American manufacturer Contol Data Corporation was to join them shortly after. ICL machines were not on the list.[17]

In contrast to the USA, where IBM had benefitted from defence contracts and was well integrated into that market, in Britain, at this stage, the divorce of the commercial data processing market and the defence market had already taken place. ICL's isolation from the defence market was not something which, at that time, seemed of immediate importance. Whilst defence expenditure declined in the 1970s, and ICL still had the public sector preference for mainframes, its isolation had little impact. But in the 1980s, with the growth of defence expenditure once again, the cut back in other public sector purchases, and the ending of preference policy, ICL's divorce from defence affected the company's solvency. Whilst companies such as Racal and Ferranti reaped the benefits of their close association with defence electronics,ICL's public sector preference was ended.

Whereas weapons procurement fell outside the preference policy, the newly formed Ministry of Defence's data processing requirements fell within it.To bring together the incompatible computer systems of the three armed services,in 1969 a Management Services Organisation (MSO) had been established within the Ministry of Defence. Since all but eleven of the 84 computers which had been installed by 1972 had to be renewed by 1975, pressure could be exerted for the Ministry to buy from ICL. By 1969 almost all the computers ordered by the MSO were for ICL machines.[18] But the

pressure on the Ministry was to rebound on ICL.

As the public sector preference policy came into effect, so ICL increased its share of central government orders, but still American manufacturers took just under 50% of the market.The reasons for their continued presence can be traced to a conflict of interest between the Civil Service Department, on the one hand, and the Ministry of Technology on the other, and to the organisation of procurement itself.Whereas the Ministry of Technology was responsible for 'sponsorship' of the computing industry, of which procurement was one feature, the Treasury's interest was in efficient administration and the protection of central government from dependence on one computer supplier. The Treasury, therefore,insisted on the use of computers for only those applications for which the particular model had been tested on private industry.[19] The restriction allowed American firms into the market.

Responsibility for computer procurement was split among several departments. Spending departments were responsible for the initial decision to purchase. The Technical Support Unit of the Civil Service Department and the Computer Advisory Unit of the Ministry of Technology were responsible for the applications required. The Stationary Office was responsible for receiving tenders. And a committee of the spending department and the two advisory units, chaired by the spending department, made the final decision. The computer purchase then appeared on the vote of the Stationary Office.[20] With so many actors involved, and the conflict of interest between the departments themselves, it was still possible to side-step the ICL preference.

Predictably, the American manufacturers, such as Honeywell and IBM, complained about the ICL preference. Honeywell argued that its machines had more British components than ICL's, and that it had invested in a factory in Scotland on the understanding that it would be eligible for public sector contracts. IBM complained that it believed a tender from itself for a central government contract had to be 25% cheaper than that from ICL. (The statement was never officially denied.)[21]

Neither was ICL happy with the procurement policy. It wanted to cut its teeth on new applications, giving it experience which it could then use as the basis for contracts in the export market. It argued that the American industry had become established and experienced through the use of 'development contracts' from the Department of Defense, and the British government should also be

159

prepared to act as the sponsoring agency for new applications. But such arguments went directly against Treasury policy.[22]

Both the American manufacturers and ICL used the public hearings of the House of Commons Select Committee on Technology to bring pressure to bear on the government to change its policy. From 1970 to 1974, the Committee investigated the computer industry. Evidence to the Committee both from civil servants and from Tony Benn, then Minister of Techology, pointed to the often incompatible goals of the Ministry's 'sponsorship' of the industry. A civil servant at the Ministry explained:

> we need to provide a sensible amount of help for the indigenous company, but to avoid injury to the 'good neighbour' policy towards American industry or alienation of the sources of advanced technology.[23]

A conflict of interest did not solely arise between the Ministry's role as 'sponsor' of the whole computer industry in Britain, and its relationship with ICL. Also, Benn acknowledged, the Minister's responsibility for regional policy and the encouragement of foreign companies into investment in the development areas, conflicted with his responsibility to ICL.[24] On the one hand, the development areas were crying out for multinational investment while, on the other, to attract multinationals in the data processing field would increase competition for ICL in the domestic market.

Before the Select Committee could report its conclusions, the General Election of 1970 returned a Conservative administration, ideologically committed to less state intervention in industry, and to efficiency in government. As far as the computer industry was concerned, the two principles did not marry happily. Much of central government was already reliant on ICL computers and, in the interests of compatibility and economy, it therefore made sense to purchase from ICL. Yet the public sector still represented a prize market sought by American multinationals. They expected the incoming government to liberalise the public preference policy. But they were to be disappointed.

The principle of efficiency won out over that of liberal ideology. The new government announced that large computers (of the capacity of Atlas and above) would be bought by single tender from ICL. So, also, would computers leading into the large machines and those where there was a need for compa-

tibility. In other cases, competitive tenders would be sought, including, as far as possible, at least one offering a system manufactured in the UK. The only alteration in the policy from that of the previous Labour Administration was the abolition of the price preference in favour of ICL. The exact effect of that price preference had never been divulged by government, so it was difficult to estimate the effect of its discontinuation. It seems likely that the change was minor, and that it was given to placate the American multinationals.[25]

In the Select Committee's reports, of both 1971 and 1973, it is possible to discern the effect of lobbying by the multinationals,and the Committee's desire to defuse their attacks on ICL. The Committee favoured the cessation of the single tender preference policy and recommended that more support should be given to the industry through grants and loans. It argued that purchase preference should be given to companies which contributed to the British economy through exports. But it also argued that in determining that contribution,the government should take into account whether the company's R&D was located in Britain, how much control the UK subsidiary had over its parent Board and the shareholding of British nationals in the company.[26] According to these criteria neither Honeywell, nor CDC,which had no R&D facilities in Britain, nor IBM,which admitted to the Committee that it attempted to balance its exports with its imports,would have qualified for preferential purchasing.[27] Had the Committee's recommendations been put into effect, the result would have been the continuation of ICL purchases by central government, and pressure on the multinationals to show that they 'qualified' under the relevant criteria for public sector contracts.

The Committee also recommended that contracts should be broken up and should allow seperate tendering for peripherals and software. In these recommendations the Committee was clearly responding to demands from the software industry for public sector support.But, in recommending these changes, the Committee overlooked the crucial fact that central government software needed to be compatible,and that standardisation on one type of software would have had to precede the introduction of the recommendations.

The Committee also commented on the lack of co-ordination in central government purchase and use of computers. In the interests of greater co-ordination,it recommended the establishment of a Computer Purchasing Board, responsible to Parliament

through the Civil Service Department. Its task would be to purchase computer equipment and services, and to develop and co-ordinate their use in Central Government.[28]

This keynote of 'efficiency' in management coincided with a similar fashion within the new Conservative administration. Under Edward Heath, the Conservatives were concerned with 'co-ordination', with efficiency through forward planning and with the hiving off of departmental responsibilities into 'accountable units'. The idea of a Central Computer Agency fitted in well with these predispositions.[29]

Moving to bring together all 'staff' sevices concerned with computers, the Government co-ordinated all central government procurement under one agency. This new agency - the Central Computer Agency - located within the Civil Service Department, received an annual vote for the purchase of computers. The responsibility for initiating computer purchase was taken away, therefore, from the spending departments.

Although the conflict between the Treasury's desire to see only proven computers introduced to central government and the Department of Trade and Industry's remit to 'sponsor' the industry remained, the establishment of the CCA allowed easier imposition of the 'Buy ICL' policy. By 1977, ICL was said to be taking two thirds of central government contracts. The easier links between ICL, which already had a department responsible for negotiations with central govenment, and the civil service agency are said to have developed into a position where the CCA came to be regarded as ICL's spokesman within Central Government. It also became ICL's defender, when complaints about failures of ICL computers became well publicised.[30]

Later hearings in the American Senate unearthed the existence of a 'Project Knock-Off' team employed by IBM to publicise criticism of ICL.[31] Also, never having taken kindly to being included within the procurement policy, the Ministry of Defence vociferously voiced its complaints against ICL. These culminated, in 1977, with allegations to the Auditor General that the use of ICL machines had cost millions of pounds in lost days and inefficiency. The allegations presented a considerable blow to ICL. The Ministry of Defence accounted for approximately half of government computing expenditure. The Auditor General then joined publicly in the argument between 'efficiency' and 'sponsorship', by castigating the government for the way in which sponsorship functions had overidden

concern with efficiency.

The matter was subsequently investigated by the Public Accounts Committee. The problem had arisen in 1972 when ICL offered to supply two of its new 2900 machines to the Ministry of Defence computer bureau. At that time the hardware was in the pre-production stage and the software was being developed. However, Ministers concluded that preferential purchasing was crucial in launching the new machine. In other words, the politicians were using the public sector preference in the form of a 'development contract' requested by ICL. But the Committee argued that, in so doing, the precondition of the preference policy of satisfactory price, performance and delivery had not been met. It roundly castigated the CCA for giving Ministers ' only a broad indication of the risks involved without any financial evaluation of those risks '.[32]

The CCA and the Department of Industry won the ensuing battle over the continuation of the preference policy. In this there is little doubt that they were helped by the ideologically favourable Labour government, which had come in during 1974. But cutbacks in public spending were to reduce the value of the preference policy to ICL. In response to the financially stringent climate, the civil service began to lease, rather than to buy computers. In 1976 ICL received 46% of the orders for procured computers from central govenment, but only 37% of the orders for leased machines.[33]

At the same time, in response to changes within the market which favoured smaller sized computers, ICL diversified into minicomputers. By 1976 its best selling product was a minicomputer, which fell beneath the size for which there was an ICL preference. This diversification, in turn, took it away from dependence on central govenment preferential purchasing. In the 1960s, central government orders represented about 20% of ICL's sales in the home market, and another 20% came from the public corporation sector.[34] By 1977, ICL received only 7% of its business from the government and over 50% of its sales were in the export market for minicomputers.[35]

At the beginning of 1980, the new Conservative Government announced that, because GATT rules came into effect in January 1981, the ICL preference would end. The GATT rules had been accepted by the EEC and were therefore enforceable by legal sanction. Effectively the rules outlawed preferential national policies in large computers.

ICL itself considered that the end to

preferential purchasing would have little effect on its turnover. By 1980 only 5.5% of its business (about £40 million)came from the preference policy. But the prospect of a complete liberalisation of trade in computers was something which the industry did not relish. The general feeling was that other European governments would find mechanisms for circumventing the new regulations - by breaking down contracts to below the size to which the regulations referred.

A new pressure group was formed - the United Kingdom Information Technology Organisation. The group consisted of British owned, British based companies. It included ICL, Nexos, GEC Computers, Ferranti, and CAP. Local subsidiaries of overseas manufacturers were denied membership. The intention of the new group was :

> to advise the UK Government and Parliament and other public bodies ..... and to monitor the implementation of international trading arrangements to ensure that any discrimination against UK interests is challenged and removed and to ensure that UK owned and controlled organisations are offered fair opportunities under these arrangements.[36]

One of its first actions was to call for an EEC preference agreement for European owned industry on the grounds that the USA controlled 86% of the world computer market and things had gone too far. Unfortunately the proposals conflicted with the GATT rules accepted by the EEC.[37]

Predictably the scheme came under fire from the UK subsidiaries of US companies, and most vociferously from Honeywell. It argued that preference policies reduced the choice of the consumer and considered that local industry should be helped by such mechanisms as grants rather than by single tender purchasing. The new organisation was also opposed by the Computer Services Association. The new group had stated that the CSA could not act as a lobby for British manufacturers because it had American companies among its membership.[38]

In the same month a new Parliamentary Computer Forum was launched - an inquiry and research service for MPs, to give in-depth briefings on computer issues. The inquiry service was to be run in conjunction with the British Computer Society, and it started its activities with a briefing on public preference policies. Both sides of the argument were

represented.[39] Given that the public preference policy was due to finish at the end of December 1980, it might seem that all the interest was somewhat belated. But the reasoning behind the interest was exactly identical to that behind the sudden politicisation of the UK manufacturers.

One large contract remained to be settled in 1980 - that of the Inland Revenue's large system for computerisation of PAYE. The debate in the Computer Forum preceded an announcement by the government that it intended to review the Inland Revenue's much publicised plan for twelve large on-line systems linked by a regional network. The plan was opposed by interests close to the American multinationals and other software companies. If, instead of the large machines originally envisaged, numbers of small machines were to be used, then the ICL preference policy would not be a consideration. On the large mainframe computer-based system, which ICL had tendered for on a single tender basis, the Chancellor announced tha there would be a review to consider 'alternative approaches'.The Chancellor also said that the Government continued to recognise the importance of the ' maximum feasible involvement' of UK companies and of ' ensuring a high UK content in the system'.[40]

The second part of the statement was especially welcomed by IBM, which had been pressing its claim on the basis that it was a British company, in the sense that it employed many people and contributed to exports and to R&D. The Government delay could itself have been due to pressure exerted by the US multinationals. IBM was known to be looking for another European site for a factory and was 'understood to be putting the word around in political circles that the UK would get the plant if the PAYE contract went IBM's way'. An expansion of its Croydon factory was promised by Burroughs,whilst Honeywell pointed to its factory in Scotland. Univac, which would have had to import all the mainframes for the system, said that, almost certainly,it would build a factory in the UK.[41]

As Parliament reassembled after the summer recess, MPs were bombarded with literature from all sides. A campaign began in favour of a distributed processing system. The attack was mainly launched, not at ICL itself, but at the technical specifications for the project. The Trade Unions also entered the argument on ICL's side. ASTMS argued in favour of ICL's workforce,and ICL mobilised sympathetic MPs.[42]

Once more the multinationals were to be

disappointed in the workings of British liberal ideology. Only days before the deadline, the government decided the contract should go to ICL. Thus ended the public preference policy of the British government - at least formally. Concomitantly, the government announced that the CCA was to be restructured into the Central Computer and Telecommunications Agency, whilst funding for computer purchases was to be transferred back to the spending departments. The possibility of a co-ordinated public sector purchasing policy for data processing was thereby reduced. [43]

Meanwhile Treasury and Conservative ideological concern had shifted to the Public Sector Borrowing Requirement and to cash limits. ICL was asked to extend the operational life of several ten year old computers for another two or three years by additional maintenance, thereby reducing the necessity for replacement computers. Cuts in public expenditure inevitably made their way through to those replacements. Although only 5.5% of ICL's turnover, central government represented 30% of its sales in large computers. Within twelve months the government was forced to bail out ICL.

5.4 PUBLIC PROCUREMENT - MINICOMPUTERS AND PERIPHERALS

During the period under review, companies manufacturing hardware other than ICL received little or no help from the Government of either party, until the appointment of Kenneth Baker as Minister of Information Technology in 1981. No Buy British policy operated in the minicomputer market and small minicomputer manufacturers struggled to raise finance. For instance, Computer Technology Ltd, a small British company sold only 90 computers to central government and 37 to public corportions up to 1974. Digico, another small British manufacturer, sold only 50 computers to the two sectors in the same period. In contrast Data Equipment Corporation (DEC), the American minicomputer manufacturer, sold 338 computers to the two sectors in the same period. Whereas Computer Technology's sales were worth £2.1 million and Digico's £0.3 million, those of DEC were worth £6 million. In 1976 it was revealed that universities had purchased 47% of their minicomputers from abroad in 1973-4 and 76% of them from abroad in 1974-5. [44]

Computer Technology complained to the House of Commons Select Committee in 1970. It said that, as far as the government was concerned, it did not

exist. But the Committee, concerned as it was with the ICL preference, made no recommendations on the procurement or support of the minicomputer manufacturers. The company again made representations to the Committee in 1974, suggesting a European policy towards minicomputers, but the Committee disbanded after the October 1974 election and no recommendation was publicly made to the government.[45]

With the demise of the Committee, there was no obvious way in which small firms could make their views felt in the political arena. The sole organisation left outside the Department of Industry nexus was that of the Electronics Committee of NEDC. But representatives on that committee came mainly from large firms and included representatives of multinationals. However, in 1977 the Trade Union element on the committee made its presence felt. The Committee recommended that a Buy British preference in the public sector should extend to all sectors of the computer market.[46]

The recommendation was greeted by the resignation of the Honeywell representative on the committee. The resignation was then followed by the threat that Honeywell would close its manufacturing facilities in Scotland, and would transfer them to France, where Honeywell Bull had public sector preference. The threats came at a bad time for the Labour Government. It was already under considerable electoral pressure in Scotland, where it was losing seats and support to the Scottish National Party. The possible closures of the two Scottish factories brought immediate pressure from the SNP, who looked set to make considerable political capital out of the issue. The Labour Government therefore did nothing to implement the recommendation, which was debunked in the Press as the notion of rabid Trade Unionists.[47] It is most likely that the political pressure, which Honeywell was able to bring to bear on the government, outweighed any economic arguments in favour of growth areas of industry, such as minicomputers.

Manufacturers of peripherals also received no help from the government of either party. Yet in 1970, NEDO had identified the imports of peripherals as the most rapidly rising component in computer imports, and responsible for more imports than complete computer systems.[48] The likely infuence against giving help to this sector was probably a combination of a fragmented industry, lack of money within the Ministry of Technology, which in the 1960s had no financial vote of its own, and fear of

competition with ICL.

In the 1960s it was common for mainframe manufacturers to buy in peripherals from outside companies, but as the peripherals took a greater proportion of the added value of an installation, so it became more economic for the mainframe manufacturers to produce the peripherals for its own machines to a standardised design. Central government therefore procured both the central processor and the peripherals from ICL. It was this practice which the Select Committee castigated in 1971.

By that time the peripherals market had diversified, responding to demands for varying tapes, discs, printers, terminals and video units. ICL alone could not meet this demand, but the British peripherals industry was highly fragmented and all but dead. Although the Select Committee recommended that the government should support the peripherals industry, the policy of both parties during this period was to leave the peripherals market to take care of itself. Fear of upsetting Honeywell may have been a factor again, but probably of as much importance were the structural constraints of the fragmented market and the civil service predisposition for a passive role towards industry.[49] In turn this style favoured those companies with existing links into Whitehall. By the 1970s, with the exception of ICL's supplier, Data Recording Instruments, there were only a few small peripherals manufacturers. A passive stance towards industrial policy almost inevitably resulted in no action towards any section of industry which did not make its presence felt. And with the demise of the Select Committee, there was no obvious way into the political arena for the small company.

By 1979, the results of this policy were clear. Eighty per cent of peripherals used in Europe were manufactured by subsidiaries of American companies.[50] Responding to this problem, in 1979, the National Enterprise Board, funded a major expansion in Data Recording Instruments. In 1980-81 the company lost £9.5 million, due, it is said, to start-up costs of a subsidiary company, United Peripherals, in which Control Data Corporation had a 24% stake and for management of which it was responsible. The DRI loss raised questions concerning the accountability of the NEB, which had concluded the deal with CDC in secret. DRI was subsequently sold to CDC.[51] The importation of peripherals by American multinationals continues to be one of the most important contributory factors to

COMPUTERS

Britain's balance of payments deficit in information technology products.

Finally the public procurement of microcomputers was ignored by government until 1980. At that time the proposed action by the French Government to purchase 10,000 microcomputers for use in schools seems to have increased Whitehall concern about the lack of computing expertise among schoolchildren. Although in 1979 the Department of Education had found £9 million for a programme to educate teachers into using computers, a Department of Industry survey in April 1980 discovered that only 1000 secondary school children (1 in 8) had access of even a limited kind to a computer.

In response, the Department of Industry announced a microcomputer scheme in which there would be 100 computer systems, of £2000 each, for winners of an essay competition.[52] These were to be made by a small British company, Research Machines. Later a further programme to provide 50% of the finance for a computer in each secondary school was announced, to be followed by a similar scheme for primary schools. These programmes, coupled with computer orientation programmes by the BBC, may have had both the intention and the effect of increasing demand for home computers. It is noticeable that those small computer manufacturerers, such as Acorn, with machines specified as suitable for these programmes, have boomed, whilst those, such as Newbrain, whose machines narrowly missed being specified, have subsequently failed. Research Machines also figured in the list of nine microcomputer, which the CCTA had drawn up for all purchases of central government microcomputers in 1981. But the company was only one of three British manufacturers to appear on the list. British microcomputer companies complained that the government was doing too little for too few British manufacturers. The same complaint recurred in 1982 with several British manufacturers complaining that, although talk about buying British came out of the Department of Industry, it had had little effect on procurement.[53]

The conflict between the Thatcher Government's free market ideology and the major role played by the state through public procurement in fostering domestic industry, is well illustrated by the actions of the new Information Technology Minister. Speaking in February 1982, the year the Department of Industry had named Information Technology year, he argued to the NEDC that the role of government was essentially that of providing the 'infrastructure and domestic environment in which IT industries can

achieve growth'. Yet, in the same speech, he called on managers in the investment and procurement area 'to take investment and procurement decisions with the long-term objectives of the UK industry in mind'.[54] But as UKITO and the microcomputer manufacturers had pointed out, these actions needed central direction.

5.5 PUBLIC PROCUREMENT OF SOFTWARE

Whether specialist software firms are used in central government depends upon the attitudes of civil servants to in-house specialism. Traditionally the civil service in Britain has preferred to have control over its own data processing facilities and to have its own data processing staff. Opposed to this practice, the software industry has claimed that it constitutes a wasteful use of scarce resources in computer personnel. Certainly as data processing skills became marketable, during the early 1970s, so government lost those it had trained into private industry. The amount of government purchasing of external software expertise and the amount which public corporations and local authorities leased out spare capacity on their computers, remained a bone of contention between the software industry and the government throughout the period.

From 1966 to 1970, the central government purchased generalised software from ICL in conjunction with its mainframes. Specialised software was either developed by the civil service itself or was bought in from Dataskil, ICL's software subsidiary. Then, in 1970, the software industry through the CSA complained of the government's failure to support the industry. It pressed the issue both with the Ministry of Technology and in the trade press. It repeated these complaints to the Select Committee in 1971, but by the mildness with which it pursued them, commentators thought that a change of policy was imminent.

In what seems to have been anticipated reaction to the Committee's recommendations, the government announced that it was reviewing its procurement policy towards the software industry. It complained, however, that the large number of software firms made the use of the industry on a consultancy basis difficult. In 1968, an analysis by the Ministry of Technology had shown that the public sector had spent approximately £4 million on the use of the services of the largest 92 computer bueaux. Some of

that work would however have included straightforward use of computer time for data processing, rather than consultancy work. A current figure of £1.5 million per annum was mentioned in 1971, as being the level of government purchasing of 'consultancy and software support'.[55]

In 1972, the Conservative Government announced that 'development contracts' would be used in future for ' advanced applications systems to meet customer requirements, involving users and software houses in addition to ICL'.[56] But the CSA commented, in 1976, that these contracts seemed to have been designed for ICL. No other member of the services industry had been awarded such a contract, a fact related perhaps to the intrinsic involvement of the Central Computer Agency in the process of issuing software contracts. Of other companies, approximately 125 had been awarded contracts by 1976, but 75% of the work had been done by forty companies. In total, by 1976, the government was reported to be spending £6 million per annum on software services.[57]

However, the CSA was able to show in a report, prepared for discussions with the Department of Industry, that the level of government support for software had decreased in real terms since 1972/3. The CSA argued that software houses were given short term contracts and that, because they were not normally able to enquire into the basic purposes for which systems were intended, or ' to test the relevance of a computer system to the needs of the organisation', they were rarely given the opportunity to use their management skills effectively.

It contrasted the situation with that in the USA and Canada where the government used external software companies for the majority of its computing work. It called for an increase in government use of consultants and a concomitant decrease of expenditure on providing in-house resources. Recognising possible opposition from the civil service trade unions, it suggested that future increases in government work should be met by a gradual increase in the use of outside resources. It pointed to experience in America where manpower had stayed constant in Federal Government employment in data processing but expenditure on processing services outside had grown substantially.[58]

Other representations for the support of software were made by the Electronics Committee of the NEDC. It proposed, in 1977, that the government should give purchasing preference to software houses, which developed systems for UK minicomputer manufacturers. This nationalistic proposal met

similar opposition to its proposals on the support for UK minicomputer manufacturers. It was not until 1978 that the software industry itself gained representation on the EDC. There followed a report from the EDC pointing to the shortage of manpower in the data processing industry, a point which underlined arguments about the wastefulness of central government in-house computing capabilities.[59] To some extent, increased use of external services was forced on the government by the economic situation of the latter 1970s. In the year 1979-80, total sales of the software service industry rose by 30%. The contribution of the public sector to those sales had risen to 10%. It is probable that cutbacks in civil service personnel and failure to upgrade computers forced changes on departments in their use of short-term support from external sources. Logically, the easing of the ICL preference for large-scale computers should also make more likely the use of software consultants. The problem of retaining data processing personnel within the public sector pay scales is also likely to increase that trend.[60]

5.6 CONCLUSIONS ON PUBLIC PROCUREMENT

In conclusion to this section one can say that the British Government policy of preference for ICL computers remained almost unchanged for fourteen years. The sole changes which occurred publicly in the policy came, either in anticipation of, or in response to, recommendations of the Select Committee of the House of Commons. These included the establishment of the Central Computer Agency and the slight extension of software consultancy use. Yet the value of the policy was itself eroded, first by the conflict between 'efficiency' and 'sponsorship', which erupted into public debate and damaged ICL's reputation, and second, by changes in the markets themselves. As ICL expanded into the minicomputer market, not covered by the procurement policy, so it became less dependent financially on the policy. However the raison d'etre of the Central Computer Agency was the procurement policy, and it is possibly not too much to speculate that the Agency's interdependence with ICL became a prime factor in the continuation of the original policy.

That policy, through which mainframe computer, software and peripherals were bought from ICL, clearly conflicted with an extension of the use of external software consultants and with government

support for peripherals companies other than ICL. It may be that the organisational weight of the CCA was effective in limiting any extension of support in those directions. But public sector preferential purchasing of British minicomputers would have favoured ICL. It is therefore probable that political pressures on the government were more potent than the possibility of influencing a growth market.

Neither ICL, nor any other computer manufacturer, could pack the political weight of Honeywell, with its factories in Scotland and backing from Scottish National MPs. It was therefore prudent of the Labour Government to allow Honeywell to portray the report of the EDC, which recommended a Buy British minicomputer policy, as being the work of a body dominated by Trade Unionists devoted to protectionism. In this instance, the Labour Government's much vaunted economic strategy, newly announced in 1976, seems to have fallen to pressure from an American multinational.

In software procurement, although the publicly announced policy changed, in practice the amount central government spent on external software services increased by only a relatively small amount over the period. Although it is possible to surmise that the CCA may have had a hand in dampening down a development which would have threatened the Buy ICL policy, a more likely cause was the traditional desire on the part of departments to have control over their own data processing. To have allowed software consultants to question whether a system was suitable would both have the endangered the ICL preference and would also have demanded that senior civil servants without expertise in the management of computer installations deal with outside specialists. Even as recently as 1980,[61] a report from the Civil Service College pointed out that administrative trainees received no training in computer use, and that, although one fifth of the 750 top civil servants were responsible for major computer systems, those civil servants perceived little need for any more training in management of such systems.

The policy of preference for ICL ended publicly because of external pressure from EEC harmonisation rules. The pressure brought by ICL and American manufacturers on MPs, in relation to the PAYE contract, suggests that industry had begun to recognise the importance of Parliamentary pressure on the outcome of government decisions. That computer companies felt it worthwhile to maintain a permanent liaison group with Parliament, whilst British

COMPUTERS

companies formed their own lobby group, is an indication of the increased role of Parliament in the policy process during the late 1970s. In this instance, and in the way in which small companies were able to have pressure exerted on Whitehall on their behalf through the Select Committee, points to the importance of political mediation in Britain between industry and bureaucracy.

5.7 RESEARCH, DEVELOPMENT AND INVESTMENT

In the case of the computer industry it is almost impossible to separate grants for research and development from grants for investment in general. One reason is that the electronics industry spends a higher proportion of its turnover on research and development than do other industries. R&D expenditure takes the place of the capital investment in buildings and machinery of other industries. A second reason is that the majority of the money spent by the Government on R&D in the computer industry has gone to ICL. Some of that money has been labelled specifically for research and development and has been administered by the NRDC (now the British Technology Group). But the majority of the money has been in the form of grants and loans wihtout specific strings attached to its expenditure. Approximately 87% of the government money spent on research and development in the computing sector has gone to ICL. The exceptions have been grants to universities and some programmes funded 50% by industry and 50% by government.

Although a Computer Requirements Board was set up within the Department of Industry in 1971, with the intention of co-ordinating research programmes with the Ministry of Aviation, and of providing a new focus for research, its importance can be estimated from its original budget of one million pounds, some of which was already earmarked. Only between £200,000 and £300,000 per year has been devoted to a joint programme with the industry on software development.[62] In 1980, in contrast, ICL requested a grant of £6 million from the Government for the development of a new Distributed Array Processor.[63]

From its inception in 1976, the National Enterprise Board pursued a policy separate from that of the Department of Industry. Its policy was to invest in the peripherals, software, small business computer mini and microcomputer markets. The Board, which was given a borrowing limit of £750 million

(later raised to £3000 million) was free to 'exercise its commercial judgement' in investments worth less that £10 million.[64] Within a year of its inception, it had bought four software companies, had set up a consortium to market software products abroad (Insac), had set up a company to produce and market automated office machinery (Nexos), and had formed a microcomputer company in conjunction with Q1(US) Corporation. In 1979, the projects were threatened as Conservative backbenchers pressed for the end to government involvement in industry, and the whole NEB Board resigned over the removal of its control over Rolls Royce. But the NEB survived under a reconstituted Board until merged with the NRDC in 1981.

The projects themselves seem to have been dogged by problems. Dissension on the Insac Board resulted in the company being split into two, with one company, Insac Viewdata, concentrating upon marketing British Telecom's Prestel system. In 1982 Nexos failed and marketing rights to its word processor were taken over by ICL. In total Nexos cost and lost £28 million. Its failure illustrates the problems of market intervention where customer base has already been lost to overseas manufacturers as in the office technology market.[65]

In the early 1980s, various small microcomputer firms were given funds by the Department of Industry. These are not published, because they fall below the lower limit set for publication of figures for government aid. Yet, even if expenditure on microelectronics is included, the NEB expenditure on computer equipment of £36.5 million up to 1980 must be compared to its investment of £700,000 million in British Leyland and Rolls Royce.[66] Even the hardware computer industry has received relatively little of the national resources that have been available, despite the fact that the computer market has been a growth market.

5.8 RATIONALISATION AND FOREIGN TECHNOLOGY

The third feature of British government intervention in the computer market has been the encouragement or discouragement of rationalisation, both within domestic boundaries and within the EEC. Faced in the 1960s with a small home market, a policy of support for rationalisation of British computer manufacturers could be said to make economic sense. It gave a larger customer base to one firm, and it allowed the concentration of R&D resources. The process of

this rationalisation had already begun to take place in response to market forces before the government gave support in 1967, to the Elliot Automation/ English Electric merger. Its support in that particular case took the form of a £15 million loan.

Similarly, at the time of government support for the ICT merger with English Electric Computers in 1968, it was said that it was no more than a hastening of the inevitable. Discussion of the need for such a merger had been public since 1966, but it was expected that the companies would delay until their generations of machines needed replacement and they could co-operate on mutually compatible technology.67 In the final merger, in 1968, 53.5% of the shareholding was taken up by ICT's former shareholders, 10.5% was taken by the Government and 18.5% each went to English Electric (later taken over by GEC) and Plessey. In return for a £3.5 million equity stake and £14 million grant aid, the government took one seat on the Board of Directors and held certain reserve powers over the company. Although ICL was assured that the Minister would not intervene in the day to day running of the company, his permission was required for any association by ICL with foreign companies or with foreign controlled companies in Britain, except for trading or licensing agreements. His permission was also needed for any major change in the nature of the business of ICL. It is not at all clear what changes would be covered by this clause in the legislation on the merger, but, legally, it opened avenues for governmental influence on marketing decisions.[68]

Stephen Young and A.V. Lowe state that the rationale underlying the creation of large companies, during the period of the 1964-70 Labour Government, stemmed from fear of entry into the EEC.[69] It was assumed that entry would lead to mergers with Continental companies, and that large size would give a whip hand in negotiations. With a small home market for computers, with exports to Eastern Europe handicapped by the strategic arms embargo and opposition from the USA, with export entry to the American market effectively blocked by the Buy American Act and the dominance of American mainframe manufacturers, the obvious place to look for an expansion of the market, and of the customer base of the UK computer industry was to the EEC. Harold Wilson even talked of a European technological community to challenge the hegemony of the States.[70] Then, in the late 1960s the French and German governments began to support their own national computer industries. For British

COMPUTERS

Figure 5.1 Some Negotiations Between UK Mainframe Manufacturers and Foreign Owned Companies.

Year	Companies involved	Attitude of UK Govt.	Type of Agreement
1965	CITEC(FR) EE-LEO	neg.	Joint production of large computer.
1965	ICT CITEC	?	Marketing of commercial computers.
1967	ELLIOT CGA(FR)	?	Exchange of information.
1969 C.O.S.T. (EEC)	OLIVETTI(ITALY) CII(FR) PHILIPS(NETH) TELEFUNKEN(FDR) SIEMENS(FDR) ICL	neg. pos. pos.	Build giant computer. European computer idex. European common standards.
1970	ICL CII CDC(US)	pos.	Plan standard interfaces and machine architecture
1971	ICL US SOFTWARE CO.	neutral.	Joint software company.
1972	ICL BURROUGHS(US)	neg.	Takeover by Burroughs.
1972-3	ICL CII SIEMENS TELEFUNKEN	pos.	French and German companies instructed by their governments to start talks with ICL on joint projects.
	NIXDORF(FDR) TELEFUNKEN ICL	pos.	Merger.
1976	ICL SINGER BUSINESS MACHINES(US)	?	Takeover of Singer in Europe by ICL.
1978	UNIVAC(US) ICL	neg.	Univac to buy 30% of ICL.
1981	UNIVAC ICL	pos. then neg.	Takeover by Univac.

manufacturers to break into the EEC market required either local manufacturing units, or marketing agreements with EEC firms.

Figure 5.1 illustrates some instances of government reaction to ICL involvement in merger and other collaborative proposals. Between 1964 and 1970, both Labour and Conservative Governments were broadly in favour of collaboration with EEC firms, although not always in favour of the particular form of collaboration proposed. For instance, the proposal to manufacture an Anglo/French large computer met with British government resistance on the basis that there would be only a very small market for an expensive project.[71] In particular, as one might expect, the 1970-74 Conservative administration was particularly enthusiastic in encouraging ICL to look for a European partner. After 1974 the policy changed. The Labour Government looked at European collaboration with suspicion, claiming that ICL was larger than its French or German counterparts and would gain little.[72]

The alternative strategy for ICL - to buy an American firm or merge with an American company - was discouraged by both parties. This discouragement was hardly surprising. ICL had been brought into existence to fight off American competition and an increased American input into ICL technology would have created further difficulties in exports to Eastern Europe. At least one American firm, RCA, could have been bought fairly cheaply, for its customer base during this period. Eventually this alternative strategy was adopted by ICL when, in 1976, it bought the European base of Singer Business Machines (US). The acquisition gave ICL three thousand extra customers, marketing bases in France and West Germany, and entry in a large way into the minicomputer market.[73] ICL also subsequently set up a subsidiary in the USA.

In 1971 the Select Committee registered its concern at the government's influence over the international policy of ICL, and it is likely that political considerations influenced attempts by ICL to join up with French and German companies. Only when, in 1973, the French, Germans and Dutch formed Unidata (a co-operative arrangement on marketing) without inviting ICL to join, may the alternative American strategy for entry into EEC markets have become politically attractive, and, therefore, a feasible policy for ICL to pursue. ICL's special relationship with the British govenment may well have handicapped its business strategy.[74]

Whether that special relationship also affected

ICL's decisions on entry into the growth markets of mini and microcomputers is less clear. The influence of ex-IBM personnel within ICL and their prediliction for large central processors rather than a distributed network of small computers is said to have been partly responsible for ICL's late entry into the minicomputer market.But, in 1978, the British Trade Press began to question the viability of ICL's manufacture of large computers.Commentators pointed out that large computers were less in favour on the Continent than medium sized computers.[75] The prime market for the large computers - the British Government - took 30% of ICL's production. Despite ICL's contention that this sector of its market was a profitable enterprise, the suspicion remained that ICL with the aid of government funding, had begun development on a new generation of large computers partly because it was caught in the trap of having to upgrade its old government 1900 machines. By the latter 1970s ICL had still not entered the small business system microcomputer markets then beginning their boom in the USA, and in the 1980s it became clear that ICL was not reacting fast enough to the convergence of technology with telecommunications.[76]

Despite these continuing criticisms and despite a government appointed director on ICL's Board, there seems to have been no intervention by government in ICL's market strategy.In fact it seems that the goverment appointed director had no specific duty to liaise with the government on ICL. That liaison took place between the Chairman and the Minister.[77] So, although ICL's links with the British government may have added an extra parameter to its decisions on whether to enter or exit from markets, the government itself seems to have interfered directly only in specifically 'political issues' such as cross-national mergers. Otherwise ICL was allowed autonomy.The effect of its special relationship with government was felt mainly through the structural interdependence created between the two organisations.

ICL's special relationship with government was thought to have ended in 1979 when the shares held on behalf of the government by the NEB were sold to financial institutions. The sell-off took place primarily to provide cash to relieve the Public Sector Borrowing Requirement and was a watershed in the history of ICL. By selling shares to institutions, rather than to other manufacturers, the government ensured there was no outside interference in the management of ICL. It also passed up

the opportunity to link ICL structurally into other markets, such as telecommunications. Among all the European computer companies, only ICL and Honeywell-Bull of France were completely dependent on the data processing market. Whilst companies, such as GEC and Plessey, were diversifying into office technology from telecommunications, ICL remained committed to 100% data processing without a telecommunications input, or a defense linkage, or coverage of the whole range of data processing machines.

Hardly had the procurement preference ended in January 1981, than it became apparent that ICL was in financial trouble. There is, in fact, some evidence to show that the government had become aware of some of these financial problems as early as October 1980, before the PAYE decision.[78] The Department of Industry was said to have held discussion with Shell B.P. and GEC in an attempt to find a private sector solution to ICL's need for cash. The company's problems became public in November 1980, with the peremptory announcement of 2,500 redundancies. ICL explained the redundancies as due to over-valued sterling, high interest rates and falling demand abroad. With 50% of its turnover in exports ICL was particularly vulnerable to exchange rate appreciation.

The full extent of ICL's problems were not revealed until December 1980, when the year's figures showed it had made a £4.6 million profit in the second half compared to a £20 million profit in the first half of 1980. The collapse took the City by surprise and within two days ICL shares had been marked down to 70p - a dramatic decline from the high of 198p earlier in the year.[79]

The figures revealed obvious problems of cashflow. ICL's new generation of computers had been introduced in a recessionary climate. Instead of upgrading existing installations by purchasing new computers, companies had reduced immediate outgoings by switching to rental. ICL had been left to pick up the huge bill for manufacture which could only be discounted over seven or more years.

Beyond these obvious problems, the collapse also demonstrated how far ICL had become isolated from those domestic public markets which were still growing. Unlike GEC or Ferranti or Racal, other major electronics companies, ICL was not tied into the defence sector. Nor like GEC or Plessey was it tied to the telecommunications sector. In fact, in 1980, British Telecom delayed announcement of its transfer of directory enquiries onto computers and

eventually bought IBM not ICL machines.[80]

The isolation of ICL into the data processing market, its manufacture of large computers, for which the public sector market had been cut back, and failure to involve the company in other markets must be laid at the door of its various managements, the NEB and the Department of Industry in previous years. Similarly, the cash problems of ICL in 1980 can be traced to the failure of the British government to act in the 1960s to provide a government-backed rental scheme. In contrast to solutions found in both France and Japan, the government had been content to allow a private sector solution, via the banks, to the problems of financing rental.

In January 1981, the Chairman of ICL was involved in a frantic round of meetings with stockbrokers to attempt to regain confidence in the company. But there was considerable doubt about whether ICL could actually afford to meet its loan commitments. By February, its shares had sunk to 37p.

Meanwhile, the Department of Industry continued to exert pressure on GEC to invest in the company. There was some comment that the intention was to bring back Geoffrey Cross, the previous manager of ICL, who had subsequently joined GEC. But the proposal had eventually been acknowledged to be a non-starter. By March, the Department was said to be looking favourably at the possibility of a 'white knight' from abroad. But such negotiations took time and, by the end of March, ICL's cash flow problems were such that it needed to raise credit which its bankers were unwilling to extend.

At the beginning of April, the Industry Minister, Sir Keith Joseph, announced a credit guarantee of £200 million. Before hostile members of his own party, he argued that the government investment in ICL, and its dependence on ICL for its own computing needs, made it necessary to provide the guarantee. But the hostile reaction of government right-wing MPs to 'creating the British Leylands and British Steel Corporations of the future' and taunts from Labour members of 'another U turn' made the possibility of asking the NEB to invest in the company a political impossibility. A private sector solution therefore had to be found. The Department encouraged ICL's existing management to hold discussions with Sperry Univac, the only foreign company, which could be found to be interested in ICL. During these discussions the Department explored the possibility of a Japanese

linkage for ICL.[81]

For a time it seemed that Univac would provide the solution. But then the terms it was prepared to offer became known. It intended to pay ICL shareholders only pence above the 37p at which the stockmarket had frozen dealings in ICL shares. Furthermore it became clear that Univac was only interested in ICL's customer base and its joint venture with Saab of Sweden in 1975 could be used as a reliable predictor of the outcome. As Saab's customers' machines had come due for renewal, so Univac had offered to convert them to its own machines, with the result that R&D and manufacturing in Sweden had soon ended. The transition to Univac machines once complete amongst Saab's customers, Univac had bought Saab out of the company. A similar scenario in relation to ICL's computers would have created a situation where Univac could have held the British government to ransom on the maintenance and renewal of its machines.

The realisation of the implications of the Univac bid seems to have caused a split in opinion within Whitehall. On the one side the Central Policy Review Staff was of the opinion that funding of R & D through mainframe computer companies, such as ICL, was irrelevant to the future of an integrated telecommunications based microcomputer technology. ICL should be allowed to go to Univac. In this outcome it seems that the Treasury concurred, worried that the commitment to bail out ICL would result in increasing amounts of expenditure (the £200 million guarantee, if taken up,would come out of the PSBR). Ranged against these two departments and Ministers ideologically committed to non-intervention were the Department of Industry, in alliance with the Central Computer Agency. Kenneth Baker, the new Minister of Information Technology, was known to be sympathetic to government intervention, and the disposal of ICL into foreign hands would have left him with only the small stock of companies under the NEB's wing, from which to construct a policy for the industry.

The proponents for keeping ICL devised an alternative strategy- a change in management with the specific task of putting ICL back into profit within two years. At that time, ICL could then be joined up as a going concrn with the highest bidder. The plan had the advantage that existing shareholders - and particularly those shareholders who had been sold their investment on the implicit guarantee of future profits made by the NEB - would at least have the chance of recouping some of their money. How far the institutional market played a role in the final

decision is unknown. But if the institutions had lost faith in the government as seller, then it might have been difficult for the government to sell other publicly owned companies such as Cable and Wireless. It may be also that the fact that Univac was also completely dependent on data processing affected the decision. That dependence on data processing might have left the British government in a vulnerable position a second time around. A further factor may also have been the government of Saudi Arabia's dependence on ICL machines - Mrs Thatcher had just returned with export orders for defence equipment which might have been cancelled if ICL had been taken over.[82]

Finally a change in the management of the company was announced. The new Chairman, a BP man, took over from the previous Merchant Banker Chairman, whilst the new Managing Director came from the microelectronics firm of Texas Instruments, known for its aggressive marketing. The new management immediately terminated talks with Sperry Univac, whilst the government pledged itself to support ICL's R&D (ICL needed £70 million) and to buy the company's products. The previous managing director, Chris Wilson, was kept on the Board. The new management went out of its way to point out that ICL's problems were not his fault. ICL had been unlucky in introducing a new product line at a time of recession.The new managing director, Rob Wilmott, also argued that distributed networks would still need large mainframe computers and ICL's ability to offer the whole range would put it at an advantage over microcomputer companies. He pointed out that ICL could also manufacture compatible products under licence from other companies, or have marketing agreements with other companies in order to extend its range of products.[83]

Within a short time ICL had announced a tie-up with CDC of the USA, a maker of very large computers, and with Fujitsu of Japan. For the first time ICL also ventured into the defence market in the USA. Later,ICL announced that it had entered an agreement with Mitel of Canada to market its large private telephone exchange, which it intended to use as the basis for development of networks of automated,integrated office equipment.ICL has not only begun to extend its product range but has also begun to integrate across markets.[84]Perhaps the most ironic part of the 'rescue' of ICL was that the NEB had sold off its shares directly to raise money to reduce the Public Sector Borrowing Requirement. The Treasury had held up the replacement of ICL large

computers for the same reason. And both actions helped to hasten the crisis.

There seems no reason to believe that the government decision to rescue ICL was related to fears of technological dependence upon America. In both the fields of microcomputers and office technology, governments of both parties have allowed the free flow of foreign technology into the country and have allowed public sector agencies to actually invite dependence. For instance, the NEB entered the automated office machinery sector, with the establishment of Nexos. This firm linked up with the American Delphi Corporation, a subsidiary of Exxon, for a licensing agreement to sell its telephone answering video machine. It also signed a contract to import Japanese products. Later the NEB formed a microcomputer company Q1 Europe, a joint venture with Q1 Corporation of America to manufacture its products in England. The NEB also developed an Anglo-American fund to provide finance for British companies wishing to exploit American technology. Hence the general tenor of the NEB in the office technology sector was to encourage dependence on American technology.[85] No complaint about its activities were heard on that score from either political party.

5.9 CONCLUSION

In his article on the European computer hardware industry, Nicholas Jequier argued that the industry was used by national governments during the 1960s for prestige purposes.[86] It is certainly true that during that decade governments saw technology as a means to national prestige. Harold Wilson was not alone in believing that a 'technological break through' was needed to put Britain ahead of the world. Nationalistic considerations, especially the fear of domination by American technology, can be seen in the British government's rationalisation of the computer industry and its original decision to support ICL. Predominant party political considerations also influenced the Conservative Government's enthusiasm for a merger between ICL and a Continental company and the Labour Government's suspicion of any such thing. But as the status stakes in the computer industry reduced, so one might have expected nationalistic sentiments towards the industry to have diminished and market strategy to have taken over in importance. Yet it is obvious that this has not been the case.

COMPUTERS

    The continuation without change by successive British governments of a policy of support for the computer industry devized in the 1960s and rapidly out of tune with changing markets cannot be explained by purely political factors. Nor can it be explained in terms of a failure of information about market growth. The Ministry of Technology, in its evidence to the Select Committee in 1972 showed that it had accurate information on the growth of the minicomputer and software markets. It undertook a survey of software bureaux as early as 1968. In addition, between 1964 and 1970, the Electronics Committee of the NEDC published data which explicitly conveyed the message that the sector of the industry in which most imports occurred was that of the peripherals market. Independent market analysis also produced forecasts which showed the growth of the software and peripherals markets to exceed that of the mainframe market. Government had access to these reports.
    It is unlikely that it was lack of information on markets, which caused successive government failure to pay attention to manufacturers other than ICL. But, judging from a comment by Tony Benn to the Select Committee, it may be that information on markets was not finding its way to the political head of the Ministry. He remarked in 1974 that the advice he was receiving on markets was different from that which he received in 1970, whereas the market forecasts in those years hardly altered.[87] One may assume from those comments that computer policy was not an area in which that particular Minister was interested and that, after the initial publicity in the 1964 government, the policy became bureaucratic rather than a publicity generating mechanism on which a minister might hang his cap.
    It seems probable that the internal policy making world of the bureaucracy took over and gradually evolving organisational structures acted to protect established policy. Within government the responsibility for a 'computer' policy was originally fragmented, and the goals of that policy were both unclear and, on occasion, mutually incompatible. The goal of support for ICL clashed with sponsorship for the industry as a whole. The goal of regional development and attraction of multinationals into regions clashed with public preference for ICL products. Whilst the Ministry of Technology was responsible for sponsorship, the departments, public corportions, local authorities and universities were responsible for procurement. Negotiations with EEC companies rested with the

Foreign Office.

In this fragmented bureaucracy the Ministry of Technology originally wielded little power. It had no vote for expenditure and had to beg for specific funds from the Treasury. Only as it accrued more functions did it gain more centrality. Its change of leadership from Frank Cousins to Tony Benn in 1966 helped towards this process, as did the recognition from 1968 that the IRC was not to be the major instrument of intervention in industry that the Labour Government had expected.

It is reasonable to assume that the original policy of support for ICL arose, first, from a political need on the part of the Ministry of Technology to make a public gesture but to do something fairly inexpensive, and, second, from the current political concern for rationalisation. It was only when organisational reform coincided with the introduction of a public preference policy that the organisational mechanisms evolved to produce a 'core' computer policy around which other policy goals were added or subtracted, Subsequently, with the entrenchment of bureaucrtic interests, other policy mechanisms came to be measured by whether they fitted in with the 'core' policy of support for ICL.

Two points seem to have been crucial to this process. The disbandment of the Department of Economic Affairs released the Ministry of Technology from competition with a department which had an overview of the import/export structure of the electronics industry. It was George Brown, not the Minister of Technology, who in 1965, started a train of political consciousness on the public sector purchase of computers. Following the demise of the DEA, the sole institution within central government with this remit of overview of an industry - NEDO - lacked centrality in the policy process. Its recommendations could be undermined or ignored and the representatives of multinationals on its committee could be expected to oppose any developments which might threaten their market share. Hence NEDO was neither an equal nor independent bureaucratic competitor with the Ministry of Technology.

The second important organisational development was the establishment of the Central Computer Agency. Seeking efficiency and co-ordination, the Conservative Government produced an organisation with its own budget, whose interests and those of its client company, ICL, coalesced around the procurement preference policy. An alliance of

interest existed between the CCA and the Department of Trade and Industry (later the Department of Industry).The CCA bought predominantly ICL computers. The Department of Industry supported ICL R&D for new generations of computers.
It should be remembered that to the Department of Industry and its political leadership 'sponsorship' of the industry meant a channel of communication and a predominantly passive role towards industrial policy. Policy involved making decisions on approaches for finance from individual companies under one or other of the Industry Acts. Compared to the fragmented software industry or to the almost non-existent peripherals industry,ICL had the virtue of ease of access. It even had a separate department within the company from which to negotiate with government. In addition, the public manner of ICL's establishment and the public 'success' of previous subvention depended upon the survival of ICL. Inevitably one subvention led to another and to the limitation of policy to that which did not threaten ICL's survival. Coupled with lack of money in the Department, it was probably the evolution of interdependent organisational structures which led,at least in part, to continued support for ICL and lack of concern for manufacturers other than ICL.
Aginst these private organisational interests of the CCA and the Department three different strategic plays seem to have been successful. The first two relied on political mediation, the second on bureaucratic competition. The first strategic play was to gain a public reassessment of policy.
The software industry achieved a public redefinition of policy in its favour in anticipation of its appearance before the Select Committee. (It fits our explanation that the policy change worked out to be less dramatic than the public pronouncement suggested, and in fact originally worked in ICL's favour). In this context the Select Committee was of considerable importance. Publicity for a cause does not necessarily generate political pressure. Constraints on time ensure that the political arena of a Minister is delineated by what reaches him through the civil service and the House of Commons. The Select Committee can be seen as an institution in the political arena through which manufacturers without an interface with the civil service can channell their discontent. Political mediation replaced direct civil service/industry negotiations. After the disbandment of the Select Committee in 1974, for several years the sole method

to achieve entry to the Minister's agenda, was through MP's Parliamentary Questions. Although approximately 20 questions per year were asked subsequently about the computer industry, few concerned markets other than mainframes. The recent formation of an Information Technology Group of backbench MPs, of the Parliamentary Computer Forum and the foundation of UKITO by British manufacturers have all testified to the growing recognition, on the part of industry, of the crucial role to be played by parliamentary political mediation between itself and the civil service.

It is pertinent that organisational interests within the civil service may also use similar strategies to gain a redefinition of policy in their favour. The Defence Ministry attempted in the 1970s to exclude itself from the ICL preference policy through the mechanism of the Public Accounts Committee. It was defeated by the weight of ideological commitment of the Labour Government to public preference, but succeeded in publicising the role of the CCA in protecting ICL interests within central government.

During the 1970s one market which was not totally ignored by MPs was that of minicomputers. That fact probably stems from the head of Computer Technology, Ian Barron, who became a political animal, eventually heading the NEB backed microelectronics firm Inmos. One might have expected that since ICL diversified into the minicomputer market in 1976, it would have been in the interests of ICL, the CCA and the Department of Industry to extend the procurement preference to minicomputers. The evidence suggests that their preference was to do just that. But in the second kind of strategic play, Honeywell, the American multinational, was able to use the Labour government's fear of electoral defeat in Scotland to outmanoeuvre the two agencies and the Trade Unionists of the NEDC. Hence party political considerations overruled industrial strategy.

The third kind of strategy which succeeded in altering established policy was the creation of a competitive bureaucracy, in the form of the National Enterprise Board. Staffed by businessmen uncluttered by established bureaucratic interests, the NEB's resources in its competition with the Department included its relative autonomy, its expertise, its confidential negotiations with business and the political commitment to its work of the Labour Government. It also held the remit, never held by the Department of Industry, to foster growth in high risk industry. It also had its own finance. Its

relations with the Department seem to have varied from individual to individual civil servant, with the NEB claiming it worked in co-operation with the Department and some civil servants claiming the opposite.

But, even under the Labour Government, the NEB was restricted in its power. It could invest in microcomputers and peripherals but concomitant policies of procurement and R&D expenditure, as well as indirect measures to finance the expansion of markets, were under the control of the CCA, the Computer Requirements Board, the NRDC and the Department of Industry. Despite regular pressure by the industries concerned, in the trade press, at conventions, and through the Electronics Committee of the NEDC, no overall computer policy, no strategy for the whole industry had come about by 1980. The issue had not made the political agenda. Nor would it seem to have been a particularly propitious time to begin to talk of a government strategic concern for industry, when the ideological stance of the government of the day was in the opposite direction.

Two opportunities seem to have presented themselves. The first was the intention, mooted in Opposition, for the Conservative Government to liberalise the telecommunications monopoly. That liberalisation was pressed for by the telecommunications companies themselves, with their close links to government. In fact they wanted limited liberalisation of the Post Office monopoly of attachments to the network. Similarly computer companies moving into telecommunications, such as IBM, again with links into government both directly to the Minister, and indirectly through backbench MPs, were in favour of liberalisation of both the attachments and transmission. Liberalisation was seen as the necessary precursor to the development of the private office technology market.

In 1979 the Computer Requirements Board of the Department of Industry, responsible for the department's funding of R&D, commissioned a report from Ian Barron, then at the Science Policy Research Unit at Sussex. The report was to review future trends in information technology. The report emphasised the crucial role to be played by telecommunications and castigated the Post Office for its tardiness in the development of digital telephone exchanges and its slow progress in providing a data network. Having been kept under wraps for twelve months, under the pressure of civil servants at the Department of Industry, the report was published in 1980.[88]

In 1980 there also emerged from the Cabinet Office an ACARD report, which pointed to the necessity for Britain to take up the challenge of information technology.[89] It is perfectly possible, given other instances of civil servants' ability to use the Whitehall organisational structure for their own interests, that civil servants in the Department of Industry were involved in some respect in the ACARD report. But coming from the Cabinet Office the report had the authority of centrality. Suddenly the issue was political. Within a month the government had appointed a Minister of Information Technology within the Department of Industry. The first appointment seems to have been a stop gap, and hardly serious, since the occupant was moved after only two months in the job. His successor was chosen, so he contends, because he had set out several times in public his own plan for the computer industry. It seems that in lieu of having any specific policy regarding the computer industry, the Conservative Government was prepared to take the pragmatic approach of appointing someone as Minister with his own ideas.

One of Kenneth Baker's first actions as Minister in 1981 was to introduce computer terminals into the Department, so that civil servants might have practical experience of what they were dealing with. His appointment linked him with a previous assistant secretary in the CCA, Reay Atkinson, responsible as Under Secretary, in the Department, for Information Technology. He had himself previously called publicly for an integrated computer policy.[90]

Since Kenneth Baker's appointment, the Department has funded studies of the office technology markets in an effort to analyse where the growth in products will be. For the first time the Department is moving away from responding to outside pressures to considering the structure of markets. Yet, the dissatisfaction of ICL, of software companies and of microcomputer manufacturers with the procurement policy points to the difficulties of a Minister appointed to foster a 'free' market.

From the point of view of those who wish to see the complete liberalisation of information technology markets, the weak link remains telecommunications and the Department's control of British Telecom. TEMA has commented:

> The experience of the past year has shown how difficult it is for a government department.. to mediate effectively between a state

corporation and private industry in such a highly technical field as telecommunications.[91]

British Telecom was able to inundate the Department with technical detail with which it was ill-equipped to deal.

From the point of view of those who are concerned about the 'public interest', in the sense of concern with the distribution of public goods to consumers, rather than in the sense of the interests of manufacturers, the co-ordination of telecommunications and computers and office technology under one political head has disadvantages. Experience demonstrates that methods of changing bureacratic policy are either through political mediation or through bureaucratic competition. The NEB has now been emasculated by amalgamation with the less contentious NRDC, thus releasing the Department from a prime source of external competition and overlapping jurisdictions. Political mediation, through Parliament, is unlikely to fully represent those who feel, for instance, that the Departmental proposals for cable television represent the interests of those businesses for whom it will subsidise the provision of interactive services, but do not either reflect public demand or consider the long-term effect of a more highly privatised society.[92] Cable television in the USA, like video in Britain, has shown itself to be eminently exploitable for pornography and violence and American companies are linking with British consortia to bid for franchises. The Department of Industry and the Information Technology Minister are now responsible for representing the interests of client industries in central government.(Only the Home Office, with its regulation of broadcasting, has competitive powers over some of the Department's territory.) The interests of client industries are likely to weigh larger than any amorphous 'public interest'.

Intimations that this is so can be found already in British Telecom's review of its tariff structure, which followed its separation from the Post office. In that review the cross-subsidisation of trunk and international calls to local calls was curtailed. International calls became cheaper whilst local calls made from residential phones became more expensive. The new tariff structure is geared to multinational, not domestic industry or private consumers. Other intimations come from the Data Protection Code, which has been signed by the British Government, not so as to give individuals protection over the misuse of information, but to

191

allow the data flows between countries necessary for big business.[93] And yet others come from the field of cable television, where the government accepted in toto the recommendations made to it by an advisory group of businessmen.[94]

Experience has demonstrated that when one government department or institution has responsibility for an industry, the tendency is for interdependence to create rigidity towards markets. By their nature, new markets are likely to involve numbers of small firms, none geared to the kind of political pressure necessary to challenge established interests. Older markets are likely to contain large firms. In turn they are larger employers, wield greater political clout and have easier access to the bureaucracy. In such a situation the interests of both bureaucracy and established industry seem likely to coalesce around a policy of clientilism and cartelisation. The very structures designed by civil service and politicians to support and aid industry may then be a factor in its eventual market failure.

This computer industry study illustates once again the weaknesses inherent within an industrial policy in which a liberal market policy is coupled with a strong political system. The concept of an autonomous company ignores the constraints imposed by dependency for sales upon central government and the distortions in marketing which that dependency may produce. It ignores the bureaucracy's responsibility for ensuring that in return for stable sales, companies put effort into other markets. Liberal market policy has the effect of legitimising bureaucratic failure to monitor the recipients of public finance, as in the case of ICL. It also legitimises attacks on specific mechanisms of support for domestic industry, attacks which in the computer industry, came from both within the bureaucracy and from multinationals. That those attacks can be successful, as in the case of Honeywell's opposition to a Buy British minicomputer policy, is attributable to the political system, which encourages Ministers to make short-term political decisions in response to pressure.

The study emphasises the incoherence of both parties' attitudes to multinationals and to American technology. Bureaucracy sees the interests of multinationals as being identical to British interests, and incorporates them on committees to plan the future of British industry. Yet, clearly, in any one market sector, the interests of those companies will be to take as large a market share as possible and to face as little competition as

possible. Liberal ideology, with its emphasis on the free flow of capital, obfuscates the real differences of interest between national governments and multinationals, and the problems generated by the domination of domestic markets by those companies and by technological dependence upon another nation.

NOTES AND REFERENCES

1. Official Report, Vol.684, col.826, Vol.730, col.35.
2. The Economist, Vol.214, 9th January 1965, p.142.
3. NEDO, Imported Manufactures: An Inquiry into Competitiveness (London, HMSO, 1965), pp.2-20.
4. Official Report, Vol.684, col.825.
5. Ibid., Vol.544, col.87.
6. NRDC, Annual Report 1963-4 (London, HMSO, 1964), p.4.
7. Official Report, Vol.707, col.924-30.
8. The Economist, Vol.214, 6th March 1965, p.1035.
9. Official Report, Vol.707, col.924.
10. Ibid., col.925.
11 Official Report, Vol.731, col.283-4.
12. Fourth Report, Vol.II, pp.26-29.
13. Official Report, Vol.731, col.283-4.
14. The Economist, Vol.225, 16th December 1967, p.1175, Vol.243, 10th June 1972, p.90.
15. Official Report, Vol.729, col.177-184.
16. Fourth Report, Vol.II, pp.26-9.
17. Ibid., QA. 980-982, 1012, 1023, 1024.
18. Ibid., QA. 1047-57.
19 The Economist, Vol.212, 26th September 1964, p.1253.
20. Select Committee on Science & Technology, Minutes of Evidence, HC.137, 1969-70, QD. 2070.
21 Computer Weekly, 2nd June 1977.
22. Fourth Report, Vol.II, QA. 865; HC.137, QD. 2070.
23. HC.137, pp.552-3.
24. Ibid., QD. 1967.
25. The Economist, Vol.238, 27th February 1971, p.56; Vol.244, 8th July 1972, p.74.
26. Fourth Report, Vol.I, paras.231-238.
27. HC.137 , QD.326.
28. Fourth Report, Vol.I, paras.231-238.
29. The Reorganisation of Central Government, Cmnd.4506 (London, HMSO, 1970).
30. The Times, 17th February 1977, 23rd Novemebr 1977.
31. New Statesman, Vol.95, 12th May 1978, p.630.

32. *The Guardian*, 6th October 1978.
33. *Official Report*, Vol.908, col.360.
34. *Computer Weekly*, 3rd January 1980.
35. *The Guardian*, 9th December 1979.
36. *Computer Weekly*, 28th February 1980, 13th March 1980.
37. *Computing*, 14th March 1980; *The Guardian*, 6th March 1980; *Computer Weekly*, 13th March 1980.
38. *Computer Weekly*, 13th March 1980.
39. Ibid., 27th March 1980.
40. Ibid., 14th August 1980.
41. Ibid., 10th July 1980, 13th December 1980.
42. Ibid., 17th July 1980.
43. Ibid., 3rd January 1981.
44. *The Times*, 25th May 1976.
45. Select Committee on Science & Technology, HC.272, pp.35-43.
46. *The Times*, 6th December 1976; *Computer Weekly*, 18th October 1979.
47. *Computer Weekly*, 18th October, 15th November 1979.
48. NEDO, *Electronics Statistics*, (London, HMSO, 1970), p.11.
49. *Fourth Report*, Vol.I, para.148, Vol.II, QA 190, 1659-60.
50. *Computer Weekly*, 18th March 1980.
51. Ibid., 25th March 1982.
52. Ibid., 13th March, 10th July 1980,
53. Ibid., 18th February, 2nd December 1982.
54. Ibid., 11th February 1982.
55. *The Economist*, Vol.239, 24th April 1971, p.77.
56. Ibid., Vol.242, 11th March 1972, p.84.
57. Computer Services Association, *Report on the UK CSI*, p.5/16; *The Times*, 11th May 1976.
58. Computer Services Association, pp.5/16, 7/16.
59. *Computer Weekly*, 18th October 1979.
60. On pay scales for data-processing staff see: *Financial Times*, 18th June 1982.
61. *Computer Weekly*, 27th March 1980.
62. *The Times*, 29th April 1975.
63. *Computer Weekly*, 17th January 1980.
64. *The Regeneration of British Industry*, Cmnd.5710, (London, HMSO, 1976), p.10.
65. *Computer Weekly*, 29th November 1979, 28th February, 27th March 1980.
66. On government support for private industry see: Expenditure Committee, *Sixth Report Public Money in the Private Sector*, (London, HMSO, 1972).
67. *The Economist*, Vol.223, 21st June 1967; Vol.225, 16th December 1967, p.1165; *Official Report*, Vol.730, col.1573.
68. *The Computer Merger Project*, Cmnd.3660,

(London.HMSO,1968).

69. Stephen Young with A.V.Lowe,Intervention in the Mixed Economy(London,Croom Helm,1974),p.62.

70. The Economist,Vol.223,21st June 1967,p.1376.

71. Official Report,Vol.730,col.1569-1570;Vol.750,col.399-400.

72. The Economist,Vol.246,17th February 1973, p.92.

73. The Times,11th May 1976.

74. Fourth Report,Vol.II,QA.1650.

75. Computer Weekly,4th March 1978,17th January 1980.

76. The Economist,Vol.265,17th December 1977,p.126.

77. Fourth Report,Vol.I,paras.647-8.

78. The Guardian,20th December 1980.

79. Sunday Times,14th December 1980.

80. The Guardian,10th February 1981

81. Computer Weekly,19th January,26th February,26th March,2nd April 1981;Sunday Times,29th March,10th May 1981; The Guardian,10th February,20th May 1981.

82. Sunday Times,11th January,3rd May,10th May 1981.

83. Computer Weekly,14th May 1981;Financial Times,9th October,20th November 1981.

84. Sunday Times,6th September 1 981, 18th December 1982;Financial Times,20th October 1981,7th May 1982.

85. On American technology see statement by Jim Lestor,Under-Secretary of Employment,'I don't think it is necessarily a question of developing the technology ourselves necessarily; it is really a question of whether we can acquire a licence to use it', quoted in Computer Weekly,15th November 1979.

86. Nicholas Jequier, "Computers",in R.Vernon ed.,Big Business and the State(London,Macmillan, 1974),pp.195-254.

87. Select Committee on Science & Technology,(UK Computer Industry Sub-committee),Minutes of Evidence1974, Q.4.

88. Computing,9th November 1978.

89. ACARD,Information Technology (London, HMSO,1980).

90. The Times,11th May 1976.

91. Financial Times,28th July 1982.

92. For the debate on the social effects of cable TV see Sheffield TV Group, Cable and Community Programming(Sheffield,GLC and Sheffield City Council,1983);GLC,Cabling in London(London,GLC,1982).See also Computer Weekly,4th August 1983,on proposals to unify telecommunications,including radar, computing and

radio under one Minister.
    93. Kenneth Baker,in seminar,Essex University, February 1982.
    94. Information Technology Advisory Panel,*Cable Systems: A Report by the Information Technology Advisory Panel*(London,HMSO,1982);*Report of the Inquiry into Cable Expansion and Broadcasting Policy*, Cmnd 8679 (London,HMSO,1982).

Chapter Six

MICROELECTRONICS

6.1 INTRODUCTION

The importance of microelectronics as a technology rests on its wide application and the changes it produces in the manufacture of products in which microchips or microprocessors form a component. Two arguments have become apparent, relating to whether governments should intervene in the microelectronics market. The first emphasises the importance of a domestic capability in microelectronics technology, arguing that only with access to advanced domestic technology will a country's industries be able to compete technologically. Linked to this argument is a further concern that, since much of the design work of a product incorporating microelectronics is taken away from the product manufacturer and placed in the hands of the microchip designer, it is necessary to retain domestic capability so that close liaison can be maintained between the two types of manufacturers. According to this argument nationally assured supplies are necessary for technology 'push', for supplies to smaller product manufacturers and to offset growing international concentration in the sector. The alternative set of arguments emphasises the importance of applications of microelectronics, contending that it does not matter whether these are domestically manufactured or not. Those who argue in this way point to the entry of the Japanese into the microelectronics industry and suggest that supplies have become more secure through their competition with the Americans. These commentators place greater importance on the domestic application of microchip technology.[1] The relative importance attached to each of these two arguments has been crucial to the policy of governments in this market.

6.2 IMPORTS, TARIFFS AND MULTINATIONALS.

The history of microelectronics policy in Britain is similar to that of data processing. By the mid 1960s, the Americans were already dominating both the world and British markets. Imports of microcircuits posed other than balance of payments problems for Britain. Imported microcircuits were 60% dearer than in the United States and were the product of previous years' designs. British industry was therefore handicapped by both costly components and technological backwardness.

By the early 1960s firms in Britain were supposed to be responding to the market with 'frenzied activity'. Marconi had begun manufacturing, although only for its own internal consumption. English Electric, one of the first computer manufacturers to use integrated circuits, relied on Ferranti. Elliot Automation also made a bid for the market and established a technical know-how agreement with Fairchild of America. By 1965, only Mullard, a subsidiary of Philips of Holland, had failed to start any production lines.

Then, in 1965 came overcapacity in the market. There followed price cutting by the three big American manufacturers. At the same time the American government announced that it would support no more than four main contractors for the space and defence industry. The immediate impact was to make the European markets prime targets for American manufacturers. The Labour government replied to the increase in imports with a 30% import duty from November 1966.

In one respect the strategy was pointless. It merely raised costs for those manufacturers in Britain who needed to use microcircuits in their products. It could only have been effective in damping down imports had there been adequate supply in Britain, or had the microchips been luxury rather than necessary goods. It seems unlikely that the intention was to increase the incentive for American multinationals to invest in Britain, but, without a policy of support for domestic industry which would have filled the market gap, the effect of the policy was to do just that. American manufacturers responded by setting up manufacture in Britain.

As a result, Elliott, which had invested in a factory in Scotland on the basis of its know-how agreement with Fairchild, found itself in competition with Fairchild, which also decided on production there. British companies reacted by collaborating in R&D, but chip yields refused to go

MICROELECTRONICS

beyond about 70% of each production batch and R&D took increasing amounts of money. British companies were said to have spent over twenty million pounds on research and development by 1967. But it seems that little government money found its way into support of that R&D. Instead the majority of government funded research was done by the Royal Radar Establishment, a government laboratory. How much the Labour Government spent on this research is not known but it is known that it received a large chunk of the overall R&D spending of £280 million by MinTech. Again,how far this research disseminated into industry is not clear,but Ferranti argued in evidence to the Select Committee in 1971 that research should be conducted in industry rather than in government research establishments.[2]

By the end of 1967 devaluation of the pound had offset the increased tariff barrier imposed by the Labour Government and imports of components were rising. British manufacturers were still struggling to get off the ground when, at the end of 1967, the American companies began a price slashing war. Prices fell by 50%. Four months later a flood of orders emerged and capacity could not catch up.

To the Labour Government, it seemed that the problems of the industry were concerned with the scattered nature of the industrial research. Through the Ministry of Technology, the Labour Government moved into the microchip industry to bring about rationalisation. In early 1968 Elliott Automation and Marconi merged their microelectronics interests. At this juncture GEC made its bid for AEI and with its subsequent takeover of English Electric gained control of Elliott and Marconi.By 1968 GEC had one third of British production of microchips under its wing.[3] The major markets for microchips were in computers, so it is not surprising that both GEC and Plessey took an equity stake in ICL in 1968.[4]

Price cutting wars began again in 1969, with Texas Instruments cutting prices by 30% on their most popular standard chip. At the same time the technology had developed so that American manufacturers were producing Medium Scale and Large Scale Integrated Circuits, which offered savings of 20% to 30% on the basic chip. The Ministry of Technology is said to have considered the possibility of fostering an alliance with an American company in order to get production going.

Ministry policy was based on support for R&D through the NRDC,which loaned £5 million to the three British manufacturers - Plessey,Ferranti and GEC - for co-operative research. The Electronics

199

Committee of the NEDC endorsed this policy, but wanted the annual £100 million spent by the electronics industry on R&D to be grant-aided in the same way that other industrial capital investment was financed through investment grants.[5]

The problem for the three British manufacturers was that the US investment in R&D from federal sources was bigger than the entire turnover of semiconductors in Britain. Cutbacks in the American space programme brought 'overspill' of their components onto the British market. Also contributing to the lower cost of the American chips was the practice increasingly adopted by American companies of sending wafers to be assembled in low wage countries. The Department of Industry did not consider that the three British firms were large enough to take advantage of the worldwide division of labour, although Ferranti did send some production to the Phillipines. British firms were faced with high capital investment, huge R&D costs and a low return on rate of capital employed. In addition companies supplying the equipment for the manufacture of microchips had no home market on which to rely.

Whilst understanding of the problem seems to have increased in the Department between 1968 and 1970, the advent of a Conservative government which felt that the adverse balance of payments trend in components and peripherals would reverse itself without any specific act of government meant there was little help available to the industry.[6] During the period 1970-1971 the only help came through regional aid and development grants, to set up manufacture in areas with high unemployment and low wages. But these grants were available also to foreign manufacturers. Britain's export/import ratio of 0.3 in 1968 had risen only to 0.5 by 1972.[7]

Casting around for a policy in the sector, the Department seems to have considered several options. In February 1971, it suggested that Britain could either allow dependency on imports or a wider grouping of European companies could be considered. This second option followed the Conservative Party's enthusiasm for loose groupings of European companies. By May of the same year other options were being considered. In order to stem the drain on the balance of payments, attempts could be made to attract overseas investment through the mechanism of regional aid. But even with development grants, the Department felt that it was no easy task to get manufacturers in to the country. And, even if they were to set up manufacture in Britain, the American

practice of assembling components in the Far East did not mean that the greatest amount of added value would accrue to the UK. Despite these drawbacks the Department felt that the most important concern was that industry in general should have ' unlimited access' to the best microchips at any one point in time.[8] No one seems to have considered that US manufacturers might not manufacture their most up to date technology in Britain, nor that imported microcircuits tended to be less advanced than those on sale in America.

The Conservative government agonised over the specific decisions necessary for any industrial policy. The new Minister for Aerospace, Frederick Corfield, pointed out:

> There are three main companies.. They have over-capacity if you add up all their production together. So how does one pick one or two out of the three firms and do it (policy) across the board, when one has over-capacity for the foreseeable future, the next two or three years even if not indefinitely?[9]

The fact was, of course, that when the Minister spoke of 'over-capacity', he referred to a domestic market of which more than 50% was met by imports, and in which demand was expanding only slowly.

Dr Maddock, the Scientific Adviser to the Department of Trade and Industry, posed the problem to the Select Committee:

> The prizes lie very heavily with those already in the business and with a very large turnover. The ability to come in as a fresh company is very difficult, except by providing highly specialised bespoke semi-conductors... In three or four years time there may well be some new technology to let in the little man.[10]

Arnold Weinstock put the problem from the manufacturers point of view:

> we now have the situation where you can buy in British markets, devices for one quarter of the manufacturing cost of the device . You clearly have to have some Government intervention or you will have no industry.. If you are not prepared to put Government money behind these sorts of projects you will not have industrial participation in those fields.[11]

He pointed to the protection given to American industry by the American govenment in the form of non-tariff barriers and demanded a similar form of protection for British manufacturers.

> In the US that situation is.. dealt with by the requirement that.. the purchaser must have the facilities to inspect the manufacture of the object on the premises, and since the American government will only inspect things in the US, if you do not make the thing in the US you do not supply the American government. this means that 60% of purchases of semi-conductor devices are sold at a very much higher price than the same thing could be bought for had they been assembled in Taiwan.. We have no such protection in this country, and if we do not get it, unless we are prepared indefinitely to support huge losses without, so far as one can see, any foreseeable prospect of improvement, there will be no integrated circuit industry.[12]

It is reasonable to assume that GEC and the other manufacturers were, therefore, pressing the government to introduce a form of non-tariff barrier,which would involve the Ministry of Defence, at least, in buying British components. Other companies made similar comments to the Select Committee. Even the subsidiaries of European manufacturers complained about lack of government help and the strings tied to that which was available.[13] But, it seems likely that, given its previous experience with GEC, the Labour Government would have been unlikely to provide finance to a sector in which that company had the largest British stake.

Despite the more or less unanimous appeal for action from the government, no response was forthcoming, with the result that in the early 1970s both Ferranti and GEC withdrew from manufacture of standard chips. The Select Committee called for an investigation of this withdrawal on the grounds that:

> Failure to manufacture the most up-to-date items and to conduct research into the latest techniques could be detrimental to our objective of fostering a viable indigenous industry.[14]

But the Department seems to have worked on the basis that for several years, whilst the price of

MICROELECTRONICS

integrated circuits remained so low, there was not much that could be done for the industry. Finance through the NRDC kept the technology alive through R&D, but by the mid 1970s all three British manufacturers were concentrating upon the production of semi-custom chips. This form of specialised production linked in with each of the company's defence work and with Plessey and GEC/Marconi's work on computer control of manufacturing processes. But, as government spending on defence increased only slowly, so increased pressure was put on the manufacturers. In addition, the development, in 1971, of the microprocessor in America raised the probability of increased imports. To keep abreast of American developments, products such as consumer durables, automobiles and electronic goods would all be requiring the new components.

6.3 DOMESTIC TECHNOLOGY OR INWARD INVESTMENT?

The 1974 Labour government's commitment to the regeneration of British industry and its intention to promote investment in growth areas of the economy, gave the opportunity for the Department to begin to reconsider aid directed to microelectronics. From 1974 onwards the Department of Industry (the successor to the Department of Trade and Industry) concentrated upon keeping the research capability in up to date circuits alive, whilst manufacturers used defence contracts as the basis for exports. In 1974 the Department approached the Treasury for funds for microchip R&D. But no money was forthcoming. The £11 or £12 million pounds eventually found was culled from other Departmental projects. In total, the Department and Ministry of Defence aid to the industry amounted to £30 million.

By January 1978, the Department was circulating a paper to industry suggesting that a further £25 million of aid should be given. £15 million was to come from the Department for the development of specific and promising applications of microprocessors. In February of that year, the Chancellor introduced the latest phase of the industrial strategy with a promise of substantial aid to microchips. The three British firms were supplying only one tenth of the £60 million market for microchips in the UK.

At this time the Department seems to have estimated that for Britain to compete in the world wide market of standard circuit production would require

an investment of £400 million, which the department believed to be impractical without the base of a large home market. It therefore wrote off attempts at British production of standard chips. An article in the Sunday Times reported that the customers were not so sure, the reason being that microchips had had a higher than average duty imposed on them by the EEC in an attempt to stem imports and encourage local production. A similar position faced those manufacturers who had to use the components as had faced them in the 1960s, when the Labour Government raised tariffs.

The article was based on a paper prepared for the NEDC Electronics Committee by the Department. The paper rejected the possibility of rationalisation of the three British companies. Instead it called for a minimum investment of £80 million over five years, to develop the sophisticated end of the market, producing complex circuits with large numbers of components on a chip. But the paper pointed out that the companies were not prepared to risk their own money on the project. It stated that 'at least half will have to come from public sources'. But since it was doubtful whether British industry would be able to contribute its share ' means should be sought for increasing the Government contribution'. The paper was therefore asking for 100% contribution from government for VSLI research.[15]

The paper also discussed the question of how much state aid should go to foreign companies in Britain. Those companies included Philips'subsidiary Mullard, American ITT's subsidiary and five multinationals with manufacturing facilities in Britain. The paper argued that Mullard and ITT should get state help because they developed new technology, rather than imported technology from abroad. They might even get support for production, as well as research, if that would encourage them to invest in the UK rather than on the continent. But American multinationals, which imported technology, would only get help for the development of special products for British customers.

The paper did not meet with wholehearted approval at the NEDC Electronics Committee. One of its working parties had reported in February with opposite conclusions to those of the paper. 'In the medium term, the lack of a strong UK semi-conductor industry... could become critical' had said the working party.[16]

Clive Sinclair, of Sinclair Radionics, then a manufacturer of calculators 'rescued' by the NEB, put the case for those who manufactured products

using microchips. Import duty of 17% on microchips contrasted with a much lower rate of duty on finished products. The combination of the differential tariffs 'meant it was hard..if not impossible, for the British producer to compete when making products with a high semiconductor content if the semiconductors have to be imported.' Finished calculators could be imported duty free from developing countries and even calculators from Japan were charged at a lower rate of duty than microchips. In the very near future, said Sinclair, innumerable products from toys to typewriters would have a high semiconductor content.' Unless we can supply that content in Britain, I very much doubt whether companies making such products will survive here'.[17]

Perhaps in response to NEDC feeling that Britain must be self-sufficient in its supply of microcircuits (and possibly in response to Trade Union pressure in particular), the Department revised its strategy. Instead of writing off British capability in standard chips, it proposed that Britain should attempt to meet its internal demand by encouraging American manufacturers to invest in Britain. The special circuits and the custom circuits would then be met from the three British manufacturers with ITT supplying chips for telecommunications. £10 million per year was already being spent on aiding this custom-built sector.[18]

The Prime Minister, James Callaghan, had already shown some interest in the subject of microelectronics. In March 1978 he announced the establishment of three working parties to study the impact of the microprocessor upon industry. These were to report to the Advisory Council for Applied Research and Development (ACARD). By this stage the civil service had already established an interdepartmental committee to consider the applications of microelectronics to employment.

But, before any of these committees had had a chance to get off the ground, the Prime Minister saw a programme in the television 'Horizon' series entitled 'When the chips are down'. The programme discussed the production and research currently continuing in the USA and pointed to deficiencies in R&D capabilities in Britain. The Prime Minister's reaction was immediate. A special showing of the programme was made for the Cabinet and within Whitehall, microprocessors were suddenly the fashion of the day. Civil servants reported that money became suddenly available as even the Treasury scrambled onto the bandwagon.[19]

Following his conversion to the cause of microchips the Prime Minister also instructed the CPRS to act as the focus in Whitehall for dealing with the social and economic implications of microelectronics. By May 1978 the preliminary outlines of a scheme for help to the microchip industry had become firm enough for it to be debated in American journals. The plan was to be two pronged - on the one hand the multinationals, Motorola Semiconductor, National Semiconductor, Texas Instruments, General Instruments and Hughes Microelectronics, all of which had wafer manufacturing units in Britain, were to be invited to increase their operations. The inducements to their expansion were not yet public. The other part of the strategy was to consist of broad collaborative research into VSLI technology between the three British manufacturers and the two British based European companies sharing the research and financial backing.[20] The Treasury vetoed this research proposal. It seems that at this juncture also that Plessey, GEC and Ferranti were involved in discussion with the Department and the EEC on a European microelectronics company, discussions which, begun in 1978, led eventually to the signing of the 'Esprit' agreement, in which R&D on computers, microchips and applications is to be shared by twelve European companies, including GEC and Plessey.[21]

It was at this juncture in time that the NEB made its intervention and caused a major upheaval to the Department's plans.

6.4 A BRITISH COMPANY OR MULTINATIONAL INVESTMENT?

Whilst the NEDC was busy discussing a strategy for the industry, the NEB had also laid its own plans to support a part British owned company, Inmos, to manufacture standard chips. It seems that the original idea of Inmos was conceived by Richard Petritz, an American microchip expert working for Mostek in America. One year later he had interested a fellow employee of Mostek, Paul Schroeder, but financing of the new company remained a problem. At this point, August 1977, he met Ian Barron, then a consultant with the Department of Industry, who suggested that the NEB might be a source of finance. The version of the plan submitted to the NEB in December 1977 was for manufacture of standard chips. But at this point in time, apparently, Inmos had no contracts, no products, had done no design work and had not decided what to design.

MICROELECTRONICS

From various sources it seems clear that the Department of Industry was unaware of the proposal until a late stage. At Cabinet Committee, the plans were blocked by the Treasury. Joel Barnett states that this block was the result of the very scanty information available on the project, the success of which rested on the abilities of the three entrepreneurs.[22] One account suggests, however, that the Department of Industry officials actually lobbied the Treasury to object to the NEB venture. Press leaks of the venture and of proceedings in the Committee, embarrassed the NEB by their prematurity.

However, Sir Leslie Murphy, Chairman of the NEB lobbied hard for the plan on the grounds that the NEB must be allowed to be entrepreneurial. In this argument he had the backing of Tony Benn, the Energy Minister, whilst Eric Varley, the Industry Minister was also in favour. Ministers eventually agreed that they must back the NEB's commercial judgment, despite what Barnett suggests were serious misgivings. [23]

As firmer knowledge of the NEB plans emerged, so they were greeted with mixed reaction. They were based on a strategy which emphasised that Britain should have its own domestically owned company in order to have access to new technology, production methods and market developments. Inmos, itself, was to be set up in America, where chips were to be taken to pre-production stage. At that point the manufacture was to be transferred to Britain, where volume production would take place. The aim was to take advantage of skilled personnel in America and to create employment in Britain. In terms of technology the new company intended to leapfrog a generation of integrated circuits to produce a 64K RAM, at that time believed to be about three years away from production. [24]

Competitors in Britain tended to write off the project as over-ambitious and under-capitalised. Although Inmos claimed that it could start the project with £200 million capital, Mullard pointed out that Philips had already spent £500 million in order to gain its share of the market. American commentators were no less sceptical. They pointed to a similar Canadian plan which had failed. But the NEB had assured the respectability of the plan by having it vetted by a group of experts including Ian Mackintosh, of Mackintosh Consultants, and the Managing Director of Plessey's microsystems.

On the political side, there was considerable unease that the NEB was intending to back a group of Anglo-Americans, who having emigrated to America,

were about to be made millionaires by the British government. In particular, the first meeting of the Cabinet to discuss the proposals showed considerable distaste for the idea that individuals would be given the right to shares in a publicly owned company from which they might make personal fortunes. Experience with Geoffrey Cross, who, as managing director of ICL, had been allowed to buy shares in the company, which he then converted at considerable personal gain when he left earlier than expected, had not been a happy precedent.[25]

Inevitably, the NEB proposals conflicted with the interests of the multinationals already established in Britain. The Managing Director of Mullard, Jack Ackerman, also the Chairman of the NEDC subcommittee responsible for an overall strategy for British micro-electronics, publicly opposed the scheme, on the grounds that ' the NEB venture could worsen the shortage of engineers by luring them from vital jobs'. Perhaps more centrally to his interests, he stated that Germany and France were wooing the multinationals. If those companies found the British government to be 'kicking them in the teeth then they might take their investment elsewhere'. He is said to have pointed this out to NEB officials who then accused him of threatening them.

Ackerman's views seem to have been reflected in the preliminary statement issued by the NEDC :

> ..it(Inmos)would have to be seen as a long-range option with success evaluated over a five to seven year program. It would require a particularly imaginative and astute plan, with wholehearted government backing to have any chance of success. It would have to concentrate on a few selected items, pehaps memories and microprocessors, where it would be confident of achieving a significant and profitable share of world markets.

In particular, the NEDC and Ackerman were unhappy at NEB secrecy. At a joint meeting of the two bodies, the NEB refused to release details of Inmos, on the grounds that members of NEDC were competitors. It was obvious that such confidentiality would infuriate Philips and the other established suppliers in Britain.[26]

GEC was also said to be unhappy with the proposal. Sir Arnold Weinstock argued that Britain could not compete on standard circuits. He contended that what mattered was building higher added value systems incorporating the circuits that were made in

MICROELECTRONICS

Britain. At this time GEC was the exclusive distributor of Intel (US) chips, whilst its own technology was in special chips for high performance products such as defence equipment. However, GEC was also considering the possibility of re-entering the market for standard chips, through a joint venture with Fairchild of America. Fairchild had withdrawn sometime previously from its manufacturing base in Britain.[27]

Foreign companies continued to actively lobby against the NEB plan. Both ITT and Mullard claimed that they wished to expand their British chipbuilding facilities. As the arguments continued, the NEB found support for its stance. Motorola claimed to be 'surprised' that the British government had not entered the standard chip market years ago, but considered it to be the fault of the three British manufacturers who 'just could not get their act together'. The Mackintosh Consultants, who had been involved in legitimising the NEB plan, argued that the existing British microcircuit companies were heavily vertically integrated, highly structured, operations entirely unsuited to 'the style of freewheeling entrepreneurial management essential to success in the integrated circuit industry.

On the 22nd of July, the NEB announced the new company Inmos Ltd and its agreement to invest £25 million in the company. The corporate HQ was to be in Britain, whilst technological and product development was to be split between the USA and Britain. Operations were to start on both sides of the Atlantic simultaneously, and a prototype production line was to be based in America. Volume production in Britain was planned for 1981. The estimate was that 4000 jobs would be created by the mid 1980s. Peak funding of the company from the British government was to be £50 million, and employees were to have the opportunity to purchase shares in the company. The founders and future employees could hold up to 27.5% of the equity in the company. Sites for the new company had not at that date been chosen, but the press release said that ' the possibility of location in an area of high unemployment will be given special consideration'.

In an attempt to placate its opponents on the NEDC, Sir Leslie Murphy, of the NEB, stated that the NEB saw 'this investment as complementary to the activities of existing British companies'. He argued that it would contribute towards the belief of the Electronic Components Sector Working Party that 'volume production of selected multi-application circuits should be expanded in the UK'.[28]

209

After the government decision to back Inmos it was clearly necessary that the multinationals and established British companies be kept happy. Department of Industry and NEDC thinking was reflected in the announcement of July 1979 that £70 million was to be spent in encouraging microchip manufacture. The money was to be spent in assisting the development of chips at the custom end of the market (British companies) and in encouraging the manufacture of selected mass market products (multinational companies). These latter products were to be selected 'with the aim of increasing exports and import substitution'. The finance was not however to be made payable in non-repayable grants as the representatives of the companies on NEDC had wanted. Instead it was to be provided in cost-shared contracts - 50% for research; 25% for development and 25% for investment in equipment. Firms supplying equipment for the manufacture of microchips were also to be included within the scheme.[29]

With start-up costs helped by this newly available aid, Plessey announced the following month that it would be producing bubble memories in commercial volume. In the same month GEC and Fairchild of America announced the joint development of a manufacturing plant to be built in Scotland, which Fairchild would use for the manufacture of microchips. GEC was to manufacture 'price sensitive standard products', such as its teletext/ viewdata set. The Government eventually paid £8 million towards this project. Rather than a venture for GEC to enter manufacture of microchips, GEC obviously saw the agreement as a form of vertical integration, with Fairchild providing the components and GEC the products. In fact GEC was later to state that the project had been a 'financial investment' not a move to assure a supply of chips, but that may have been rationalisation after the project's failure.[30]

Whatever GEC's motivation, its agreement with Fairchild was specifically lauded in a paper presented to the NEDC in December 1978, in which the government announced its overall strategy for microelectronics. An indication of the political backing given the strategy came from the Prime Minister's presence at the meeting.

The government's strategy fell into two parts-one concerned with industry, the other with employment. Plans for industry reflected the various policy announcements over the previous twelve months. First would be production of standard chips. Despite the NEB's Inmos, here the government insisted there was room 'for inward investment by the

established multinational companies, either on their own or in collaboration with UK owned companies'.

Second, the government wanted to create capacity 'to provide user companies with special micro-electronic products and with essential research, development, design and test services'. This part of the programme was to be based on UK owned companies or on multinationals willing to become 'committed to the UK user industries'. In other words, there was to be support for special and custom-chip manufacture, where microchip manufacturer and product manufacturer had to work closely together on design and production.

Third, the government wished to support the microelectronics infrastructure industry so as to supply production equipment and computer aided design and test facilities for home and overseas.

Fourth, the government aimed to increase awareness of the potential of microchips, thereby creating a demand for them - a strategy which we will come to later.

Finally, to do all these things, the government intended to provide financial backing and also use public sector procurement so that the public sector would ' be in the lead in applying microelectronics wherever this is possible and economically desirable'.[31]

There is little doubt that in all this activity the British government was influenced by developments in other industrialised countries. In defending the scale of support Eric Varley pointed to the schemes for state aid to microelectronics in America,Japan,West Germany and France. Microelectronics was one of the least free markets in the world economy, he argued. Certainly in America, the Defense Department looked set to fund microcircuit technology for its weapons systems in a manner unseen since the days of the Space programme.

There is little doubt either that the NEB backing for Inmos coupled with government funding, spurred the multinationals into increased investment in Britain. Texas Instruments, which in September 1978, announced that it was about to produce the first 64K RAM had almost simultaneously announced the redundancy of 300 of its British workforce, who were employed on the manufacture of outdated technology. Suddenly it announced new products it intended to manufacture in Britain. ITT also decided to go ahead with a $10 million expansion of its plant at Foots Cray,of which part was to come from the Department of Industry. This plant was to make one of the first 16K RAMs. At Mullard a major

expansion of integrated circuit manufacture was planned for its Southampton plant, and following the takeover of Signetics in America by Philips, the British plant was to be upgraded in equipment to American standards. It was rumoured that Mostek intended to build a plant in Britain or Eire to beat any Inmos venture. And in Scotland, Motorola and National Semiconductor were bringing in new technology for manufacture. It was also reported that the manufacturers were establishing R&D teams in Britain. In all this inward investment, the Department of Industry was crucially concerned that those companies benefitting from investment grants should also bring in technology which was up to date. Civil servants reported projects turned down because they did not meet this criterion. It was suggested, at the time, that it was the possibility of Inmos, backed by the government, gaining market dominance which galvanised this competitive investment. The multinationals wanted to be ahead of the British company in market share by the time its production facilities came on-stream. Far from harming the Department's strategy Inmos seems to have aided it.[32]

6.4 THE BATTLE FOR INMOS

If the NEB Board was wholly satisfied that Inmos was a viable proposition in 1978, then in retrospect it made two mistakes. First, it fudged the issue of where the Inmos factories should be sited. And second, it did not ensure that the aid promised to Inmos reached it before there was a change of government. In both mistakes the NEB betrayed a lack of political 'nose' which was to lead to considerable controversy and cost to Inmos.

It seems that in its contract with Inmos the NEB got agreement only that 'consideration would be given' to the siting of factories in the development regions. The siting was not a condition of financial backing. But in its public pronouncements the NEB continued to give the impression that the factories would definitely be within development areas.[33]

However, when Inmos announced that it wished to site its technology centre in Bristol, the Board agreed to support its decision. Inmos presented the argument that the engineers needed would not be prepared to work in a development region. The technology centre, mainly concerned with R&D and pre-production technology, would not provide the same employment opportunities as the manufacturing units

212

themselves. The news was broken to the press during the Christmas recess of Parliament, timing hardly designed to improve MP's tempers. At the same time, as a sweetener, Inmos announced that it had hired the firm, PA Consultants, to recommend where it should establish its four production centres.

The decision by Inmos to house its technology centre outside the development areas caused outrage amongst the areas themselves. A concerted campaign began among MPs to have the decision changed. On Parliament reconvening, the Prime Minister, himself, assured the House that the factories would go to the development areas.[34] Upon this news the regions began to compete with each other in setting up technology centres and such like, in a bid to attract Inmos. No decision had been reached on those sitings when the Conservative Government was elected in May of 1979.

It seemed that the microelectronics programme would be doomed under a non-interventionist government. Tory fundamentalists were said to reject the view that there was a structural hole in British capital down which high technology projects seemed to disappear. The Conservatives were expected to axe the NEB, sell off its stake in Inmos, and discontinue the Department of Industry's microelectronics support programme.

In the event, the civil servant who was quoted as saying that, ' The way to get something past a Minister in this government is to call it high technology,' was proved partially correct. The evidence suggests that working within the prevailing political climate, Department officials sought to persuade Sir Keith Joseph, the Industry Minister, that government support of microelectronics was a feature of all industrialised countries' economic strategy. At least one civil servant seems to have risked his neck by publicly announcing that the £125 million aid programme, launched by the Callaghan government, would continue, although the official word from the Department was that 'Ministers were still reserving their position'.[35]

In fact the programme was cut back. The aid to industry was cut from £70 million to £55 million, with the infrastructure industry bearing the brunt of the cuts. Support for custom chips declined from £33 million to £29 million and aid to multinationals and GEC/Fairchild stayed at around the £22 million mark.[36]

The future of Inmos was by no means assured. But with some political perspicacity, the American part of the company had taken steps to ensure that

it could survive, even if the British government decided to back out of its guarantee of finance. The company had used the implied guarantee of NEB ownership to extract cash from the market. Also, helped by the fact that other manufacturers who had announced the 64K RAM had experienced delays in production, it looked as if Inmos might find the market ready and waiting for its product. However, the British end of the company was not so far ahead with its design work. It was unlikely therefore to be able to raise the necessary backing from the City. Under these circumstances, had the government withdrawn its financial backing, it is likely that the British part of the company would have closed down, whilst the American part would have survived. It may well have been considerations such as these which eventually helped to tip the scales in Inmos' favour.

Following the mass resignation of the NEB Board over the monitoring of Rolls Royce, Sir Keith Joseph seems to have switched his idea of the NEB as an institution for aiding lame duck industries to one where he saw its function as being geared mainly to high technology industries. When the Inmos second tranche of £25 million came up for approval, it seemed as though it would be a fairly straightforward decision. The NEB made the recommendation to Cabinet in January 1980. But this second tranche proved to be a lever over the siting of Inmos factories.[37]

The controversy over these factories was aroused once more by the announcement, again during the Christmas recess, that the first Inmos factory would be sited in Bristol. Once more, the reaction was outrage. The decision was particularly infuriating to Labour MPs, who saw it as the NEB going back on its commitment to foster growth industry in development areas. The new Chairman of the NEB, Sir Arthur Knight, later stated that the NEB had supported Inmos' decision basically on commercial grounds.[38] The argument was that it would be more efficient to have the factory sited near the technology centre.

In retrospect, it seems that Inmos had deliberately attempted to circumvent location in the development areas by placing its technology centre in Bristol, later to claim that the presence of the centre precluded building a factory elsewhere. The company clearly made a political mistake in announcing the siting of its factory before it had received the second tranche of government finance. That it did so seems to have stemmed from visits by the Industry Minister to its technology centre, from

which the impression was gsined that the Minister was in favour of continued government funding.

When Parliament returned after the Christmas recess, the row over the Inmos factory escalated. Even James Callaghan called for the Industry Department to refuse Inmos an Industrial Development Certificate, on the grounds that the NEB had given a commitment to himself. Meanwhile Sir Keith argued that he had no power to direct Inmos as to where it should go and that it was a matter for the NEB and Inmos itself.

It seems that Sir Keith himself was prepared to accept the consultants' and the NEB's recommendations. Since his ideological belief was that political intervention in the commercial decisions of industry should be kept to a minimum, it would have been difficult for him to reject advice given on 'commercial' grounds. But the Treasury, still not convinced that Inmos should receive more government finance, now found new allies. The Ministers for Scotland and Wales insisted that any further government money for the company should be conditional on the siting of its first factory in a development area.[39]

Inmos fought back. In Parliament, the Chairman of the all party computer group, Ian Lloyd, who had visited Inmos in the States and had come back impressed, arranged lobbying meetings for the company. At the same time the news that the market for microchips was booming and that there were waiting lists of as long as ten months favoured the company.

Into this politically fraught situation stepped GEC. It approached the NEB with the proposition that it might be interested in buying into Inmos. Rumours had it that GEC's own deal with Fairchild of America was in trouble. Fairchild had been taken over by Schlumberger, the French company, a competitor of GEC's in consumer products. The possibility that GEC might take a stake in Inmos must have looked like a way out of the ideological cleavage for Sir Keith. Inmos was asked to provide GEC with the necessary information, but was unco-operative, on the grounds that GEC was a competitor. In fact it had already objected to the presence of the head of GEC's Electronics Division on the new NEB Board, although he was barred from discussion of any electronics business. Faced with minimum information, GEC turned Inmos down in twenty four hours flat.[40]

It may be that GEC was playing a political game. Inmos described the GEC questions as 'impertinent' from a competitor. It could be that

GEC's intention was to ask questions which it knew would not be answered, and then, by turning it down, to use its own established status to undermine Inmos. The immediate effect of the GEC withdrawal was to cast doubt on the viability of Inmos. It was only later that the failure of GEC's agreement with Fairchild was announced. The factory in Scotland, to which the government had contributed £7 million was used by GEC to build a submarine. Following the failure GEC claimed that it was not interested in assuring a supply of chips for itself, which, it argued, was assured by the entry of the Japanese into the market.[41]

Six months after the request for the second tranche of government finance, no decision had been taken. In May 1980 Inmos announced that its 16K RAM was three months ahead of schedule. An NEB team was sent over to Inmos in June to reassess its prospects, followed by Department of Industry officials. The NEB review, coupled with backing down on the part of Inmos and a decision to site its factory in South Wales, seems to have clinched the Cabinet's mind. Inmos was given its money.

Basking in this success, the NEB turned to attack the established UK companies, which, said the Chairman, were failing to achieve their own targets for the production of integrated circuits - an implicit criticism of GEC.[42] In fact, one of the odder stories circulating during the Inmos saga, was that the Department had decided to back Inmos in order to galvanise GEC into microchip production, because GEC was thought to be the company most likely to make a success of the venture. If this were the case, then the Department was guilty of some rather muddled thinking. By attempting to tie itself to Fairchild technology, which was acknowledged to be the least up-to-date of the American companies, GEC showed itself to be less than aware of the market.[43]

Ironically, during the seven month delay in approving the second tranche for Inmos, a delay which was said to have cost the company £300,000 per day, the Department distributed £14 million without fuss, to multinationals establishing chip production in the UK. ITT Semiconductor, National Semiconductor, Motorola and General Instruments, all received over £2 million each for expansion. For the £14 million which the Department had invested by the end of 1980 it anticipated an output of £300 million of microchips by 1984, and claimed to have attracted £150 million pounds of investment. The cost effectiveness of the scheme was contrasted with that of Inmos.

MICROELECTRONICS

Under the second part of the aid package £28 million went to multinationals and British firms for the manufacture of special chips. But British firms were slow to take up the aid,and by the end of 1980 had put forward only two projects. In contrast Mullard, Siliconics, National Semiconductor and Motorola all benefitted from the money available. The problem arose because British companies wanted funding on a one-off basis, without presenting too much detail as to their plans. The Department admitted in 1981 that the response of the British companies had been disappointing.[44] Although GEC and Plessey licensed Mitel (Canada) technology for chips to use in the System X telephone exchange, both companies and Ferranti had established markets in the now growing defence sector and seem to have had little incentive to pursue the manufacture of microchips for the open market. Plessey subsequently withdrew from the manufacture of bubble memories, an activity which had been aided by government funds at the beginning of the scheme, unable to compete against the volume production of Rockwell of the USA and NEC, of Japan.[45]

In 1983 the argument over whether Britain should manufacture VSLI chips resurfaced again, in the context of the Thatcher Government's decision to fund research on the Fifth Generation Computer.Once more product manufacturers such as Sinclair have argued that 'the only way to have a leading edge product will be to design the silicon from scratch'and that the British industry should now be based around the three British companies — Ferranti,Plessey and Inmos.[46]

6.5 CREATING DEMAND

Throughout the development of Department of Industry policy, there has been a conflict between those who argue that it was crucial for Britain to have its own source of microelectronic technology and those who argue that more important is the rate of use of microelectronic components within other products. The first argument was put forward by those who backed the NEB (although Inmos technology is at least half-American). The second argument was used by those,such as GEC, who were unenthusiastic about the financial prospects of the standard chip market. In point of fact, the arguments are not contradictory,but complementary. An industrialised country may need to have its own technology,may need to stabilise its own internal supply of components and also, in order to improve its manufactured

products and create the possibilities of volume production, may need to create domestic demand for those components.

But at central government level, responsibility for supply and demand was fragmented until 1981. Responsibility for Inmos rested with the NEB,and, within the Department of Industry,responsibility for supply (the micro-electronics industry support programme) and demand rested with different sections. That they did so was more a feature of personnel policy within the Department, than anything else,and,following the retirement of the head of the MISP programme, they were integrated under the same Under Secretary. But,one can see,in the creation of the demand side programme, some jockeying for position within the Department.[47]

Established before Callaghan's espousal of microelectronics, but following up that interest, in late 1979, the interdepartmental committee on microprocessors produced recommendations subsequently approved by the Cabinet. At almost the same time as the NEB announced the setting up of Inmos, the Government announced a £15 million support scheme to foster applications of microelectronics in industry. Behind the new scheme lay the rationale that industry had to adapt to new components if it was to survive in competition with Japan and West Germany, both of which had such support schemes.

The scheme consisted of three separate initiatives. The first part, for which £2 million was made provisionally available, consisted of a campaign to promote awareness of the importance of microprocessors and to train key people in their use. The second initiative supported company feasability studies into the applications of microprocessor technology. The minimum size of a project which could be considered for support was fixed at the relatively low level of ten thousand pounds, to encourage smaller companies to apply. The third part of the scheme, expected to cost in the region of £10 million, gave financial support to the use of microprocessors in end products and manufacturing.

Following on the footsteps of the initial MAP scheme came a report from the Cabinet Office [48] on applications of microelectronics to manufacturing industry.What Hugh Heclo and Aaron Wildavsky, in their book on the Treasury, refer to as the 'Cabinet Office network', allows departmental civil servants the opportunity to put forward ideas into the central core of the political arena.[49] Coincidentally, the ACARD report favoured projects

MICROELECTRONICS

almost identical to those already announced.
The report argued that the important consideration was not whether microcircuits were manufactured in Britain, but whether they were used by industry. A survey funded by the Department of Industry had shown that only 5% of British firms were already using microelectronics in either equipment or processes. A further 45% were aware of the potential, but either lacked money or expertise to start applications development work. It was this latter group at which the Department of Industry was aiming the third prong of its MAP programme.
Following the publication of the report, more government money was promised to the MAP programme. This was forthcoming in mid 1979, when the MAP's project funding was increased from £15 million to £55 million. The MAP programme seems to have been quite successful. By 1981,34,000 people had attended seminars and demonstrations,predominantly from the South of England, demand for seminars being lower in the North.[50] By 1982,30% of companies were using or intending to use microelectronics. However, demand for microchips remains a problem. Compared to Japan, where use of them is predominantly in products and not in computers, demand in Britain is still very much lower.[51]

6.6 CONCLUSION

Microelectronics policy in Britain has been dominated by the structure of the world market. The 1964 Labour Government attempted to protect the domestic economy from the flood of American components by tariff barriers. Their lack of effect illustrates the importance of the flows of international capital. High tariff barriers encouraged multinational companies to circumvent those barriers by inward investment. As a corollary, it can be argued that when the 1974 Labour Government wanted to increase the inward investment of multinationals it would have been more effective to raise tariff barriers beyond the 17% imposed by the EEC. Without that increase,by 1980,regional incentives were no longer sufficient to attract the multinationals from lower cost areas of the world, whilst the high tariff imposed burdens on product manufacturers and led to overseas manufacture.
But the study illustrates also the dangers involved in relying upon inward investment without control of the technology imported. For instance,ITT was manufacturing outdated technology in

Britain, until government intervention induced it to update its facilities and the threat of Inmos loomed on the horizon. Bureaucratic control from 1979 has been important in monitoring the technology imported in return for government money, but there is no guarantee that that technology will stay up-to-date.

Other characteristics of the world market have also affected domestic market structure and government policy. The American government's funding of R&D helped to create the microelectronics industry. Its cutbacks in defence and space procurement similarly flooded the British market with microchips and made it impossible for British companies to compete. Factors which helped the establishment of Inmos were the shortages which developed in the American market, particularly for 16K chips, and the failure of several American manufacturers to develop a 64K RAM. These factors provided the gap in the world market which had not previously been available. The government's chief scientist in 1970 was correct in predicting that development, but wrong in the timespan he predicted. It took, not three or four years, but nine, before new technology and demand were sufficient for new entrants to the market.

For many years, therefore, the options open to the British government were delineated by the world market and American dominance of technology. One wonders, however, whether financial aid might not have been forthcoming from the 1964 Labour Government, had it not been GEC which was the dominant domestic company in that market. It may be that the government considered its £5 million of R&D funding to be adequate. Or it may be that, following GEC's takeover of AEI and English Electric, the large numbers of redundancies created alienated the government from GEC.

It seems certain that successive governments had little political interest in the microchip industry, and that it was the bureaucracy which kept the technology alive until political interest awakened in 1978. The immediate impact of Prime Ministerial concern for the sector demonstrates the importance of political backing for industrial strategy within the British system of government. Political weight is necessary to offset the withholding hand of the Treasury and its dominant liberal market ethos.

Microelectronics policy also illustrates well, the pluralism and fragmentation within the British state. Competiton may operate, as perhaps in the MAP case, within the Department of Industry itself. But

competition from outside in the shape of the NEB and Inmos had the effect of galvanising compensatory activity from the Department. Although that activity was at first directed against the NEB, the overall effect seems to have been positive. Civil servants' pride in pointing to the amount of overseas investment attracted for a small expenditure of money in comparison to Inmos, attests to the competitive perceptions of the NEB, held at least by some civil servants.

The battle for Inmos points once more to the illogicality of British liberal market ideology. Whilst opponents of Inmos were demanding that the State stop its support, there was no murmur from the Conservative fundamentalists about the amounts of government aid going to multinationals. Ironically, also, Treasury control, which insists that the activity for which government money is provided must not be one which would have taken place without that provision, is more easily used for the benefit of multinationals than for domestic companies. It is also ironic that, in its concern for market freedom, the British political system has incorporated multinationals onto committees designed to 'plan' domestic industrial structure, and that their position can be used as a launching pad for opposition to government policy with which they disagree. In this respect, the microelectronics sector has considerable similarities to that of data processing.

In Britain, the centralised political system demands Ministerial or Prime Ministerial backing for a particular policy to be given financial resources. One is led to the conclusion, that when, as in the case of microelectronics, a policy for an industrial sector is developed by the bureaucracy, it will lack those resources. But for a policy to attain Ministerial backing it must become public. Not only must the issue to which it is related reach the political agenda through publicity, but the policy announcements themselves become part of the self-presentation of Ministers seeking to further their own political role. When a policy becomes political, it gains resources, but brings onto itself opposition from both the 'free marketeers' and the multinationals with domestic subsidiaries. Ministers are then forced back by liberal market ideology to review their previous political decisions in the light of the publicity they have generated and to placate established interests.

The battle for Inmos also illustrates how the

concepts of state control and liberal ideology may be used within political issues. Those who opposed the state funding of Inmos were able to use its failure to locate its technology centre and its first factory in development areas - i.e. its failure to do the state's bidding - as reasons why funding should be ended. The company was posed with the choice of either obeying the state or being 'liberalised'. In other words, liberal ideology became a weapon to enforce compliance by Inmos. For others,such as Sir Keith Joseph,liberal ideology and the supremacy of markets meant that the company should be allowed to manufacture where it chose. It is interesting that in both this case and that of telecommunications, the proponents of 'state control' won the argument. Both examples illustrate the impossibility in a centralised political system of governments actually implementing a liberal ideology towards markets.

In this situation, where industrial policy is the subject of tension between the political system and the liberal market ideology, governments of both parties have attempted to defuse opposition to government intervention by pointing to the huge scale of aid given to their industries by other industrial countries. It is to the comparison of those other countries strategies with that of Britain to which we turn in the next chapter.

NOTES AND REFERENCES

1. For these two competing views see: Labour Party,Microelectroncis(London,Labour Party,1980), pp.19-21;ACARD,The applications of semiconductor technology(London,HMSO,1978).
2. The Economist,Vol.217,27th November 1965,p.979;Vol.224,2nd September 1967,p.808;Select Committee on Science and Technology,HC 272,Appendix D,p.77.
3. The Economist,Vol.225,30th December 1967,pp.1311-2;Vol.226,30th March 1968,p.76.
4. The Computer Merger Project,Cmnd 3668,1968.
5. The Economist,Vol.224,2nd September 1967,p.808.
6. Fourth Report,Vol.II,QA 618,1666,1672, 1678,1700.
7. Figures compiled from NEDO,Electronics (London,HMSO,1972).
8. Fourth Report,QA.1666-1691.
9. Ibid.QA.1668.
10. Ibid.QA.1673.

11. Ibid.QA.1293.
12. Ibid.
13. HC 137,pp.86-7.
14. Fourth Report,Vol.I,Recommendation 266.
15. Sunday Times,5th February 1978 and interviews.
16. Sunday Times,28th May 1978; The Guardian,12th June 1978.
17. The Economist,Vol.269,7th October 1978, Letter, p.8.
18. Ibid.;Vol.269,2nd December 1978,p.111.
19. The Guardian,12th April 1978;Sunday Times, 5th February 1978.
20. Electronics,Vol.51,11th May 1978.
21. Sunday Times,4th June 1978,19th December 1982.
22. Joel Barnett,Inside the Treasury(London, Deutsch,1982),pp.152-3.;W.B.Wilmott,"The NEB Involvment in Electronics and Information Technology",in Charles Carter ed.,Industrial Policy and Innovation,pp.10-12.
23. Sunday Times,28th May,11th June 1978.
24. New Statesman,Vol.95,28th May 1978,pp.696-7;Financial Times,30th June 1978.
25. Ibid.
26. Electronics,Vol.51,6th July 1978,pp.86-7; The Guardian,15th June 1978.
27. New Statesman,Vol.99,20th June 1980,p.927,The Guardian,3rd July 1980.
28. Financial Times,30th July 1980;NEB Press Release,22nd July 1978.
29. The Guardian,22nd July 1978 and interviews.
30. Electronics,Vol.51,17th August 1978,p.63.
31. Financial Times,7th December 1978.
32. The Guardian,27th July 1978;Sunday Times, 21st May 1978,3rd September 1978.
33. NEB Press Release,22nd July 1978.
34. The Guardian,24th January,23rd December 1979.
35. The Economist,Vol.272,30th June 1979,p.92; The Guardian,20th September 1979,18th March 1980.
36. Interviews with civil servants.
37. The Economist,Vol.273,20th October 1979,p.102;Computer Weekly,13th March 1980.
38. Sir Arthur Knight,The National Enterprise Board,(London,mimeo,1981).
39. Computer Weekly,20th January,30th March 1980;The Guardian 28th December 1979,28th June 1980; New Statesman,Vol.99,20th June 1980,pp.926-7.
40. Sunday Times,28th May 1980;The Guardian 3rd April,3rd July 1980;The Economist,Vol.275,17th May

1980,pp.47-8.

41. New Statesman,Vol.99,20th June 1980,pp.926-7;The Guardian,17th May 1980.

42. Sunday Times,25th May 1980;Financial Times,30th July 1980.

43. On Fairchild's technology see The Economist, Vol.274,2nd February 1980,p.80.

44. Computer Weekly,7th August 1980,and interviews.

45. Computer Weekly,6th December 1979.

46. Ibid.4th August 1983.

47. The Guardian,2nd October 1978,and interviews.

48. ACARD,The Applications of Semiconductor Technology(London,HMSO,1978).

59. Hugh Heclo & A.Wildavsky,The Private Government of Public Money(London,Macmillan,1980),p.6.

50. The Economist,Vol.271,2nd June 1979,pp.122-3;Department of Industry,Microprocessor Application Scheme:Summary of Achievements and Future Plans(London,Department of Industry,1980).

51. For instance the IC market in Japan reached $927 million compared to $888.4 million for West Europe as a whole in 1978.Electronics,Vol.51,5th January 1978,pp.125-148,See also House of Lords,New Information Technologies,pp.124-146.

Chapter Seven

COMPARATIVE STRATEGIES AND ALTERNATIVE MODELS OF INDUSTRIAL POLICY

7.1 INTRODUCTION

It was argued in the last chapter that the actions of other governments in support of their domestic industries have been an important factor in determining the response of the British government to markets. It is worthwhile therefore to consider the strategies adopted towards information technology markets by Britain's major overseas competitors. This chapter gives an overview of policies in the USA, France, West Germany, Japan, and some other industrialised nations.

7.2 MAINFRAME COMPUTERS

The American government was the first to support its mainframe computer manufacturers through its defence and space programmes. It is estimated that between 1949 and 1959 IBM received $ 396 million and Sperry Univac received double that amount in federal contracts.[1] In Western Europe the overall strategies of governments can be partly related to the penetration achieved by IBM and other American multinationals in their domestic markets by the mid 1960s. It was pointed out in Chapter 3, that by 1964 IBM took over 70% of the American market, 74% of the French, 73% of the West German, 40% of the Japanese, 50% of the British, 70% of the Belgian and Italian and 60% of the Dutch markets.[2] Faced with such market dominance, some domestically owned manufacturers failed. In Italy, for example, Olivetti was taken over by General Electric of America, which later sold its interests in both France and Italy to Honeywell of America. In Holland, after consistent

225

losses in the data processing field, Philips withdrew in 1977, selling its interests to Siemens of West Germany. In Belgium, a small country without its own data processing industry, an attempt to defend itself against market domination by IBM failed in 1975. It did not renew the agreement with two European multinationals,[3] Philips and Siemens, which was intended to provide them with 50% of the public sector market. In Belgium, Holland, Italy as well as in Ireland, where a policy of attracting inward investment from multinationals has been pursued, the mainframe data processing market is mainly taken by American multinationals.

French strategy towards mainframe computers changed direction in 1965. Until that year it had relied on American companies to supply its data processing needs. When Machines Bull, the major French manufacturer, found itself in financial difficulties, the French government refused aid and it was taken over by first General Electric and then Honeywell of America. Then the American government's refusal to allow Control Data Corporation computers to be used for French nuclear research provoked a row which dragged on until 1967. The political strings attached by the Americans to these exports, made obvious the dangers of dependency on American manufacturers, and, in 1966, the French announced their Plan Calcul, under which £40 million was to be invested over five years in building up a domestic main frame industry. Two small French owned companies were merged into CII and direct support of this company continued until 1975.[4]

But CII had too small a share of the domestic market to be a viable proposition. In 1973 the French joined with the West Germans and the Dutch in forming Unidata, a European company. The company was formed out of the computer interests of CII, Siemens and Philips. It was originally to concentrate upon joint marketing, but attempts were also made to develop a European technology. Because of French fears that it might dominate the new partnership, British ICL, the largest European data processing company, was excluded.[5]

French strategy changed once more with the break up of Unidata. CII ran into trouble again and, in 1976, the French government entered into an agreement with Honeywell-Bull(US) for a joint company CII-Honeywell using American technology. Financial support for CII-Honeywell continued until 1980, but on its ending in 1981 the company registered a trading loss.[6] During the latter 1970s the majority of the French govenment's holding in

the company was sold to a French multinational St.Gobain Pont a Mousson, but under the Mitterand administration that company has been nationalised. Although French owned,the company continues to use American technology. [7]

Japanese strategy has differed from that of Britain, France and the USA. It originally borrowed technology from America, controlled imports and foreign investment, and retained control of foreign licensing of technology through the Ministry of International Trade and Industry (MITI). In 1961 it began support of its domestic mainframe industry through a joint research project towards a large computer and with the establishment of an organisation to provide funds for computer rentals. In 1966 a MITI backed structure plan for the industry set out as objectives 'an independent technological excellence and increased domestic share' for Japanese manufacturers. Galvanised by the failure of Machines-Bull in France and the introduction by IBM of its third generation of computers, the level of support to the industry increased. In particular, Fujitsu, which had no licensing agreement with American companies, benefitted from this support. Until 1975 the only computer companies allowed entry to Japan was IBM, whose technology Japan needed and RCA,which had manufactured there prior to the war. [8] Liberalisation of imports and of foreign investment took place only after international pressure and Japanese manufacturers retain 70% of the domestic market. In 1979 IBM took 23%, Nippon Univac took 5%, and NCR Japan took 2% of the Japanese mainframe market.[9]

West Germany began funding its domestic computer industry in 1967. As in France and Japan a multiannual programme for the data processing industry is publicly announced. The first West German programme was mainly devoted to support of the industry through R&D and was financed by reduced interest loans and subsidies repayable when the project became profitable. In similar fashion to the first British programme, the government also financed the purchase of computers by universities.[10]

In this comparison there is considerable similarity in the time at which governments began to support their domestic mainframe ndustries. Japan was slightly ahead of France in its initial support,but later than France or Britain in upping the amount of financial support given to the industry. In turn Britain was slightly ahead of West Germany in beginning a 'computer policy'.The USA

227

was, of course, ahead of all. It may be that it was not until the mid 1960s that European governments became politically aware of the extent of American subvention of its computer industry. By that time, the dominance of the market by American manufacturers was such that, either domestic manufacturers had to be supported, or the product market had to be handed to multinationals. The political problems of complete dependence on America also became evident at this time.

In each of the countries which decided to support domestic mainframe manufacture there was already some domestic industry to support. In none of the countries did the government set out to create a domestic industry from scratch, although, in the case of France, CII was formed from two small French manufacturers. With the exception of the USA, in each country, the government took a direct hand in restructuring the industry. In Britain, the IRC restructured ICL in 1968. In West Germany, restructuring took place slightly later, after the government had failed in its attempts to join AEG-Telefunken data processing division with that of Siemens. In Japan, an attempt by MITI to restructure the industry in 1971 was foiled by the technological agreements of the Japanese manufacturers with American multinationals. Subsequently, MITI fostered co-operative research agreements. Consolidation of the manufacturers into three groups, then finally, two groups, followed in 1975.[11] In Sweden also, the government restructured the industry in 1978, when Data Saab, 50% owned by the Swedish government and 50% by Saab-Scania was formed. That particular company was bought by Ericsson, the Swedish telecommunications multinational in 1980.[12]

All the countries surveyed here used grants and loans for R&D and public procurement preferences to support domestic manufacturers. But the balance between the two mechanisms has differed as has the directness or indirectness of R&D support itself. The American government funds the electronics industry primarily through defence contracts, and through R&D support. In total it provides 60% of industrial R&D. Although, according to National Science Foundation figures, in real terms, federal R&D expenditure fell by 20% between 1967 and 1979, the USA still spends 4% of GNP on R&D.[13] Of this amount approximately 50% goes to defence related R&D.

In the public sector, as detailed in Chapter One, the American government relies upon the series of Acts and regulations referred to as the Buy

STRATEGIES AND MODELS

America Act. These preclude foreign manufacturers, without local production facilities in the USA, from gaining entry to the public sector. After GATT regulations on public sector contracts came into force in 1981, it seemed that one or two foreign manufacturers with American subsidiaries were gaining contracts as sub-contractors on projects, but the defence market in particular was further closed to overseas suppliers in 1983.[14] In general, the American public sector market is supplied by American companies.

Without the benefit of legal protection, the Japanese government also procures over 90% of its public sector computers from Japanese firms. Direct R&D support is less important as a mechanism in Japan, than it is in the USA, West Germany or Britain. Research projects are mounted through consortia of companies brought together by MITI and funded on a 50/50 basis with industry.

West Germany is the Japan of Europe with no formal policy of public sector preference. The formal policy of preference for Siemens and AEG-Telefunken was widened in 1971 to include all European suppliers. However, there is a de facto preference in favour of Siemens and Nixdorf (which took over AEG-Telefunken's data processing interests). Siemens takes 44% of the public sector.[15]

In contrast to Britain, where public sector preference has never been complete, in France it plays an equally important role to that of R&D support. Up to 1976 CII was given preference wherever possible, and, where it was not possible, then equipment manufactured in France by Honeywell or IBM was used. The French also adopted an indirect method of support for CII. All government software had to be supplied in the CII source language thereby making other manufacturers' software available to CII users.[16] Following the government's agreement with Honeywell for its takeover of CII, it entered into a contract which guaranteed the new company $800 million of public sector business or compensation in lieu. At one point, as a result, the French government found itself buying Honeywell machines, made in Britain, in preference to IBM machines, made in France.[17]

Although the EEC Commission itself began to formulate a policy towards the data processing industry in 1973, and has consistently pointed to the dangers of European domination by American multinationals, its direct impact on the industry has been limited. It has supported some research projects, including some directly related to its own

needs, such as machine translation of languages, but it can act only in so far as member countries have allowed it to do so. The multi-annual programme on data processing, conceived in 1973 was not agreed to by the Council of Ministers until 1979, when it was passed with a budget approximately halved. The staff requested by the Commission were reduced in numbers from 39 to seven (including secretaries)and the whole programme has subsequently suffered from delays.[18] In point of fact West Germany,Britain and France have not been keen to see EEC co-ordination in a market area in which they have been supporting national companies.However, in response to the technological challenge from Japan, the EEC agreed in 1982 that R&D among twelve firms should be supported. These included Siemens, CIT-Alcatel (France),Philips,Olivetti, ICL,Plessey and GEC.In the words of Christopher Layton,special adviser to the European Commission on Information Technology:

> Europe has to leapfrog the existing technologies and move on fast to the technologies which will be the products in the 1990s.[19]

Research is to concentrate upon the next generation of computers, microchips,robotics and computer aided design, and is to be funded half and half by the EEC and the companies themselves.

Ironically, whilst the Commission has been the most strident institution in its attempts to foster a European owned industry and technology, and to promote the whole EEC area as a domestic market for European owned manufacturers, the indirect effects of its competition policy and its attempts to open national markets have had the opposite effect. As mentioned in Chapter One ,from the end of 1980, EEC members have been limited in their normal procurement preference for domestic manufacturers of data processing equipment. American multinationals may take governments to the European Court if they exert a policy of public preference in favour of domestic manufacturers. Both Burroughs and IBM in 1982 attempted to take the British government to court over alleged breaking of the provision by an Area Health Authority and an Area Water Board.[20] Similar action may also be launched in France where officials have indicated that they intend to carry on procurement preference as before.[21]

7.3 MINICOMPUTERS AND PERIPHERALS.

In contrast to their response to the mainframe market, the response of governments to that of peripherals, minicomputers and software has been diverse. Whereas in Britain there was a very late response to the growth in those markets, in Japan, again within a system of import controls, MITI acted to rationalise production of peripherals in 1969. Japanese firms control almost 100% of the mini and microcomputer market. Japanese companies already market small computers in Europe and manufacture in France.[22]

The French government had a policy directed towards the peripherals industry as early as 1966. West Germany, like Britain has had no specific policy of support for peripherals.

The differences are probably related to market structure. In Germany the major computing firm, Siemens, was a large company with its own peripherals manufacture. As in Britain, support of the major supplier also entailed support for its peripherals manufacture. In Japan each of the seven computing firms (six from 1966) also had their own peripherals suppliers. It was only when it became clear that in some sectors technological innovation had ended, that MITI acted to standardise those peripherals and to cartelise a stable market.[23] In France, on the other hand, CII was formed from small computer manufacturers without their own internal peripherals manufacture. To supply CII, it therefore became necessary to form a viable peripherals manufacturer. The French government therefore brought together two small firms for the purpose and the ensuing firm was integrated with CII in 1970.

The French policy of support for minicomputers developed out of its support for peripherals. In its Sixth Plan the French government financed the development of small processors and calculators and gave aid to small peripherals manufacturers.[24] But following the merger of CII and Honeywell in 1976, the two policies began to collide.

Although the French government had guaranteed $800 million worth of public sector contracts to the new firm, in fact this figure proved difficult to achieve. Some government agencies had already bought computers from IBM and to change software would have been expensive. By 1979 the procurement plan had fallen short of target. Meanwhile Honeywell, responding to changes in the expansion of markets,

231

diversified into minicomputers and took a controlling interest in a French microcomputer firm. The simplest way for the government to make up the shortfall in public sector ordering was for it to purchase minicomputers from Honeywell. But, in turn, that procurement conflicted with its policy of support for small mini manufacturers. The French government was faced with buying from Honeywell, in competition with itself, for its own contracts. That it did so, seems certain. In 1980 the small mini manufacturers claimed that whereas the government had spent 3000 million francs on CII-Honeywell between 1975 and 1980, they had received only 220 million, half of it in loans. [25]

The importance of software was recognised earlier in France, Japan, and West Germany than in Britain. French government support of the industry was partly indirect through support of CII. That company's policy was to buy in software expertise from consultancies. From 1971 the Delegue a l'informatique, in charge of French computer policy, encouraged the placement of contracts by central government departments with software firms. Recent government policy also provides that the money devoted to applications of information technology should be channelled through private software houses. [26] In West Germany, software support has increased as a proportion of total government expenditure on data processing since the first programme of 1967-1971. In particular, the West German government has concentrated on the supply of software for industrial application. [27]

Because the major source of financial aid to the CSI industry itself is through public procurement, the use of software consultants depends upon civil service attitudes and the software expertise available 'in-house' to governments. In Britain, and to a lesser extent in West Germany, the civil service has preferred to use its own expertise and train its own people rather than use outside help. Whereas, in 1976, the USA government contributed 10% of domestic CSI revenue, the French government contributed 15%, the West German government 11%, the proportion of CSI revenue contributed by the British government was 4%. [28] The French CSI is now the strongest in Europe, and the Japanese CSI is growing at 100% per annum. [29]

Whereas the British government is concerned that software exports should increase, a recent trend in the opposite direction is evident in the USA. There, software export controls are now in force, even for software exported to Western Europe.

STRATEGIES AND MODELS

In order to control the transfer of, what the Pentagon believes to be, 'critical technology', companies must specify the level of software included within computer exports as well as any training package involved. Defence interests are thereby overruling commercial interests. [30]
   As in the field of data processing, the EEC Commission has been active in pointing to the dangers of a situation where 80% of European peripherals are supplied by American manufacturers. It has put forward a policy for what it terms the peri-informatics sector. [31] But just as in its programme for data processing, so the difficulties of achieving consensus on the direction and funding of a policy have as yet precluded any firm decisions. At a time when member governments wish to reduce their budget contributions to Brussels, funding for new avenues of co-operation is not easily found.

7.4 MICROELECTRONICS

In Japan and in West Germany, the markets for components, computers and telecommunications are integrated, in the sense that the major components manufacturers are also suppliers of computers and telecommunications equipment. One can therefore suppose that the support directed by those governments to such firms as NEC, Fujitsu and Siemens, from the 1960s onwards also went towards the development of components. In the USA, the markets of data processing and microelectronics overlap, both because of the process of increasing vertical concentration, and because IBM is a major manufacturer of microcircuits.[32]Although IBM has diversified into private telephone exchanges (PABx), the markets of telecommunications and data processing have been dominated by different companies. In France and Britain, all three markets have been autonomous to a large degree.
   The USA has traditionally been the world leader in the manufacture of integrated circuits. But gradually, during the 1970s, American companies not only began to lose their technological lead over Japan, but also lost market share to the Japanese both in the USA and abroad. From 80% of the world market, American companies' market share decreased to 60% and imports of Japanese microchips increased to 50% of the American 16K RAM market. [33]The US military, worried at the threat to American interests by the influx of Japanese micro-chips, stepped into the ring with a proposal for a $200

233

million research project to produce Very High Scale Integrated circuits.[34] Of the fourteen contestants for the project, IBM, Honeywell,Texas Instruments and Sperry Univac were among the winners. The rest of the industry were less pleased, pointing to the oligopolistic influence of the research contract, and to the way in which it would increase the influence of the military over the industry. They have called for an 'industrial policy' for the industry, which has not been forthcoming.

In addition, the American government placed pressure on Japan to release civilian technology to the US under its defence agreement with America. The technology wanted was that of microcircuits and optic fibres. The demand was made in 1979 as part of the pressure on Japan to increase its defence spending in return for less American protectionist pressure against Japanese imports. The Japanese government eventually agreed to the transfer of technology in June 1982.

The particular research project backed by the Japanese government which so worried the American administration was that of the VSLI circuit. In 1976 MITI brought together the four major integrated circuit manufacturers into a co-operative research project which, funded 50/50 by government and industry was scheduled to cost in the region of $350 million over four years. $250 million of this money consisted of government loans. Under the aegis of MITI's research laboratory, the manufacturers lent several hundred research personnel to the project. Whilst these personnel co-operated in basic R&D the resulting processes were to be used competitively by the four manufacturers. Between 1976 and 1979 over 1000 commercially useful processes were developed by the VSLI project, whereas the usual method of American research funding, through defence expenditure, is estimated to produce spin-offs of commercially useful patents of only 5%. The Japanese were concerned enough about protectionist pressures in the USA to end the VSLI project ahead of schedule.[35]

The Japanese government also lowered its tariff on semiconductors. At the same time it agreed to open to the public both patents held by the Japanese government alone and those held jointly with private industry, all of which had resulted from the VSLI project. These measures were followed in 1981 by a further lowering of the tariff barriers on semiconductors,which at about 10% in 1983 were lower than EEC tariffs.[36]

French support for microchips began in the

1960s when financial aid went to their industrial production through a subsidiary of Thomson Houston.[37] The programme does not appear to have been particularly successful, partly, no doubt, because the market for microcircuits was swamped at the time by American multinationals with surplus capacity. It was the prospect of the modernisation of the French telecommunications network which created the conditions for the French government, in 1978, to attract multinationals into France on a joint venture basis with a transfer of technology taking place. The policy was unpopular among the multinationals. One company is quoted in 1980 as:

> talking to the French government for about a year and a half about setting up a marketing and technical support office there ...but new conditions and new delays are coming up.. The French government is insisting on a joint venture arrangement that would allow a transfer of the company's N/MOS technology.[38]

American companies also complained that the French government was ensuring over-capacity in the French market in certain technologies in order to assure itself that companies would export a proportion of their production.[39]

French policy has mainly been directed towards the special market of telecommunications chips. But French production of all chips has not expanded as fast as anticipated. In 1980 French owned manufacturers took only 30% of the domestic market compared to the expected 37%.[40] The shortfall was expected to lead to increased pressure on companies aided by the public sector to 'Buy French'.

French, British and West German policy have all coincided in utilising American technology in the standard chip market. In Britain, this takes place through inward investment, in West Germany through licensing agreements and in France through joint ventures. Both France and West Germany were reported in 1980 as spending in the region of $400 million on the support of microelectronics.[41] In West Germany, support has mainly been through R&D and through aid to product development and VLSI development. It has gone to both Siemens and AEG-Telefunken and to foreign owned companies. Unlike France, West Germany has not sought joint ventures with American companies, but as in France, public sector preference operates against the multinationals.

Once again the dominance of American multin-

ationals over the West European market has concerned the EEC. Tariffs on microcircuits have been kept at 17% in order to decrease imports and increase local manufacture. The tariffs have been used in a variable fashion, being lowered when no local production of a particular technology was available and then raised as soon as there was a local source of supply.[42]

In 1979 the Commission put forward a programme of support for the infra-structure industry which services the microchip manufacturers. Its intention was to bring together those firms producing equipment for microchip manufacture and the European owned microchip manufacturers, in order to develop a European capability in the industry.[43] Once more it has proved difficult to get the policy off the ground. In addition, it seems that the trend is for imports of microcircuits to the EEC to increase. Alterations in exchange rates alter the impact of tariff barriers, and they are no longer high enough to make it worthwhile for multinationals to locate production in Europe.

7.5 TELECOMMUNICATIONS AND OFFICE TECHNOLOGY

Telecommunications is the market where, until recently, most governments have operated a system of preference and protection. In the USA that protection has operated through a near monopoly of the network by AT&T and its subsidiary companies, regulated by the Federal Communications Commission under the 1934 Communications Act. In other countries the operation of the network and a monopoly of transmission has rested with the PTTs.

In the USA, a move towards liberalisation of AT&T's historical monopoly came in the late 1960s with the Carterfone decision. The decision allowed consumers to buy handsets from stores and to attach them to the network. The only conditions imposed on their sale was that they should pass safety standards set by the FCC.[44]

Pressure continued to build up for a complete liberalisation of all data communications as computer companies fought with AT&T over the transmission of data and the attachment of modems to the network. A series of anti-trust cases against AT&T, and criticism that it was using its monopoly to forestall expenditure on modernisation of the network, eventually led, in 1981, to the decision to deregulate all but the basic telephone network. It had become impossible to distinguish legally between

STRATEGIES AND MODELS

the transmission of voice and data, rendering perpetual anti-trust cases or infringement cases inevitable.The decision was expected to boost the office technology and data transmission markets. It has allowed companies, such as Satellite Business Systems, a consortium headed by IBM, to put up a satellite to provide data transmission between business premises. This particular company has had the advantage of by-passing the AT&T land lines necessary to get the signal from earth station to consumer. It has done this by using small dish aerials on the roofs of customers' buildings. For other companies attempting to use satellites it has been possible for AT&T to delay transmission by witholding the use of its land lines.It is noteworthy that British Telecom later adopted a similar strategy against the Mercury consortium.

Within the new deregulated network, AT&T has had to divest itself of its manufacturing subsidiaries. But it is allowed to compete in the data communications and data equipment market through arms length subsidiaries. It is also allowed to market equipment overseas. Both it and Western Electric (its manufacturing arm) are now competing in overseas markets. [45]

The fact that there has been a private monopoly of the telecomunications network has allowed the American government to claim that it operates a liberal market policy, whilst allowing discrimination against foreign manufacturers.In 1981 the Japanese firm Fujitsu had a bid for optic fibres for the AT&T network turned down in favour of a higher bid fom Western Electric. It is said that AT&T acted under pressure from the FCC and producer groups and that it turned down Fujitsu's bid in the 'national interest'.[46] It was possible for the American government to plead innocence whilst, simultaneously, pressuring the Japanese government to open its telecommunications market to American companies.

In France some liberalisation of the PTT monopoly in telephone handsets has taken place. In Japan there was also some liberalisation of the data processing network following a confrontation between MITI and the Ministry of Posts,which has overall responsibility for communications. Under pressure from the USA, the Japanese government agreed in 1979 to open up their telecommunications procurement to American companies.[47]The president of NTT who suggested that Japan might be able to buy broomsticks and buckets from America was quietly dropped. NTT's retention of control over standards of equipment proved a delaying non-tariff barrier and it was

not until 1982 that American firms actually gained entry.

The modernisation of the telephone network to electronically controlled exchanges is of crucial importance. On it depends the growth of the new markets of office technology and the possibility of the cheap provision of these services. Ideally the new technologies, such as facsimile and interactive computing, need a digital network for their cheap provision. France's network was the first to adopt a digital technology which allows integrated speech and data networks. But the internal telephone system in Japan is also well advanced,with the introduction of electronic telephone exchanges,a full public data network and a nationwide facsimile service. Communications satellite development has been given a great deal of attention and is said to be ahead of America.[48]

The telecommunications network in France was elevated to a matter of national priority in 1974 by the French President. Not only were the non- French owned subsidiaries of Ericsson and ITT bought out with government support, but investment in telecommunications was increased. The French, like the Japanese,use public procurement as a mechanism of support for domestic industry, as a means to reduce unit costs and as a vehicle to promote familiarity with new technology among the population at large. The NORA report of 1979 on telematiques, with its emphasis on the development of an information society, was followed by a further increase in resources to the sector.[49] Facsimile service on a nationwide scale is to be introduced and video terminals are to be installed instead of paper telephone directories. The intention is to reduce the cost of the VDUs through mass production and thus to produce cheap products for export, in the same way as the Japanese have done in relation to facsimile machines.

Japan, Germany and France are all attempting to create a domestic demand for information technology products. Whereas in Britain the demand side has been mainly through the microprocessor awareness scheme of the Department of Industry and lttle attention has been given to education, in France and Germany education is emphasised. In Germany programmes also stretch to assisting firms with first installations of data processing machines and to increasing amounts spent on education and training. Training and education account for approximately one third of the Federal Government's budget on computers. In France, the emphasis is on

giving the general population 'hands on' experience through operation of VDUs and to providing each lycee with a computer. Neither Britain, nor the USA, nor Japan match this expenditure on education. But, in Japan, research into pattern recognition is expected to produce a voice driven computer for use by the general population and experiments in interactive networks of computers and television have been run on a community wide basis. In total, the Japanese government will spend $210 million on the development of such leading edge technologies between 1972 and 1985.[50]

The French, German, British and Japanese PTTs have all developed the equivalent to 'viewdata' - a mechanism for information retrieval using television sets and the telecommunications network. In Britain, development of a mass market was held up by the cost of adapted television sets and the growth of the service, although quickening in 1983, has not been as fast as anticipated. In contrast, in France, the political importance and publicity given to information technology resulted in the early adoption by French TV manufacturers of a standard set incorporating an attachment. The standardisation has meant larger production runs and lower unit costs for adapted sets. Heavy government support for the national systems in the export market is aimed at achieving dominance of the world market. From that dominance would come the de facto recognition of one national system as 'standard', in the same manner as IBM's standards became world standards. The three Western European countries and Canada battled it out in the export market and the confrontation became so bitter that the whole question of compatibility and standards was referred to the CCITT.[51]

In 1979, the EEC Commission recognised, in its policy statement on telecommunications, the crucial part the network played in the development of information technology products. The Commission had been interested in the market since 1973, first attempting to generate interest amongst the European PTTs in standardisation of equipment. The Commission acted as a catalyst to discussions between the PTTs on possible harmonisation of data processing networks, and it supported the development of Ethernet - a data processing network for European· scientific institutions.[52]

In 1979 the Commission suggested that what it called 'telematics' should be open to competition. The areas it suggested for that liberalisation included those which were not in already established

service. Hence, telephones,modems,teleprinters and PABx would remain within PTT monopolies.It suggested that 10% of PTT's annual purchases should be open to competitive tender. These 'annual purchases' could include such things as vehicles and furniture as well as telecommunications equipment.[53] The British government expressed its desire for the liberalisation of 'telematics' markets to go further than that proposed by the Commission,on the grounds that the British liberalisation of the market would allow EEC and American companies to compete in areas from which Britain would be disbarred on the Continent. But,early in 1983, the EEC member countries decided against even a 10% liberalisation of telecommunications.[54]

7.6. STRATEGIES COMPARED

Coalescing technology and the demands of new markets have pressed governments into rethinking their role in the regulation of telecommunications and their support of computer and microelectronics industries. Response has varied from increased indirect funding of computer and microelectronics companies and liberalisation of telecommunications in the USA to a more state controlled reaction in France and Japan. In the first chapter it was argued that the response of governments in aiding markets will be related to such factors as the 'core' ideology, the political system (whether it is decentralised or centralised) and the structure of markets. Hence the USA, with its 'core' liberal ideology and its decentralised political system could be expected to use methods, such as tariff barriers and indirect mechanisms of giving aid to industry, which did not undermine the 'core' ideology. In contrast,Japan,with its 'core' mercantilist ideology and its centralised political system could be expected to institute control over imports and an 'industrial policy' based on subventions to industry, as a method of gaining comparative advantage in world trade. These differences in approach are particularly marked in the various countries' approach to the patterns of global investment and international market structure in the information technology sector.

First, only the Japanese appreciated at an early stage, the impact of foreign investment and the licensing of foreign technology upon domestic industry, and then took steps to control it. In Western Europe, the French alone have attempted to control the transfer of technology through joint

240

ventures with multinationals and through state/multinational holding companies. Yet French policies have differed from the Japanese.
Whereas the Japanese have concentrated recently upon domestic technology and its development, the French have been content to rely on American technology and to establish domestic ownership. Equally the West Germans have relied on licensing agreements with the Americans.The British and Irish have been xenophilic towards multinationals, providing investment incentives but retaining little or no control over the technology imported.GEC has argued that by attracting that inward investment the British government has weakened and fragmented the UK market.
The importance of European markets and access to them by American companies is underlined in a report by the American Semiconductor Association in 1980.

> To keep production costs as low as possible, American firms need to produce for the largest possible market. The large up-front R&D costs associated with new product development can be more easily recovered with a larger potential market. Further,since foreign semi-conductor product life cycles may lag, and,in some instances,extend over a longer period, U.S.producers can capture additional returns on their initial R&D investments through access to these markets. 55

It is interesting that the Americans are now concerned at the possibility of local production by Japanese microelectronic companies, which will retain R&D facilities in Japan. The Americans,like the British have few mechanisms to control the inward transfer of technology by multinationals.
The American response to this threat has been threefold. First they have indirectly funded the microelectronics industry through defence R&D, possibly with the dual purpose of not only giving financial aid to the industry,but also gaining a greater measure of state control over the market. Second, they have put pressure on Japan through its defence agreement to release VSLI and optic-fibre technology to America's defence industry, thereby transferring it directly to the Japanese companies' American rivals. And, third, they have attempted to control the outward flow of technology,in order to give American companies a longer lead time to gain ascendancy in the market

before technology is transfused overseas. This concept of 'critical technology' was originally applied specifically to technology which had potential for use in weapons systems. But it has proved difficult to define that technology with any precision. The trend is towards labelling commercial technology 'critical', and to a general tightening of technology transfer by multinational corporations. Given the mobility of personnel, it is unlikely that these mechanisms can be successful in the long run, but the transfer of knowledge, for instance through conference papers, can be slowed down.[56]

The mechanisms used to support manufacturers differ with institutional structures, market structures and the role of multinationals within the domestic economy. The Americans can rely on tariffs and export controls partly because of the low penetration of foreign multinationals in their economy. But the demand and supply of products can also be manipulated by governments through the mechanism of public procurement. In particular, the French, Japanese and American governments have used the mechanism to create a home market to a much greater extent than the British or German governments have done. The French have also used central government power to direct effort into exports.

There are obvious explanations arising from ideological, historical and institutional factors. The American Buy American Acts are the product of the depression years, and subsequently of producer pressure within Congress. The highly centralised administrative system in France, coupled with a history of state involvement in industry, create conditions favourable to the central direction of demand and supply. In Japan the relative formal autonomy of local government is countered by a similar history of state involvement in industry and informal networks of communication.

By comparison, the federal structure of West Germany and the local autonomy of Britain do not lend themselves to central control of purchasing. However, the West Germans do seem to operate informally a policy of preference to Siemens, although it is not officially stated. And the British government has recently attempted to introduce a procurement policy, the guidelines for which are worded so as to avoid EEC repercussions. The presence of multinationals in certain markets and their importance as local employers (IBM in West Germany, Honeywell in Britain) has also limited the use of public procurement preference as a policy

STRATEGIES AND MODELS

instrument. Its use is further limited by EEC regulations, although exemptions from those regulations on such grounds as the need for continuity of supply, can be ,and are being, made.

Market structure also affects the extent and mechanisms of intervention. All those countries, except Belgium, which intervened in the mainframe computer market had domestic manufacturers to support. Those, such as France, which intervened in peripherals, did so because a separate supply was necessary or,as in Japan, because too many suppliers competed for a low technology market. Multinational investment has been sought, for instance in microelectronics, where no domestic capability existed. Aid has also tended to go to large rather than small firms and to reflect ongoing organisational links. German policy cannot be separated from support for Siemens, or Japanese from support for Fujitsu, or French from CII-Honeywell, or British from ICL.

In the process of coalescing markets and converging technology, existing horizontal stratification of national companies has eased the organisational problems of government support. Siemens, Fujitsu, NEC, Hitachi and now Ericsson, straddle the markets of telecommunications, components and computing. CII-Honeywell and ICL did not. The French attempted to overcome this problem by integrating CII-Honeywell into the telecommunications market. The British did not.

Recently the diversification of ICL, GEC and Plessey into office technology and Ferranti into telecommunications, has eased the constraints of autonomous markets upon British policy, but it is noteworthy that the major pressure for liberalisation has come in those countries, such as Britain and the USA, where the telecommunications and data processing companies have not been integrated. In the USA, IBM having diversified into telecommunications, was excluded from transmission of data until the liberalisation of the network. In the early 1970s commentators were predicting that IBM's intention was to create a transmission system which, taken in conjunction with its world market in computers, would give it a world domination of data processing. It can be argued that its SBS satellite, now linked by a gateway to to British Telecom's satellite service, is the first step in that direction.[57] It is less likely that France, Germany or Japan will liberalise their telecommunications markets except under international pressure. Whereas in Britain and the USA the telecommunications net-

work could not handle fast data transmission cheaply, in France the technology of the public network is such that it can. In Japan and West Germany, the major data processing companies are also telecommunicatons suppliers. These countries are therefore less likely to liberalise their telecommunications markets under domestic pressure, although the British government seems to hope that they will.

Finally, institutional and organisational frameworks affect responses to markets. An appreciation of changing markets seems to be quicker in those countries where plans or programmes for industries are published and attract public attention. France, Germany and Japan all have coherent strategies for the information technology industry. So also does the EEC, although it does not possess the political powers to implement its strategy.

In comparison to the industrial strategies adopted by France, West Germany or Japan, British strategy towards information technology has lacked coherence. It has lacked the Japanese commitment to foster domestic industry and technology. It has also lacked the French commitment to produce French ownership and increased exports. British policy has been modelled in terms of markets on that of America. A 'free market', inward investment by multinationals and foreign technology have been welcomed, whilst the highest proportion of funding of R&D in the electronics sector has been through the defence industry. Competition within the market and formal centralised responsibility for policymaking have been the tenets underpinning British policy. But, unlike Japan, where competition takes place within an overall consensus about the importance of Japanese industry, within Britain, no overriding consensus fuels policymaking and implementation. Pluralism within the state itself, conflict over the proper role of the state within industry, the autonomy sought by various units of the state and the decisions made in terms of political priorities, have produced incoherent policies. The conflict between state control and the 'core' ideology has been primarily contained in the markets discussed here by limiting the state's role to 'technology push' and by adhering to a liberal approach to markets - i.e. ignoring the importance of market pull on economic success. This approach has been largely modelled on American experience. But then, perhaps there is no alternative to the British government either supporting American technology, or aiding the development of British

STRATEGIES AND MODELS

technology, which then cannot be marketed either because it lacks volume production to make it cheap enough, or because of the dominance of multinationals within the domestic market? In the following section we look at possible alternative models for British industrial policy.

7.7 AN ALTERNATIVE MODEL FOR INDUSTRIAL POLICY

7.71 The American Model

The American model of the role of the state in relation to markets has been adopted by Britain in such measures as the liberalisation of telecommunications. Yet, in fact there has been a failure to appreciate major differences between the image and reality of that model. Although claiming to run a free enterprise economy, the American government actually runs one which is highly protectionist towards domestic industry. Legal controls are retained over purchasing for the public sector, whilst quota restrictions and countervailing tariffs are imposed on commodities whose import either threatens local producers, or is thought to be subsidised by foreign governments. In the past, Canada, in particular, has suffered from these tariffs, when its governments has attempted to build up domestic industry against American competition.[58]

Defence spending, a form of industrial subsidy, funds commercial R&D and the Federal Government also provides about 50% of all industrial R&D funds. Direct controls have been exerted over the export of technology, and, in the case of the Soviet pipe-line, over American subsidiaries abroad and foreign companies' use of that technology. None of these mechanisms are those of a 'free market' economy. They have arisen because America is also a de-centralised state, in which producer pressure can be easily and effectively levelled at Congress. They have arisen also because a decentralised bureaucracy does not allow the specific intervention necessary for a more direct 'industrial policy', whilst the weakening position of America within the international economy demands that the government protect itself from the domestic repercussions of that weakness.

7.72 The Japanese Model

Just as the American model put forward by liberal ideologues has tended to be a partial one, so the model of Japanese policy put forward by mercantilists has also tended to be partial. The

version tends to stress the linkages between the bureaucracy, the parties and big business and regards those linkages as being the primary determinants of Japanese economic success.[59] The version tends to emphasise the power of MITI and its role in altering the industrial structure of Japan. It tends to underestimate the role played in postwar development of Japanese industry by the Ministry of Finance, the Japanese banks and the individual Japanese consumer Where other elements have been stressed, such as the importation of technology, the Japanese propensity to upgrade that technology and to develop its own has been downgraded in importance.[60]

It is clearly not possible to review here, in depth, Japanese industrial policy, so three elements have been selected which bear on British experience. First, the importance of the bureaucracy will be discussed, then the role of the banks and finally the role of MITI.

1)The Japanese bureaucracy.
Within a vertically structured society,the government ministries play a role at the pinnacle. Japanese bureaucrats hold a very high social status stemming from the fact that they comprise the best graduates from top universities. Their power in the immediate post-war period stemmed both from the disarray of the parties and from the fact that they alone remained unpurged during the American Occupation. As in the case of business, bureaucrats retire in their fifties. The whole of the year's entry to a ministry will retire when one of their number becomes Vice-Minister(Permanent Secretary). The most able will retire into businss or into finance - the Ministry itself arranges the transfer. The destination of the retiree will depend on the Ministry's client groups. Some will retire into politics to become Dietmen. The least able will be found sinecures in public corporations or quasi-governmental agencies.This practice of what is called 'descent from heaven' provides an interlinking network between parties,business and bureaucracy,which is reinforced by informal ties between those who graduated from the same university. It functions in the same way as the 'old boy network' functions in Britain.[61]

Ministries are organised vertically,there being approximately twelve,with the Ministry of Finance and MITI being the most important. In similar fashion to other elements of the vertical social structure,they act in competition with each other.

Co-ordination between ministries is a considerable problem, compounded by a weak political leadership structure. Ministers stay only one year, posts being shared around between factions of the ruling party. Competition between Ministers from different factions may exacerbate conflict between Ministries. In contrast to British experience, the permanent secretary of a Ministry, the Vice-Minister, is a public figure. He will have his own programme for the Ministry which will be publicly stated. The political system is a combination of elements of the British Cabinet system and the American Congress, so that officials may be called before the Diet, as in America. But, in general, the bureaucracy is probably no more accountable to Parliament than in Britain.

Similar political control over top appointments in the bureaucracy is wielded as in Britain. But unlike Britain, no changes in the organisation of Ministries can be made without legislation. Whereas, in Britain, Ministries tend to be organised along functional lines, possibly with the odd working party, task force or planning unit slotted into the functional line of command, in Japan, there may be both horizontal and vertical co-ordination. For instance, MITI, which until 1973, was organised on the basis of industries, now has a mixture of both industry bureaux and co-ordinating bureaux. This form of organisation has been widely considered by organisational theorists to allow a quicker response from the organisation to its environment.[62]

2) The Banking Sector

Japanese consumers save approximatley 15%-20% of their annual income, compared to 5% in the USA and Britain. Part of the reason for this higher rate of savings may be the tradiional bonus system in Japan, where employees receive lump sums at New Year time. Traditionally this money has gone to the banks and thereby into capital investment. Savers have been paid a low rate of interest and until recently were content to accept that state of affairs because real incomes were growing and taxes remained low.

Traditionally the Ministry of Finance has encouraged firms to finance capital investment through bank loans rather than through equity. This has led to the majority of large firms being capitalised predominantly by bank lending, which in turn has meant that they have been less geared to short-term profits than their Western counterparts. In general, although specialist banks have developed for small business, credit has been easier for large

companies. Banks seem to be prepared to take more risks than their Western counterparts.[63] The American Semiconductor Industry Association claims that some Japanese companies earn only a 7% return on capital, whereas 9% would be needed to finance their bank loans. It argues that Japanese banks are prepared to forego interest if the company is expanding its market share, and consider this practice to be a form of subsidy.[64]

Since the banks are dependent, in the long run, on the Bank of Japan, the system has allowed the Ministry, through the Bank of Japan, to control the level of company loans. Central control of credit is also made easier by the dual structure of the Japanese economy. Around the large firms revolve satellite companies. Each banking group has its own trading company, which acts as a go-between, buying goods and services abroad and selling in Japan and vice versa. Each banking group tends to extend credit more easily to its own affiliates and, in recessionary times, affiliates will help each other out.

Within this system of predominantly private credit, MITI has encouraged high growth industries. The overall consensus in favour of growth developed by MITI has had a direct effect on the financing of industries through the private banks and through the state-owned Japan Development Bank. Coupled with Ministry of Finance 'window guidance' to private banks and control of interest rates, easy credit has gone to both those industries targeted as 'growth' industries by MITI and to the larger, faster growing companies within them. Hiroya Ueno has demonstrated that private banks tend to have followed the example of the public Japan Development Bank in the industries to which they have lent most money.[65]

The economic structure in Japan, with increasing wages, life-time employment and a large supply of young people has meant the advantages on wage costs have gone to those firms which have grown fastest, thereby taking in young workers and decreasing average wage costs. These advantages built into high growth have yielded an increasing divergence between the most successful and least successful companies, even within a growth sector. In the immediate post-war period preferential loans went to basic industries such as steel, shipbuilding, coal mining and fertiliser producers. Similar preferential treatment was extended to automobiles and petrochemicals in the 1960s and to computers in the 1970s.[66]

3) MITI'S ROLE

MITI's direct involvement has been mainly in fledgling or depressed industries. In both cases its philosophy has been to promote cartelisation and rationalisation. In some industries it has gained legal backing for such policies, for instance in cotton spinning, shipbuilding and software. But mainly, given its lack of legal controls, such rationalisation has come about through consensus with industry. Where there has not been that consensus and in industries where growth and easy long-term profit made even marginal producers viable, MITI's influence has been limited. Nor does competition between the banking groups or the difficulty of merging two companies each with life-time employment systems ease matters. In such industries as automobiles, steel and computers, MITI's influence in the past has been limited.[67] It has been most successful in industries which were highly fragmented such as textiles, car components and computer peripherals. In general, MITI's policy has been to protect fledgling industries, to allow their development in the home market and then to encourage exports. [68]

Inward investment into Japan was strictly controlled until the 1970s. Then, under increasing international pressure, Japan allowed foreign investment, in other than joint venture format, although MITI and the Ministry of Finance still prefer the joint venture. The Anti-Monopoly Law is now the major vehicle through which foreign companies are controlled. They are not allowed to gain a dominant share of the market. In 1978, for instance MITI exercised administrative guidance to state that foreign computer companies were not to take more than 50% of the domestic market.[69] But foreign capital still takes a low proportion of total domestic capital formation. In 1980, MITI found in its annual survey that there were only 1,600 firms with 25% or more of foreign capital in Japan. Recent entrants have included American semi-conductor companies, such as Texas Instruments, Motorola and Burroughs.[70]

Until recently export of capital was also controlled. The majority of overseas investment went to securing raw material resources. But with the increase of tariff barriers and protectionism in the West, MITI has actively encouraged industries to locate manufacturing production outside Japan. In particular, the car and semiconductor industries have been encouraged to locate in the USA and EEC.

MITI has also encouraged technological links between Japanese companies and foreign firms. Hence outward investment and technology exchange have been subordinated to the wider needs of the national economy and are used as a strategic resource. Helped in periods of yen over-valuation against the dollar, overseas investment has increased,to more than 0.5% of GNP (compared to the USA's 0.9% and Britain's 1.4%), but there are fears that increased overseas investment causes unemployment at home.[71]

A further strand of industrial policy pursued by MITI has been that of increasing domestic capability in R&D. The policy has been linked to its nurturing of high-growth technological industries. Present policy contrasts with that of the immediate post-war years,when technology was predominantly imported under the strict control of MITI and the Ministry of Finance. On an annual basis,since 1973,Japan has exported more industrial technology than she has imported,and companies receive tax advantages for its export.[72]

From 1971,when she overtook France in the league table,Japan has ranked fourth in the world,slightly behind West Germany,in expenditure on R&D. In contrast to either the USA or British governments,however, the Japanese government has consistently provided less than 40% of total research expenditure. The majority comes from private industry,backed by government tax incentives for technology development. These incentives provide tax credits of a 25% year to year increase in R&D expenditure,accelerated depreciation on R&D capital investment and a lower rate of tax on income received from overseas licensing of technology. Of the government proportion of 30% of industrial R&D,approximately 50% is spent on three 'national interest' projects of space, nuclear development and ocean development, and of the three agencies responsible for R&D, MITI has the lowest proportion of finance.

MITI's preferred method of research and development sponsorship has been to bring together consortia of private industry and academics with MITI's own research institutions,with funding on a matching basis. Thus the project for a Very High Scale Integrated Circuit brought together manufacturers and MITI in this way. So also does the Fifth Generation Computer Project currently in progress. But the MITI funding is limited. Only £11 million will be put into the project by the government over three years. It is expected that the project will be spread over ten years.Both these projects have

stemmed from concern in the latter 1970s on the part of MITI and the Economic Planning Agency that R&D expenditure should increasingly be directed towards the information technology sectors of the economy. MITI is aiming for independence from the West in basic technology and an increase in R&D expenditure to 3% of GNP by 1985. [73]

There seems little doubt that the strength of Japanese research lies firstly in its direct relationship with industrial production, and secondly in the method of organisation of MITI's sponsorship. The first element in this dual strength means that unlike research in the USA or Britain, research in Japan is linked to growing industries. The second element allows R&D and growth to be tied together at minimal cost to government. For instance, although the government put in only 70 billion yen on the VHSLI project, over 1000 new processes were developed in the four years by the hundred or so engineers loaned by industry to the consortia's project.(700 were patented in the USA) This form of organisation is also used by other public bodies, such as Nippon Telegraph and Telecommunications Corporation. The results are marketed competitively by the manufacturers participating in the project. [74] Research cartelisation reduces costs, while technology is transferred to the fastest growing, more successful companies in the sector. One can contrast this method of organisation with that of the American government, where money goes to individual companies, and to that of Britain, where, for instance, research on System X or the Fifth Generation Computer was and is carried on in several scattered locations.

Nor in the past has MITI pulled back from utilising overseas investment to gain access to technology. The investment of Fujitsu in Amdahl(US) was pointed out by MITI as the turning point for the Japanese computer industry, because it gave the Japanese company access to up-to-date technology. Some of the Japanese investment in microelectronics in the USA may be for the same reasons, although as mentioned previously, overseas investment has also been accorded higher priority by MITI to overcome tariff and quota barriers. [75]

Perhaps the role of MITI most emphasised by Western commentators has been that of 'co-ordinator' of industry through its various advisory committees and through what have been called 'Public and Private Sector Forum'. [76] These forum combine representatives from specific industries and include civilian 'experts'. According to Masaya Miyoshi,

these forum discuss capital investment based on estimated future demand and provide guidelines for company operations. But the decisions of the Forum are not binding on individual companies. However, through these committees MITI has been enabled to press on industry its views on product markets. In particular it has emphasised the necessity for Japanese goods to move to the higher value added products, and, more recently has urged companies to co-operate with foreign firms to ease protective pressures against Japanese goods.[77] The upgrading of products to those of higher value added content has been of immense importance to the Japanese economy in the past. Specific export markets, such as those in electronic typewriters and cash registers and in the 64K RAM have been created by the failure of Western companies to upgrade their technology as fast as the Japanese.

This system of committees and conferences produces a series of indicative micro plans, which in turn are co-ordinated first by MITI and then by the Economic Planning Agency. Each year a White Paper from the Ministry sets out future trends and expectations for the industrial sector. The emergent economic plans act as a target for industry to aim at, already armed with information from MITI on current market trends, international competitiveness of industries etc. But in so far as Japanese economic plans have successively been overshot or undershot, they cannot be said to have been 'successful' in meeting targets. However, at the individual industry level, the network of conferences and committees, not only ensures that information reaches companies, but also allows responsive and incremental policymaking on the part of both bureaucracy and business.[78] R&D plans are similarly co-ordinated and published.

Some of the elements contained in this outline of the Japanese model have altered in the 1980s as international and domestic factors have caused shifts within the domestic industrial structure. But the elements discussed above were those pertaining when Japanese economic success was unparallelled. That is not to suggest that these elements alone were responsible for that success, but to suggest that they aided the Japanese in gaining comparative advantage within the world trading system in certain products, including microelectronic components and the products which incorporate them. In telecommunications and computers, Japanese exports are also increasing.

In this section we have looked at two possible

future models for British industrial policy. In the next section we consider the implications of the adoption of either of these or more extreme models of industrial policy.

7.8 THE ALTERNATIVES AVAILABLE TO BRITAIN.

There are several alternative ways in which British industrial policy might develop. It might take the path of 'liberal ideology', or that of the real American model, containing elements of protectionism. It might take the path of the ideal mercantilist state, or it might take the path of Japan, with elements of decentralisation involved. Before discussing these alternatives there are first some points which should be made. Both the American and Japanese economies differ from Britain, in that neither is so reliant on exports and neither is so concentrated in its industrial structure. Although Japan has no natural resources of its own, neither it, nor America, are so open to changes in comparative advantage between countries in the manufacture of goods. Neiher is so penetrated by foreign capital as is Britain, and neither invest overseas to the same extent.

One way in which British industrial policy might develop is to take the path of decentralisation of the political system to match the 'core' liberal ideology. To do this would however run contrary to the trends of the last forty years, during which power has increasingly accrued to the centre. In particular, during the 1979 Thatcher Government, this centralisation became more, rather than less, pronounced. This path would also run counter to the trends in the international economy over the last ten years, with its increasing politicisation of markets and increased managed trade. Particularly in the export of capital goods, governments are needed more, rather than less, for the financial packages which they provide.

Further, to reiterate Locksley's point, a free domestic market would mean the domestic replication of the international market.[79] Those companies with the largest share of a particular product in the world market could be expected to take the largest share in the domestic market. Since, in the information technology sector, those companies with the largest world share are American or Japanese, one would expect the domestic market to be dominated by them.

Proponents of free trade argue that Britain,

with 30% of GNP in exports has more to lose by
tariff barriers than any other country.Yet free
markets depend upon other countries' actions and the
trend in the USA and France, in particular, is
towards protectionism, whilst Japan has always
proved a particularly difficult market to penetrate
through exports rather than local production. The
argument given is that Britain should set the lead,
both in the world and within the EEC. But where that
lead has been taken, as in telecommunications, it
has not been followed by other EEC members. The
difficulty is that free trade within the EEC
benefits the strongest country - West Germany -
whilst free trade outside the EEC benefits Japan and
the USA.

A second path which British industrial policy
might take would be to adopt the 'real' American
model. To take this model and espouse the American
variant of free trade would be to acknowledge that
protection is a legitimate device. Britain would
impose countervailing tariffs against governments
which supported their domestic industries through
subsidies - involving action against other EEC
countries. Public sector purchasing would be
protected by legal means, giving a price advantage
to domestic industries and insisting that products
be manufactured in Britain. Preference would be
given to small business within the public sector.

The disadvantage to this model is that American
separation of powers allows Presidential policy to
favour free trade, whilst Congress passes protective
legislation. No such evasion of responsibility would
be possible in Britain, nor would countervailing
tariffs or public sector preference through legal
means be possible without withdrawal from the EEC.
The application of such a model is also dependent on
the capital structure of the country concerned, and
the proportion of output of multinational subsidiaries. Tariffs would be ineffective as a protective
device for Britain.

A further disadvantage to this model is the
emphasis within American policy on defence R&D and
production. Not only is technology slow to be
diffused from defence to civil applications,
limiting its value to manufacturing industry in
general, but the policy relies on huge defence
purchases by the state and the use of scarce
scientific personnel within the defence industry. To
a great extent the American government has been able
to utilise its defence hegemony over Western Europe
and Japan to export its defence products. For
Britain there is no such guaranteed market.

Therefore, unless technological investment in the defence industry found its way into civilian applications, which could be exported, upgrading of the civilian sector would not take place and eventually, the defence industry would be cut back by th state as too expensive. Alternatively, the British defence industry would become the largest export market.

A third path which industrial policy might follow would be to take that of the 'ideal' corporatist model, and opt to change the 'core' ideology for one which believes in the control of markets by the state and the subjugation of industry to the national interest, as defined by politicians. According to this model, imports would be limited by tariff barriers and exports supported by government political and financial assistance. The inward movement of technology and capital and the outward movement of capital would be controlled. Capital and R&D would be directed towards export industries, and to building national champion companies in those industries. Close relations between government and industry would lead to cartelisation where government decided that it was necessary.[80]

The problem once more for Britain would be that tariff barriers would conflict with GATT and the EEC. Leaving these aside, the model would require that the mechanisms of the state should be strengthened. The bureaucracy would need to become technocratic and more insulated from Parliament and public pressure. Ministerial Responsibility would have to be modified, so that Ministers were less prone to make short-term decisions for electoral or other reasons, and so that long term policy could be developed towards exports. Increased centralisation would rule out local authorities and geographically differentiated units of the state from making autonomous decisions. In short, the bureaucracy would become stronger, but less accountable and more hierarchical, whilst cartelisation might lead to further stagnation within industry.

A fourth path for industrial policy would be to take the 'real' Japanese model. Whilst government and industry would work together within a consensus which placed exports high on the agenda, competition between companies would be high in expanding markets. In declining markets the state would take powers to cartelise capacity and re-equip the industries to become more competitive, whilst employers took primary responsibility for keeping their workforce employed. Cheap credit would be directed through the banks to companies in expanding

market sectors, and the government would support R&D through tax relief programmes and, in particular sectors, through intensive, geographically concentrated research programes.

In fact, the British government has had a Japanese style industrial policy recommended to it by both the Select Committee on Science and Technology and the NEDC, amongst others. It is noticeable that the NEDC's recommendations on 'picking winners', in terms of technology for future R&D support, were accepted by the government, but that those concerned with an increased role for the government in providing a market for British industry were rejected. In each case the government accepted the legitimacy of a government role in 'technological push', but regarded a role in 'market pull' as illegitimate.[81]

Yet the 'real' Japanese model implies both components, and, indeed, structural adjustments at central government level. It implies increases in bureaucratic expertise in market structure, the collection of data and the publication of long-term structure plans for each industry, explaining what changes in technology and products are to be expected in the short and long-term. These would be put together by the Ministries and co-ordinated through the Prime Minister's Office, thereby ensuring that they gained centrality. The model implies an increase in civil service status, and, to compensate for the Japanese system of early retirement and the informal networks with industry built up through that practice, it implies more interchange between civil service and manufacturing industry. It implies that civil servants be made more accountable to Parliament. It implies that there should be competitive bureaucracies in central government with overlapping jurisdictions, much as the Department of Industry and the NEB overlapped, in order to increase responsiveness to industry and to compensate for the consensual orientation of Whitehall. It involves a diminution of status of the Treasury within Whitehall, in so far as Treasury officials would no longer work in other departments. It involves the Treasury, in conjunction with the Department of Industry and Trade, and the Prime Minister's Office, in arriving at agreed sectors of industry which should receive increased funds, bearing in mind their relation to export performance. It involves the co-ordination of public sector purchasing through the bureaucracy, so that the public sector would be expected to Buy British and to justify exceptions to that norm. It involves

STRATEGIES AND MODELS

the control of imports in some growth sectors and the limitation of multinationals' entry and market shares. It implies the control of the export of capital, ensuring that those exports serve, and do not conflict with the needs of the domestic economy. It implies less capital export and less spending on defence or defence related R&D. It implies fewer public research institutions and the co-ordination by the bureaucracy of joint government/industry projects in one geographical location. It implies commitment to education as a national resource, a commitment to a numerate, highly skilled workforce, and a commitment to managerial expertise. Above all the model implies that cheap credit should go to fast growing firms in growth sectors of the economy and that emphasis should be placed on market share, not profits. Firms would be grouped around banks to compete with each other on market share.

One problem in this model for Britain, would be that banks are no longer the major recipients of private saving. It would therefore be necessary to give some form of tax advantage to the individual saving through the bank. The model implies levels of both centralisation and decentralisation. It implies a liberal ideology in markets, but a central role for the state in co-ordination and leadership and control of inward and outward investment. It implies less of a direct state role in disbursing funds to industry via the Minister, and by making technology the subject of public long-term strategy, it overcomes the problems of big technological decisions taken for charismatic reasons.

Finally, British industrial policy could stay as it is, with a 'core' liberal ideology and strong centralised state control. The penalties for remaining in that position have been illustrated in the previous chapters in incoherence and confusion over the aims of industrial policy. If the past were to be replicated in the future, then the state would continue to finance some growth markets, where the technological component provided a flag for nationalism. But to provide support for industry through public sector purchasing, although possible through the centralised, if fragmented, state, might either lead to further examples of bureaucratic autonomy or remain based upon exhortation. The activities of multinationals would go unchecked within the domestic economy and the balance of trade would worsen. As in the past, the existing customer base of multinationals would erode the possibilities of small companies entering the market, which would be taken by American and Japanese companies. These

would import components in unchecked quantities, further eroding the domestic industrial base. Meanwhile state control would operate through indirect policies of financial aid and through the defence sector. As has become evident from American experience, the defence industry, under state control, provides a mechanism for the aid of industry which allows the two competing ideas of liberal market ideology and state control of markets to be legitimate. If the past were to be repeated, then R&D in defence related projects would not find its way into civilian applications. One scenario, based on the past, is that the defence industry would continue to be primarily home centred, in which case history would suggest the the industry could not be supported for long to the same extent. A second scenario, again based on the past, is that firms, such as electronics companies, would shift into the defence industry and arms would become the target export market. The state would retain control of certain markets and industry would accommodate to these markets.

In the information technology market one would expect American interests and technology to predominate. The domestic market would come to reflect the world market. In this case the promotion of liberal ideology would be the promotion of American capital and technology. And, because the provision of capital and technology gives power to the controller, Britain would become more dependent on America and American good-will. Yet with the weakening of the American economy, American intentions towards Europe cannot be relied upon. Increased protectionism and increased political efforts to control European economic competition can be expected.

NOTES AND REFERENCES

1. Fourth Report, Vol.III, Appendix 29, p.82.
2. OECD, Gaps in Technology, pp.161-7.
3. Computer Services Association, p.6/33.
4. The Economist, Vol.220, 13th August 1969, pp.659, 662.
5. Select Committee on Science & Technology, UK Computer Industry Sub-committee, Minutes of Evidence (1972-3), pp.29-30.
6. Financial Times, 6th February 1982.
7. Ibid., 30th June, 7th July 1982.
8. Ira Magaziner & Thomas Hout, Japanese Industrial Policy, pp.39-42.

9. Computer Weekly,6th November 1980.
10. Computer Services Association,pp.6/23, 6/25.
11. N.Jequier,in R.Vernon ed.,Big Business & the State,pp.214-9.
12. Computer Services Association,pp.6/28,6/29.
13. Electronics,Vol.53,17th January 1980,p.81.
14. Financial Times,20th November 1981.
15. Computer Services Association,pp.6/23,6/24.
16. Ibid.
17. Computer Weekly,6th December 1979.
18. House of Lords,New Information Technologies,Q.66-7,fn.p.17.
19. Sunday Times,19th December 1982.
20. Ibid.,11th July 1982.
21. House of Lords,Q.63.
22. Computer Weekly,22nd January 1981.
23. I.Magaziner & T.Hout,pp.72-81.
24. P.Goodman,French Sixth Plan (1971-5) Research and Development(London,Dept.of Trade & Industry,1971),p.7.
25. Computer Weekly,10th January 1980;The Economist,Vol.263,23rd April 1977.
26. Computer Services Association,p 6/22.
27. Ibid.,pp.6/25,6/26.
28. Ibid.,passim.
29. Financial Times,10th February 1981.
30. House of Lords,Q.354;Electronics,Vol.50, 17th January 1980 p.26 on 'critical technology'.
31. Computer Weekly,18th September 1980; European Commission, New Information Technologies; First Report (COM (80) 513 final).
32. Charles B.Lecht,The Waves of Change. A Techno-Economic Analysis of the Data Processing Industry (New York,McGraw Hill,1977),passim.
33. US International Trade Commission,Competitive Factors Influencing World Trade in Integrated Circuits(Washington D.C.,Govt. Printing Office,1979),pp.9-15.
34. Electronics,Vol.51,14th September 1978, pp.81-2.
35. For a lengthier discussion of this series of events see: Jill Hills,"Foreign Policy and Technology: the Japan-US,Japan-Britain and Japan-EEC Technology Agreements"Political Studies,Summer 1983,pp.205-233.
36. "US-Japan Semiconductors Issue",Oriental Economist,Vol.48,March 1980,pp.10-11.
37. The Economist,Vol.231,12th April 1969.
38. US Semiconductor Industry Association, pp.39-40.
39. Ibid.,p.40.

40. Financial Times,12th January 1981,12th March 1982.
41. Labour Party,Microelectronics,pp.18-19;US International Trade Commission,p.76.
42. House of Lords,Q.369.
43. European Community,Proposal for a Council Regulation (EEC) Concerning Community Action in the Field of Microelectronics Technology,9361/80 (COM (80)421 final).
44. Report of the Post Office Review Committee,Cmnd.6850,pp.107-8.
45. Financial Times,5th September,1st December 1981.
46. Ibid.,19th January 1982.
47. Computer World,13th August 1980.
48. Electronics,Vol.53,28th February 1980, p.56.
49. J.Nora & A.Mino,The Computerisation of Society(Cambridge,Mass.,MIT Press,1980).
50. Current State of the Information Industry In Japan (Tokyo,MITI,1980),roneo; Optical Visual Information System Hi-Ovis(Tokyo,MITI,undated), roneo.
51. House of Lords,Q.106.
52. "Council Resolution of 15th July 1974 on a Community Pricing Policy on Data Processing", Official Journal of the European Communities, No.C 86/1,20th July 1974; Bulletin EC,2-1975, points 1501-7;9-1975,point 2236;7/8-1976, point 2263; 10-1976,points 1021-5.
53. European Commission,Recommendations on Telecommunications(COM (80)422 final).
54. House of Lords,Q.57,125.
55. Semiconductor Industry Association,p.21.
56. Electronics,Vol.50,17th January 1980,p.26.
57. A.G.W.Biddle,"IBM versus AT&T.Its Meaning to the User and the Public",Computers and People,Vol.24,No.1,1975,p.21.
58. Caroline Pestan," Revising the GATT Approach to Subsidies:a Canadian View",in S.J.Warnecke,ed.,International Trade and Industrial Policies,p.99.
59. See: Ezra Vogel,Japan as Number One,passim.;Sir Arthur Knight,"UK Industry in the Eighties",Journal of Fiscal Studies,Spring 1981,pp.4-5; For an overview of the "power elite" thesis,see: G.L.Curtis,"Big Business and Political Influence",in Ezra Vogel ed.,Japanese Organisation and Decisionmaking(Berkeley,University of California Press,1975),pp.33-41;H.Fukui,"Studies in Policymaking: a Review of the Literature",in T.J.Pempel ed.,Policymaking in Contemporary Japan

(Ithaca & London,Cornell University Press,1977), pp.24-59.
60. Select Committee on Science & Technology, 2nd Report,1976-77,Innovation,research & development in Japanese Science Based Industry ;Innovation,R&D in Japanese Science Based Industry,Cmnd.7779 (1979).
61. Ezra Vogel,pp.54-64.
62. H.Kataoka,"The Administrative System of the Japanese Government",Waseda Political Studies, 15,1980,pp.1-52.
63. Tait C.Ratcliffe,Japanese Corporate Finance 1977-80 (London,Financial Times,1977),passim.
64. Semiconductor Industry Association,pp.19-21.
65. Hiroya Ueno,"Conception and Evaluation of Japanese Industrial Policy",Japanese Economic Studies,White Plains,75,(2),1976/77,pp.32-3.
66. William V.Rapp,"Japan's Industrial Policy",in Isiah Frank ed.,The Japanese Economy in International Perspective(Baltimore,John Hopkins University Press,1975),pp.35-6.
67. I.Magaziner & T.M.Hout,pp.31-44.
68. N.Amaya,The Ministry of International Trade and Industry,Socio-Economic Instituto Bulletin No.24 (Tokyo,Sophia University,1970).
69. Nihon Kogyo Shimbun,26th May 1978, in Daily Translations of the Japanese Press (Tokyo,American Embassy,1978).
70. Nihon Keizai Shimbun,Industrial Review of Japan(Tokyo,Nihon Keizai Shimbun,1981),p.55.
71. Ibid.,1979,p.28.
72. T.Dixon Long,"Japanese Technology Policy: Achievements and Perspectives",Research Policy 4,1975,pp.2-86.
73. "Japan's Plans for the 1980s Pose Global Challenge for Western Firms",Business International,14th November 1980,p.364;Computer Weekly,7th October 1982.
74. Hiroshi Inose,"Government Policy and Innovation in Japan",in Arthur Gestenfeld & Robert Brainard eds.,Technological Innovation: Government/Industry Cooperation(New York,John Wiley,1979),pp.141-58.
75. MITI,Current State of the Information Industry in Japan (Tokyo,MITI,1980),roneo.
76. See Jill Hills,"Government Relations with Industry: Japan and Britain. A Review of Two Political Arguments",Polity,Vol.14,No.2,1981, pp.222-248.
77. M.Miyoshi,"Government/Industry Co-operation",Paper prepared for the Japanese Chamber of Commerce in London,undated.

78. V.D.Lippitt,H.Fukui & F.Gibney,"Japanese and Planning",Center Magazine,Vol.9,No.11,1976, pp.66-71; H.Fukui,"Economic Planning in Postwar Japan; a Case-study in Policymaking",Asian Survey,Vol.12,No.4,1972,pp.327-348.
79. Gareth Locksley,p.46.
80. These types of relations already exist within the EEC in relation to steel. See for instance:Sunday Times,5th June 1983,on reduced quotas for British Steel.
81. The NEDC has considered Japanese industrial Policy on several occasions. See for instance: Roger Gibbs, Industrial Policy in More Successful Economies - Japan,Discussion Paper No.7 (London,NEDO,1980); See also: Financial Times,10th February 1981,on 'picking winners'; Select Committee on Science and Technology,Second Report1976-77,passim;Cmnd.7779 (1979).

Chapter Eight

CONCLUSION

This book began from the point that the international economic structure has become interdependent. All countries in the industrialised West have seen their economies become more open. Exports as a proportion of GNP have increased. This rising interdependence in trade has been mirrored by interpenetration of capital and technology.[1]

In the 1960s it was argued that American multinational capital had colonised Europe. but since that time capital penetration of the United States has also increased.[2] The mid-1970s with a low dollar exchange rate, saw numbers of European and Japanese companies investing in the USA. Much of this foreign investment took place in high technology sectors, such as microelectronics, in response to companies' desire to ensure in-house supplies of crucial components. Some were also concerned to gain access to the technological know-how of American companies.

These flows of capital and technology also redistribute power between nation states. The exporter accrues political as well as economic power. For instance, in recent years, the USA has attempted to utilise the political power given it by these capital and technological flows in order to retain its economic power. From the European's point of view, the most obvious instance of this conjunction of American political and economic power, has been the ban on the use of American technology for the USSR pipeline, and the imposition of American law upon subsidiaries of American companies operating in Europe. But other examples exist of the combined use of American economic and political power against the economies of other industrialised countries. For example, American concern that Japanese R&D funding has taken place as the result of its lack of spending on defence, has

263

CONCLUSION

led to American pressure on Japan to increase its defence expenditure and to hand over fibre optics and microelectronics technology, developed for Japanese civilian use,to American defence interests. That technology will thereby be transferred to companies such as IBM and Honeywell.

These recent American actions are particularly interesting, because the concept of international free trade was built up to benefit American interests. Krasner has established that international free trade was a product of the hegemony of the USA.[3] Yet as he has also pointed out, the ideals of free trade were built upon the domestic precondition of higher productivity than the rest of the industrialised world and American technological leadership. The policies were relatively costless in the domestic context.[4]

More recently, as Samuel Brittan has demonstrated, productivity in the American economy has been traded-off against rising unemployment. Japan is now almost as productive as America, and,is more productive in certain manufacturing industries. America is losing both its lead in productivity and its technological leadership.[5] Concomitantly, it is moving towards greater protectionism at home and to the use of political power abroad to shore up its weakening economy.[6]

The American case presents in dramatic form the need for national governments to take control of the flows of capital and technology, when those flows limit rather than extend its power. The impact of imports and multinationals upon a domestic economy varies according to the sectors in which they operate. The penetration of Japanese imports of microcircuits and Japanese capital into the American domestic economy is considered of critical importance to that economy. In particular, defence interests see the domination of the microchip industry by Japanese companies as a matter of grave concern. Foreseeing that the control of this technology and leadership in it, increases the political dependence of the USA upon Japan, defence interests have sought to limit the problem by subvention of the microchip industry. Similarly, the Justice Department,in 1982, investigated possible collusion by Japanese companies in controlling the flow of exports of the 64K chip to the USA. It can be hypothesised that the concern was not with the establishment of higher prices through that collusion, which the American microchip industry welcomed, but the knowledge in government quarters that if the Japanese withdraw their supply of this

chip, the American computer industry would be likely to come crashing down.

One can perceive in these examples the way in which the American ideology of free trade is gradually being eroded by its economic decline, and by its government attempts to limit the vulnerability of the domestic economy to international pressures. All governments have had to face a diminution in their power over their domestic economies brought about by international factors. The methods by which national governments have been able to control their domestic economies has been weakened through GATT and, in the case of member countries, by the EEC. Both have reduced the possible use of tariff barriers as a mechanism of protection for domestic industry. In their place have been substituted a variety of bi-lateral agreements on particular products, and non-tariff barriers. These in turn have led to an increased politicisation of the international trading system and, in turn to an increased need for government intervention within the domestic industrial structure.

Coincidentally, as tariff barriers have been reduced, so they have become less effective as protective devices. The inward investment of multinationals has allowed foreign companies to evade tariffs. So, for instance, the increase in tariffs on microchips, imposed by the British Labour Government in the 1960s was met by an increase in local manufacturing by American multinationals.

The central argument of this book is that governments have not ceased to protect their domestic economies with the disappearance of tariff barriers on manufactured goods. With the decline of the efficacy of tariff barriers has therefore come an increase in non-tariff barriers. These have taken on a variety of guises, but policies have been aimed at giving market advantage to domestic industry. This market advantage may come from subventions under the guise of R&D policy, or defence policy or regional policy, or through instruments of an 'industrial policy'. Aid may be given to industry though indirect mechanisms, such as tax concessions, or through direct mechanisms, such as grants. But in each and every case, the overall effect is for the government to manipulate the workings of the international capitalist economy to its domestic benefit. The question of major importance, is why governments have opted for differing mechanisms of industrial policy.

The explanation of these differences, contained

CONCLUSION

in the first chapter, suggests that they are not simply the product of the ideological predispositions of governments. An exploration of the linkages between 'core' ideologies, the centralisation of the political system, the relationship of government to finance and industrial capital, and the structure of particular markets, provokes the explanation that the mechanisms of industrial policy are related to these variables, which are themselves rooted in historical experience within the country concerned. In Britain and the USA, the 'core'ideology is liberal, whilst in Japan the 'core' ideology is mercantilist, but in each ideology is shifting as short-term economic and political interests challenge the prevailing ideology. The USA is moving towards mercantilism, Japan is moving towards liberalism, but at the moment both preserve the legitimacy of their 'core'ideologies.

Because industrial policy, based on non-tariff barriers, geared to the aid of particular sectors or companies, relies upon close relations between state and industry, the mechanisms of a mercantilist ideology are suited to centralised states with centralised bureaucracies. In these states a range of direct grants and subsidies to specific companies and sectors will be given overall direction from the centre. In contrast, liberal ideology, with its emphasis on the autonomy of the company, is suited to states with devolved institutions and a weak bureaucratic/industrial relationship. In the liberal ideological state, industrial policy will tend to be mainly through indirect policies of financing industry, such as R&D and defence policy, or through the mediation of private sector institutions with industry. In the decentralised state, protection is best afforded through tariff barriers, quotas and legal mechanisms limiting market entry. The 'core'liberal ideology of the USA is in accord with its decentralised state and the 'core' mercantilist ideology of Japan and France is in accord with their centralised states. In West Germany, industrial policy, based on non-tariff barriers may be carried on, despite its 'core' liberal ideology, through its banking sector, which supplements the indirect policies of aid, such as R&D.

Britain sits between. She has both a 'core' liberal ideology and a centralised state, although, crucially, the bureaucratic element within the state is more fragmented than in France or Japan. There are two sets of ideas which have legitimacy in Britain. The first, that the state should 'govern',

CONCLUSION

that governments are responsible for the workings of the domestic economy, lends political credence to actions by central government to alter market arrangements. The second idea, that business should be allowed to act in its own interests, gives legitimacy to political action which retains the autonomy of the firm. It allows the state to eschew bureaucratic forms of control over companies which receive public money. Hence, British governments accrue the right to give public funds to industry and the firms receiving that cash have the right to remain non-accountable for the money received.

The conflict between the two sets of ideas is structured into the British political system. On the one hand, the responsibility and autonomy of Ministers to decide affairs in the 'national interest' is emphasised. On the other, that very concept of Ministerial Responsibility allows appeals over the heads of the bureaucracy to the Minister, in turn reducing the insulation of the bureaucracy from societal constraints.

Taken together, Ministerial control and responsibility and the ideoloy of company autonomy undermine the strength of the bureaucracy. On the one hand civil servants are geared to looking upwards to the Minister to ensure that their actions have no unfavourable repercussions upon him or her. Access for large firms through the Parliamentary arena, provides an incentive to consensual, rather than conflictual, decision making. Ministerial and Parliamentary accountability demand that decisions be made unchallengeable and therefore to concern for the fine print of the law. Even so, disgruntled companies may appeal over their heads to the Minister and may gain a redefinition of the relevant criteria. Centralisation of decisionmaking on borderline cases creates delay. Monitoring of what happens to government aid, once it is disbursed, finds no ready constituency within the machine. And monitoring itself may lead to appeals, as in the case of the NEB and Rolls Royce, on the grounds that company autonomy is being disturbed. In the British centralised system, the civil service is vulnerable to pressure from companies, Parliament and the public in general.

Because the centralised system allows, and Ministerial control invites, short-term decisions taken for electoral reasons, considerable sums of money can be disbursed to both companies and individuals. The clash of ideology and political system acts to the advantage of the major actors in the domestic economy - large domestically owned and multinational

CONCLUSION

enterprises. But, on occasion, as with the Anglo-American Venture Fund, it acts to the benefit of individuals also.

This conflict between liberal ideology and state control is further exacerbated by the structure of the British economy. Of all the European countries, Britain is the most heavily penetrated by foreign capital, and, in particular, by American companies. On the whole, overseas investment has been welcomed as a boost to employment, reflecting the national consensus which regards each person as having a right to employment. As a result of these factors, no controls have been taken over multinationals, which are most heavily represented in growth sectors of the economy.

The legitimacy allowed to their demands for autonomy and a 'free' market, has hidden the extent to which their interests conflict with those of the nation state. As global actors they may balance imports with exports, and their focus of interest extends beyond the national territory. In Britain, their geographical location in development regions, brought about by government financing under regional aid schemes, has given an extra dimension to their power. In particular, against Labour governments, more likely to espouse industrial policies of preference to domestically owned industries, the multinationals have been able to use their geographical location and employment related potential, to pressure the government into ' free' market policies. In so doing they have been able to appeal both to electoral concern with employment and to liberal ideological principles of company autonomy. No study has been undertaken to determine their true value in terms of R&D, or in terms of their contribution to the balance of payments over the last ten years.

Whilst the legitimacy attached to liberal ideology allows those international companies with an economic interest in free markets to challenge decisions which do not meet those interests, the concept of Ministerial Responsibility allows Ministers the autonomy to make decisions in the 'national interest', which alter markets. These decisions may be based upon ideological grounds, such as the funding of co-operatives by Tony Benn, or the various acts of nationalisation, denationalisation and privatisation by the Thatcher Government, or they may be based on grounds of national chauvanism and government charisma. Many of the decisions on government support for high technology can be seen as falling in this third

category. Concorde and the British nuclear powered reactor are obvious examples, but so also may be the 1983 decision to fund the Fifth Generation Computer.

The difficulties of combining the 'core' liberal ideology with state control of markets, increasingly demanded by the politicisation of the international economy, has led governments not only into these technological pronouncements, justified on the basis of what other governments are doing, but also, particularly in the case of the Conservative Party, into increased indirect policies of aid to industry. Regional aid, employment policy and, more recently, defence policy can be seen in this light. In particular, defence policy, where the state is completely autonomous, allows both liberal ideology towards individual companies and complete state control of markets to flourish.

The conflict between 'core' ideology and state control is also evident among the fragmented units of the state, both on a geographical and functional basis. The Treasury, the major department in Whitehall, has been charged with a hard-line liberal ideological approach to industry.[7] Even within the Department of Industry, itself, opinions vary as to the correct role of the state in relation to industry. In the field of telecommunications policy one can see the variation over time from consensus to confrontation on the Department's part. Just as industry may at one point emphasise the responsibility of the state to act and the next demand its autonomy, so government may at one point demand action in the 'national interest' and the next may insist on the paramountcy of the market.

Amongst the bureaucratic fragmentation of the British state it is possible for individual units to develop autonomous links with industry to their mutual benefit. These are based on interdependence of supply and demand for certain products, or on the interdependence created by previous financial aid by the state. This form of corporatism may in turn create a company dependency, stultifying industrial response to markets.

The evidence of the industries in this book suggests that in the field of industrial policy, corporatism of this kind, based on interdependency between particular sectors of the state and industry may develop, but that the consensus is always under threat of public confrontation. Other large companies have access to the political arena through Parliament, the Minister or Prime Minister. Alternative routes of access to power prevent too close an association between particular companies

CONCLUSION

and the bureaucracy, unless there are both no interests threatened by that association and the particular unit of the state can retain its autonomy. The cartelisation of telecommunications can be seen as the product of the years between the wars, when, as a civil service department, the Post Office was insulated from Parliamentary investigation, and, also, as a result of the incorporation of the major multinational then in the field (STC) into the cartel. Only when the telephone service degenerated to such an extent that it became a political embarrassment was the cartel challenged. It was finally broken when another multinational, (IBM), moved into the field and wanted admission. But it has subsequently been re-established to some extent, because government and industry are interdependent in terms of exports. The interdependency between ICL and the Central Computer Agency was finally ended by the EEC directive on public sector purchasing. But it had already come under pressure from multinational interests such as IBM and Honeywell. Only within defence has the cartelisation been completely stable.

Because many of the information technology markets are dominated by multinational and large domestic companies, whilst others are fragmented, the sector is prone to variations in policymaking. Where markets are fragmented, industry is often ignored by government. There is no set pattern of interaction within the sector, and policy swings as the concepts of either state control or the 'core' liberal ideology gain ascendancy.

The telecommunications market demonstrates the clash between public control and market ideology in the interventions of government in Post Office finance and organisation. Almost in the same breath governments have demanded both political control and a commercial return on capital used. The clash is reflected also in government intervention in the relationship between suppliers and the Post Office. The Labour Government of the 1960s instituted competitive tendering for public exchange equipment, and thereby increased the costs of the Post Office. The Thatcher Government's liberalisation of the telecommunications monopoly in 1980, was partially concerned with the 'too cosy' relationship between suppliers and the Post Office/British Telecom.

In the first case, market liberalisation ignored the exigencies of the telephone network which demanded compatible equipment. In the second case, the cartel has been partially restored as government has pledged financial support to the

CONCLUSION

companies for the marketing overseas of System X. Although the provision of that finance undermines the concept of liberalisation, the reality of international competition in this field demands competitive financial packages from governments to back industrial export efforts. Hence the politicisation of world markets, in turn, has pressured a liberal ideological government into recognition of the interdependence of the state and telecommunications manufacturers. Interestingly also, British Telecom can threaten to implement liberalisation in its public exchange ordering, against the interests of the state. By using liberal ideology against the Thatcher Government and threatening to buy abroad, it can indicate its autonomy from the state and seek to lessen other aspects of state control. In other areas, such as its directory enquiry system and a computerised billing system, British Telecom has bought American systems from STC and IBM.

The telecommunications industry study also illustrates the way in which state agencies may gain autonomy and impose their decisions to the benefit of particular companies and against the interests of the community at large. The intervention of the Industrial Reorganisation Corporation in the industry, although accidental, gave public backing to GEC. Yet there seems to have been no consideration of the possible impact upon the monopoly buyer of switching equipment - the Post Office. The autonomy allowed GEC by the state, after its merger with AEI, legitimised its subsequent disbandment of AEI's research team and its scrapping of reed relay research, which resulted in delay in modernising the telephone network. GEC and Plessey's subsequent lobbying at Cabinet level against a technical decision taken by the Post Office, emphasises the power of large companies in the British political system and the difficulties and weakness of bureaucratic control. But, equally, the way in which the Post Office, after that decision was taken in GEC and Plessey's favour, went ahead with ordering exchanges from STC as fast as it could, illustrates the possible autonomy which can accrue to technological orientated units of the state.

The various attempts by the Department of Trade and Industry, first to vet that decision, and then later to hold a technological audit of System X illustrate the problems of a non-technocratic civil service when faced with technical details. Similar weaknesses have been illustrated by the efforts at the Department of Industry to liberalise the tele-

CONCLUSION

communications network. Part-time academic consultants substitute for technical expertise within the civil service.The very concept of the supremacy of markets over politics undermines the rationale for a technocratic bureaucracy, whilst the actual practice of state control of markets demands one.

The computer market study illustrates the organisational pluralism of the civil service and the way in which the clash between state responsibility and control and liberal ideology is played out within it. The public preference policy for ICL came under fire from the Treasury, maintaining its stance on efficiency and demanding that computers must be proven first in the open market before receiving preference. The Treasury was also against the rescue of ICL in 1981,preferring to see it fail rather than increase demands on the public sector borrowing requirement.

But, within the Department of Industry there were also splits of opinion. In what must be a classic case of muddling objectives, the Department is responsible not only for the sponsorship of domestically owned industry, but for sponsorship of all industry located within Britain. Inevitably there is a clash of interests between sponsoring an industry to the benefit of multinationals and that sponsorship to the benefit of domestically owned industry. The clash of interests plays out within the civil service itself,between free markets for foreign multinationals entering a market and non-tariff barriers for the benefit of domestically owned industry.

Most noticeable within the computer industry study is the way in which the NEDC, in attempting to work out policies in favour of British industry,has been handicapped by the presence of the representatives of multinationals upon its committees. Again the clash of interests was not perceived. As a result, it was possible for Honeywell to use its membership of the Electronics Committee as a pawn in its pressure on a Labour Government. More crucially it could also threaten to withdraw employment from a development area if the government adopted a pro-British preference policy for minicomputers. IBM also had an anti-ICL team operating in Britain, utilising problems with ICL computers to undermine the company. Both were able to operationalise the liberal market ideology of 'free trade' and 'the best products for the job'in their favour.

The fact that preference for ICL was maintained despite this ideological battering, and despite

CONCLUSION

attempts to show its illegitimacy, can be put down to the organisational interests involved in its retention. The co-ordination of public sector purchasing into one department and the building up of interdependence between it and ICL was crucial to the continuation of the preference. But, inevitably, because ICL was dependent upon government for 30% of the orders for its large computers, its linkage with government had some impact upon its marketing policy. In fact the 1970 Conservative government, specifically recognised ICL's dependence and the impact that dependence would have on its marketing structure.[8] But, until 1981, and ICL's crash, despite its various links with the company, there seems to have been little conception in Whitehall that ICL was vulnerable because it relied for all its turn-over on data processing. Nor, when ICL shares were sold to financial institutions were attempts made to link ICL with other markets. Yet the government was involved in ICL's various negotiations with foreign companies. Finally it was possible for the Treasury to cut back on ICL orders, contribute to its downfall and then attempt to deny it rescue. At the same time, state control of markets was favouring other companies, such as Ferranti (a company 45% dependent on defence work).

The computer study also illustrates the importance of political mediation within the British system. Parliament played an important role in publicising the discontents of minicomputer manufacturers and software houses. That, in general, the Select Committee was ineffective in altering government policy to any substantial extent, does not detract from its position as a mediator. With the demise of the computer committee, entry onto the political agenda for small companies depended upon individual MPs and the companies' own resources. On the whole small companies do not have the resources to become political animals, and they can therefore more easily be written off that agenda.

Only when the NEB came into existence could those companies look to an alternative institution to alter policy in their direction. The importance of the NEB lies not so much in what it did in the computing sector as in the fact that it created competition within the state's central government sector. For the first time, since the demise of the Department of Economic Affairs, the Department of Industry was faced with a rival with money and autonomy enough to question its overall policy for the industry. This is not to say that the two institutions did not work in co-operation at times,

CONCLUSION

but that overlapping jurisdictions brought more responsiveness in policymaking.

The microelectronics industry study illustrates how the NEB allowed the entry of alternative solutions to the problems of the British microchip industry than those proposed by the NEDC and the Department of Industry. The NEDC plan relied heavily upon increased production by existing multinational subsidiaries and the entry of others. Once again their representatives were enabled to utilise their positions on the NEDC to launch attacks against Inmos in their own interests.

The NEB, staffed by businessmen, was not a politically attuned institution, in a political system where there is little bureaucratic insulation from the political. To make a commercial profit from Inmos it allowed the company to dictate where first its technology centre and then its factory should be located. Parliamentary confrontation on the issue of those sitings then allowed those interests in favour of liberal market ideology to team with those in favour of state control to bring pressure to bear on the Minister. In contrast, neither set of personnel challenged the bureaucratic policy of aid to multinationals.

The microelectronics study also illustrates the importance of Prime Ministerial or Ministerial backing in the British political system. Although a bureaucratic policy for the industry had been continuing, it was the political weight of Jim Callaghan which produced the money for the programme to be developed. Similarly, the increased prominence given to the information technology sector under the Thatcher Government, can be traced to the appointment of an Information Technology Minister. A Minister, responsible for a particular sector, provides the means of leadership and conflict resolution which is not open to the civil service. That such a Minister was appointed can be traced, not so much to industry and civil service pressure, but to pressure for the liberalisation of the telecommunications network, the conjunction of that liberalisation with the liberal ideology of the government and the possibility of presenting information technology in charismatic terms.

Yet, once in power, the Minister has been handicapped in promoting domestic industry. Demands have arisen from small business, from microcomputer manufacturers and from the NEDC for a more co-ordinated approach to public sector purchasing, which would favour British industry. Although the public sector is considerably larger than that in

CONCLUSION

Japan or West Germany, it is highly fragmented and public purchasing is unco-ordinated. The microcomputer manufacturers drew attention to the fact that the Computer and Telecommunications Agency's list of approved supplies to government contained, at first, more American than British names. Small business has also cited the example of the USA, where a proportion of public sector contracts is reserved to that section of industry.

It is clearly contradictory to fund small business and small microcomputer manufacturers and yet deny them a market within the public sector. But there are several problems to the policy of public sector preference for a liberal ideological Minister, as previous Conservative administrations have admitted. To take into account the numbers of institutions involved needs preference to be either legally enforced or to be co-ordinated centrally through the bureaucracy. The 1979 Thatcher Government attempted the latter. A 'positive'form of public purchasing was to be adopted in which the buyers were to inform the suppliers in good time of their specific requirements.[9] The model to be copied was that of the defence industry.

Yet the defence sector cannot be considered a perfect model for emulation. Not only Sir Ieuan Maddock, but also evidence to the Defence Committee, has shown how a bureaucracy may grow up around public purchasing, leading to over-specification and high costs to suppliers.[10] A similar problem arose in telecommunications. No solution to these problems of dependency, control and market responsiveness, no middle range mechanisms between liberal markets and complete state control have yet been found in Britain. The result has been that the extension of public sector preference has had mainly to rely on exhortation to 'Buy British' and on provisions through British Telecom. And, despite the Minister's formal control over British Telecom, because of the legitimacy accorded to the 'core' liberal ideology, it has been able to purchase computerised systems abroad and to threaten to do so for public telephone exchanges.

It was suggested earlier that markets influence government policy. Where markets are fragmented, as in British software, government is less likely to act than in markets where there is more concentration. Similarly, where there has been inaction over a period of years, the point may come where imports take a large proportion of the domestic market. If no control is to be taken over those imports, then it is hardly worth funding

domestic industry. The microelectronics sector in the 1960s and the office technology sector of the 1980s are cases in point. The probability is that where government does intervene in these markets with large proportions taken by overseas suppliers, unless the public sector is used as a basis for sales, the proportion of the market which can be captured is too small for viability. The NEB's backing of Nexos is an example of a sector where customer base did not exist for British industry.

Where there is no existing market, or a depressed one, government may set out to create demand - as in the case of Prestel, microprocessors, robotics and cable TV. In the case of Prestel the creation of demand is only beginning to succeed. In the case of microprocessors, the importance attached to British products has overridden concern about increased imports. Since no domestic source of microprocessors exists, except custom built, to create demand also increases imports. And in the case of robotics, the creation of demand with grants for installation, has brought 75% of installed robots from overseas. One wholly owned British manufacturer, using British technology, ceased business in 1982, whilst funds have gone to Unimation (US controlled) and to the importation of Japanese technology. The creation of demand seems to have been divorced both from the creation of supply and the development of British technology.

Nor does it seem that the EEC 17% tariff on microchips makes sense in present circumstances. Because there is a 9.7% tariff on finished goods, those companies which are predominantly in the business of packaging chips into black boxes, as in the case of microcomputers, are encouraged to assemble them abroad. The British Microcomputer Manufacturers Group has lobbied government on this trend. The tariff is not now high enough to offset the comparative advantage of manufacture of microchips in the USA and Japan. If the purpose of the tariff is to increase local manufacture, then it actually needs to be higher, but that then penalises domestic manufacturers of products using microchips, until local manufacture has been established.[11] The problem is similar to that faced in the 1960s.

To conclude, British information technology policy has been no more coherent than British industrial policy in general. The goals are inconsistent. Whilst exhorting industries and the public sector to 'Buy British', the policies have done as much to bring multinationals a greater share

CONCLUSION

of the domestic market and to increase imports. Whilst supporting British technological R&D on the one hand, the policies have taken no consideration of the importance of customer base, and set out to limit the market open to foreign competition. The emphasis has been on 'technological push',leaving 'market pull' to take care of itself. The policies reflect the same failings as those which were identified in the 1964 Labour Government's original policy towards computers. On the one hand the state intervenes, citing the 'national interest' in the technology, on the other it refuses to intervene citing the paramountcy of the market. Together, in the past the result has been that British technological expertise has not been converted into manufactured exports.

The alternative paths possible for British industrial policy are outlined in the penultimate chapter of this book. Two options would retain the 'core'liberal ideology. Either the political system could be decentralised to 'fit' the ideology, or the American model could be adopted. A further option is to alter the ideology to that of mercantilism and adopt ostensibly nationalistic policies, controlling imports and financing exports. The fourth alternative is to adopt a variant of the Japanese model, decentralising intervention to private sector institutions and providing indirect subsidies for R&D,whilst,at the same time, introducing competition within central government administration and producing overall strategic plans for industrial development and R&D. It seems highly unlikely that either a completely free market with little state responsibility, or the American protectionist pattern, could work within the British centralist tradition or within the present EEC framework. Nor does it seem likely that the 'core' ideology, giving autonomy to the company and weakening the bureaucracy, will be an early candidate for alteration. The final possibility is therefore to follow Japanese practice in limiting concentration and market dominance,in allowing cartelisation in certain declining markets,in using banks for industrial finance directed by government,in reducing defence expenditure and defence related R&D, in developing institutions with overlapping jurisdictions so as to produce a bureaucracy more responsive to industrial trends, in taking away from Ministers the big technological decisions by producing long-term strategies and publishing them and in controlling foreign investment. To follow Japanese practice would involve the geographical

concentration of research teams where projects were to be funded on a 50/50 basis with industry.

The alternative, a continuation of the present conflict between state control and the 'core' ideology , has results which have already been documented.It is inevitable that a free market will reflect world market structure. Given the technological and world market dominance of America in the information technology sector, Britain will have to accept a worsening balance of trade in information technology products. For Britain the weakening of the American economy has starkly presented the political costs of technological dependence. The economic costs attached to Britain's liberal ideology and failure to implement effective non-tariff barriers cannot be quantified. But one may assume that, if multinationals continue to invest in Britain without any form of political control,then the options open to British governments will foreclose. The intention of previous governments may have been to selectively intervene to promote domestic industry. The result, in the information technology market, has fast become a handing over of markets in both products and technology to American companies. We may not see an official 'Buy American' or 'Buy Japanese' policy,but if governments are not to intervene to protect domestic industry, to allow it to build up within the domestic market, then the world market structure will impose itself upon the domestic economy. In turn Britain becomes the Trojan Horse for multinational interests in Europe, and for the supremacy of American firms in the European market.

In case the reader should think that this represents a distortion of the overall picture, IBM alone leads the British market in private telephone exchanges, has a link with British Telecom via its SBS consortium, which gives entry into voice and data transmission in Europe, has entered the public telephone exchange market, and has a link with Mitel, which is also inside the British telecommunications market, for an automated office network. In addition it has a 40% market share in European mini and mainframe computers, takes 30/40% in the world market in word processors and 25/30% in that of interactive word processors. It also supplies a majority of the data processing terminals in Europe and has recently entered the robotics market. This one company alone has enormous economic power within Europe and Britain. Without effective non-tariff barriers, one may expect IBM and other American and Japanese multinationals to prosper at

CONCLUSION

the expense of British and European owned industry. And,as these large firms spread into each fast growth market, so smaller domestic firms will be squeezed out,further eroding the possibility of government action to stem economic decline.

NOTES AND REFERENCES

1. On economic and political power and interdependence see: Robert O. Keohane & Joseph S.Nye,*Power and Interdependence. World Politics in Transition*(Boston,Little Brown & Co.,1977).
2. Raymond Vernon,*Sovereignty at Bay:The Multinational Spread of US Enterprises*(London, Longmans,1970),passim.
3. Steven Krasner,"State Power and the Structure of International Trade",*World Politics*,Vol.28,1975-6,pp.319-343.
4. Steven Krasner,in P.J.Katzenstein ed.,pp.54-5.
5. Samuel Brittan,"Clues to World Stagnation",*Financial Times*,22nd July 1982.
6. *Financial Times*,28th July 1982.
7. Mr Geoffrey Chandler quoted in Financial Times,21st October 1982:"We need an industrial Rayner Committee within the Treasury and Whitehall. At present the Treasury can devise policies without understanding their impact on industry".
8. *Fourth Report*,Vol.II,Q 1650.
9. Committee of Public Accounts:Third Report 1981-2,*Introduction of a New General Policy for Public Purchasing*,HC29,ppv-vi.
10. Sir Ieuan Maddock, *Civil Exploitation of Defence Technology*,Part II,Comment by the M.O.D.,pp.21-30; Defence Committee, Minutes of evidence, *Ministry of Defence Organisation and Procurement* , HC22i; Memoranda,*Ministry of Defence Organisation and Procurement*,HCiii(London,HMSO,1981-2)
11. *Computer Weekly*,4th August 1983.

SELECT BIBLIOGRAPHY

Neville Abraham,Big Business and Government(London, Macmillan,1974)
ACARD,Industrial Innovation(London,HMSO,1978).
ACARD,The Application of Semiconductor Technology(London,HMSO,1978)
ACARD,Information Technology(London,HMSO,1980)
N.Amaya,The Ministry of International Trade & Industry,Socio-economic Institute Bulletin No.24 (Tokyo,Sophia University,1970)
Artur Attman & Wolf Olsson,L.M.Ericsson,100 years. Rescue,Reconstruction,Worldwide Enterprise 1932-6 Vol.II (Stockholm,Jacobaeus,1976)
Jack Baranson,Technology and Multinationals Corporate Strategies in a Changing World Economy (Lexington,Mass.,D.C.Heath,1978)
Richard J.Barnet,Real Security.Restoring American Power in a Dangerous Decade(New York,Simon & Schuster,1981)
Joel Barnett,Inside the Treasury(London,Deutsch, 1982)
Ian Barron & Ray Curnow,The Future with Microelectronics(London,Frances Pinter,1979)
Samuel Beer,Britain Against Itself(London,Faber & Faber,1982)
Tony Benn,Arguments for Socialism(London,Penguin, 1980)
Tony Benn,Arguments for Democracy(London,Jonathan Cape,1981)
J.R.Besant,J.A.E.Bowen,K.E.Dickson,J.Marsh,The Impact of Microelectronics(London,Frances Pinter,1981)
A.G.W.Biddle,"IBM versus A.T.&T.Its meaning to the user and the public",Computers and People,Vol.24, No.1,1975,pp.20-23
John Black,The Economics of Modern Britain,2nd

SELECT BIBLIOGRAPHY

edition (London,Martin Robertson,1980)
F.T.Blackaby ed.,De-industrialisation(London, Heinemann,1978)
——— ed.,British Economic Policy 1960-74 (Cambridge,Cambridge University Press,1978)
G.Boyle,D.Elliott & R.Roy,The Politics of Technology(London,Longman,1977)
David R.Cameron,"The Expansion of the Public Economy:A Comparative Analysis",American Political Science Review,Vol.72,1978.pp.1243-1261
Charles Carter ed.,Industrial Policy & Innovation (London,Heinemann,1981)
Gian Casadio,Transatlantic Trade,USA-EEC Confrontation in the GATT Negotiations (Farnworth,Saxon House,1973)
Richard Caves ed.,Britain's Economic Prospects (Washington,D.C.,Brookings,1968)
——— ed.,Britain's Economic Performance (Washington,D.C.,Brookings,1980)
A.Cawson,"Pluralism,Corporatism and the Role of the State",Government and Opposition,Vol.13,1978, pp.187-199
CPRS,Social and Employment Implications of Microelectronics(London,HMSO,1978)
W.Cline,N.Kawanabe,T.O.M.Kronsjo,T.Williams,Trade Negotiations in the Tokyo Round(Washington,D.C., Brookings,1978)
Stephen Cohen,"Coping with the New Protectionism", National Westminster Bank Review,November 1978,pp.2-15
Computer Services Association,Report on the UK Computer Services Industry(London,CSA,1976)
W.M.Corden & G.Fels,Public Assistance to Industry.Protection and Subsidies in Britain and Germany(London,Macmillan,1976)
Counter Information Services,Private Line.The Future of British Telecom,CIS Report No.32 (London,CIS,1982)
Colin Crouch ed.,State and Economy in Contemporary Capitalism(London,Croom Helm,1979)
Michael Crozier,The Bureaucratic Phenomenon (Chicago,University of Chicago Press,1964)
Edmund Dell,Political Responsibility and Industry (London,Allen & Unwin,1973)
W.Diebold Jr.,Industrial Policy as an International Issue(New York,McGraw Hill,1980)
Marshall Dimock,The Japanese Technocracy.Management and Government(New York,Weatherhill,1968)
T.Dixon Long,"Japanese Technology Policy:Achievements and Perspectives",Research Policy,4,1975, pp.2-26
Mattei Dogan ed.,The Mandarins of Western Europe

SELECT BIBLIOGRAPHY

(New York,Halsted Press,1975)
John W.Dower,*Origins of the Modern Japanese State. Selected Writings of E.H.Norman*(New York,Random House,1975)
John Dunning,"The UK's International Direct Investment Position in the Mid 1970s",*Lloyd's Bank Review*,No.132,April 1979,pp.1-21
Electronics EDC,*Policy for the UK Electronics Industry*(London,NEDO,1982)
Policy for the UK Information Technology Industry(London,NEDO,1983)
Tom Forester ed.,*The Micro-electronics Revolution. The Complete Guide to the Silicon Chip and its Impact on Society*(Oxford, Blackwell,1980)
Isiah Frank ed.,*The Japanese Economy in International Perspective*(Baltimore,John Hopkins University Press,1975)
H.Fukui,"Economic Planning in Postwar Japan;a Case-Study in Policymaking",*Asian Survey*,Vol.12,No.4, 1972,pp.327-348
Andrew Gamble,*Britain in Decline*(London,Macmillan, 1981)
Roger Gibbs,*Industrial Policy in More Successful Economies:Japan*,Discussion Paper No.7 (London,NEDO,1980)
Robert Gilpin, *US Power and the Multinational Corporation. The Political Economy of Foreign Direct Investment*(London,Macmillan,1975)
P.Goodman,*French Sixth Plan (1971-1975)R&D* (London,Dept.of Trade & Industry,1971)
John B.Granger,*Technology and International Relations*(San Fransciso,W.H.Freeman,1979)
Wyn Grant,"Comment,Analysing Industrial Policy", *Public Administration Bulletin*,1980,No.32, pp.50-6
The Development of the Government Relations Function in UK Firms: a Pilot Study of UK Based Companies(Berlin,Institute of Management,1981)
The Political Economy of Industrial Policy(London,Butterworths,1982)
"Studying Business Interest Associations: Does Neo-Corporatism Tell Us Anything We Didn't Know Already",Paper to Annual PSA Conference, Newcastle,1983
Wyn Grant & David Marsh,*The CBI*(London,Hodder & Stoughton,1977)
D.C.Hague,W.J.M.Mackenzie & A.Barker,*Public Policy and Private Interests*(London Macmillan,1975)
Hansard Society,*Politics and Industry-the Great Mismatch*(London,Hansard Society,1979)
Nigel Harris,*Competition and the Corporate*

SELECT BIBLIOGRAPHY

Society.British Conservatism,the State and Industry 1945-64(London,Macmillan,1972)
J.Haslam,"An Appraisal of Micro-electronics Technology"National Westminster Bank Quarterly Review,May 1979,pp.55-63
Ian Hargeaves,"The Dilemmas of Job Subsidies", Financial Times,4th August 1982
C.Harlowe,Innovation and Productivity under Nationalisation.The First 30 Years(London, Allen & Unwin,1977)
Jack Hayward,"The Politics of Planning in Britain and France",Comparative Politics,7,1974-5, pp.285-298
Jack Hayward & R.Berki,State and Society in Contemporary Europe(Oxford,Martin Robertson,1979)
Hugh Heclo & Aaron Wildavsky,The Private Government of Public Money(London,Macmillan,1974)
A.Helou,"Japan and the Tokyo Round",Journal of World Trade Law,Vol.15,1981,p.450
Jill Hills,"Government Relations with Industry:Japan and Britain.A Review of Two Political Arguments",Polity,Vol.14,1981,pp.222-248
        "Foreign Policy and Technology:the Japan-US,Japan-Britain and Japan EEC Technology Agreements",Political Studies,1983,pp.205-233
        "Government policies towards the Telecommunications and Computer industries", Physics in Technology,Vol.13,no.3,1982, pp.105-112
M.T.Hills,"A Comparison of Switching Systems Development in the UK & Japan",Telecommunications Group Report,No.116,Essex University,1977,roneo
Michael Hodges,Multinational Corporations and National Governments: A Case-Study of the UK's Experience 1964-70(Farnborough,Saxon House,1974)
Brian Hogwood,"Monitoring of Government Involvement in Shipbuilding",Public Administration, Vol.54,1976,pp.409-424
        "In Search of Accountability: the Territorial Dimensions of Industrial Policy",Public Administration Bulletin,No.38,1982,pp.20-42
        "Analysing Industrial Policy: A Multi-Perspective Approach",Public Administration Bulletin,No.29,1979,pp.18-42
Independent Commission of International Development Issues,North South,a Programme for Survival (London,Pan,1979)
IRC,First Annual Report(London,HMSO,1968)
Clive Jenkins & B.Sherman,The Collapse of Work(London,Eyre Methuen,1979)
J.K.Johannson,Japanese Export Management. The Organisational,Institutional and Market Forces

SELECT BIBLIOGRAPHY

Behind a World Force(Stockholm,Marknadsteknikst Centrum,1981)
Mary Kaldor,The Disintegrating West, (London,Penguin,1979)
Eugene Kaplan,Japan,The Government:Business Relationship(Washington D.C.,US Dept. of Commerce,1972)
P.J.Katzenstein ed.,Between Power and Plenty.Foreign Economic Policies of Advanced Industrial States (Wisconsin,University of Wisconsin Press,1978)
Robert O.Keohane & Joseph S.Nye,Power and Interdependence. World Politics in Transition (Boston,Little Brown & Co.,1977)
Sir Arthur Knight,"UK Industry in the Eighties",Journal of Fiscal Studies, Spring 1981,pp.1-14
Stephen Krasner,"State Power and the Structure of International Trade",World Politics,Vol.28,1975, pp.319-343
Labour Party,Microelectronics(London,Labour Party,1980)
Simon Lavington,Early British Computers (Manchester,Manchester University Press,1980)
Gerhard Lehmbruch & P.C.Schmitter ed.,Patterns of Corporatist Policymaking(Beverly Hills & London,Sage,1982)
Gareth Locksley,A Study of Evolution of Concentration in the UK Data Processing Industry With Some International Comparisons (Brussels,Commission of the European Communities,1981)
Sir Ieuan Maddock," Science,Technology and Industry" 7th Royal Society Technology Lecture, Proceedings of the Royal Society(Mathematical & Physical Sciences),Vol.345,1975,pp.285-326
"Putting Technology to Work",The Radio & Electronic Engineer,Vol.46,No.12,1976,pp.624-630
"The Future of Work",New Scientist, Vol.79,1978,pp.592-5
Civil Exploitation of Defence Technology (London,NEDO,1983)
R.Major ed.Britain's Trade and Exchange Rate Policy (London,NIESR,1979)
Peter Maunder ed.,Government Intervention in the Developed Economy(London,Croom Helm,1979)
Keith Middlemass,Politics in Industrial Society (London,Deutsch,1979)
Michael Moran,"Banks and Politics: an Anglo American Comparison",Paper to PSA Annual Conference, Newcastle,1983
"Monetary Policy and the Machinery of Government",Public Administration,Vol.59,1981,

SELECT BIBLIOGRAPHY

   pp.47-61
        "Finance Capital and Pressure Group Politics",British Journal of Political Science, Vol.11,1981,pp.381-404
        "The Politics of International Business", British Journal of Political Science,Vol.8,1978, pp.217-236
Michio Morishima,Why Has Japan Succeeded? Western Technology and the Japanese Ethos, (Cambridge,Cambridge University Press,1982)
NEDO,Electronics(London,HMSO,1970-72)
    Imported Manufactures:An Inquiry Into Competitiveness(London,HMSO,1965)
J.P.Nettl,"Consensus or Elite Domination - the Case of Business",Political Studies,Vol.13,1965, pp.27-44
Nihon Keizai Shimbun,Industrial Review of Japan (Tokyo,Nihon Keizai Shimbun,1979-81)
J.Nora & A.Mino,The Computerisation of Society (Cambridge,Mass.,MIT Press,1980)
Eric A.Nordlinger,On the Autonomy of the Democratic State(Cambridge,Mass.,Harvard University Press,1981)
Jim Northcott,John Mati & A.Zoilinger, Microprocessors in Manufactured Products(London, PSI,1980)
OECD,Gaps in Technology-Computers(Paris,OECD,1968).
    International Investment and Multinational Enterprise(Paris,OECD,1976)
    Gaps in Technology - Electronic Components (Paris,OECD,1968)
    Transfer of Technology by Multinational Corporations,Vol.II (Paris,OECD,1975)
Keith Pavitt ed.,Technical Innovation and British Economic Performance(London,Macmillan,1980)
G.Peninou,M.Holthus,D.Kebschull,J.Attali,Who's Afraid of the Multinationals. A Survey of Opinion on Multinational Corporations(Farnborough,Saxon House,1978)
John Pinder ed.,National Industrial Strategies and the World Economy(London,Croom Helm,1982)
Douglas Pitt,The Telecommunications Function in the British Post Office(Farnborough,Saxon House,1980)
D.Pitt & B.C.Smith,Government Departments: An Organisational Perspective(London,Rutledge & Kegan Paul,1981)
S.J.Prais,The Evolution of Concentration of Giant Firms in Britain.A Study of the Growth of Concentration in Manufacturing Industry 1909-1970(Cambridge,Cambridge University Press,1976)
Tait C.Radcliffe,Japanese Corporate Finance 1977-80 (London,Financial Times,1977)

SELECT BIBLIOGRAPHY

W.B.Reddaway,S.T.Potter & C.T.Taylor,*Effects of UK Direct Investment Overseas*,(Cambridge, Cambridge University Press,1968)

RIPA,*Allies or Adversaries?Perspectives on Government and Industry in Britain*(London, RIPA,1981)

SPRU.*Microelectronics & Women's Employment in Britain*(Sussex,SPRU,1982)

Semiconductor Industry Association (US),*The International Microelectronics Challenge. The American Response by the Industry, the Universities and the Government*(Washington D.C.,SIA,1980)

Philippe C.Schmitter & Gerhard Lehmbruch,*Trends towards Corporatist Intermediation*(Beverly Hills & London,Sage,1979)

Andrew Shonfield,*Modern Capitalism*(Oxford,Oxford University Press,1965)

J.Sleigh,B.Boatwright,P.Irwin & R.Stanyon,*The Manpower Implications of Micro-Electronics Technology*(London,HMSO,1979)

Bruce L.Smith & D.C.Hague,*The Dilemma of Accountability in Modern Government. Independence Versus Control*(London,Macmillan,1973)

Joan E.Spero,*The Politics of International Economic Relations* (New York.Martins Press,1977)

David R.Steel,"Review Article:Government and Industry in Britain",*British Journal of Political Science*,Vol.12,1982,pp.449-503

M.J.Steuer et al.,*The Impact of Foreign Direct Investment on the UK*(London,HMSO,1973)

Telecommunications Equipment Manufacturers Association,*Annual Reports*(London,TEMA,1956-70)

TUC,*Employment and Technology*,Report by the TUC Council to the 1979 Conference. (London,TUC,1979)

Hiroya Ueno,"Conception and evaluation of Japanese Industrial Policy",*Japanese Economic Studies*,White Plains,75,Winter 1976/77,pp.3-63

UNESCO,*Case Studies on Technological Development* (Paris,UNESCO,1971)

US International Trade Commission,*Competitive Factors Influencing World Trade in Integrated Circuits*(Washington D.C.,Govt.Printing Office,1979)

D.Van deb Buelcke,J.J.Boddewyn,B.Martens,P.Klenner, *Investment and Disinvestment Policies of Multinational Companies in Europe*(Farnborough, Saxon House,1979)

Raymond Vernon, *Storm over the Multinationals:the Real Issues*(London,Macmillan,1977)

"International Investment and International Trade in the Product Cycle",*Quarterly Journal of Economics*,Vol.80,1966,pp.190-207

ed.,*Big Business and the State*(London,

SELECT BIBLIOGRAPHY

Macmillan,1974)
Norman J.Vig,Science and Technology in British Politics(Oxford,Pergamon Press,1968)
Ezra Vogel,Japan as No.One(New York,Harper & Row,1979)
    ed.,Modern Japanese Organisation and Decision Taking(Berkeley,University of California Press,1975)
Helen Wallace,W.Wallace & C.Webb ed.,Policymaking in the European Communities(London,J.Wiley,1977)
William Wallace ed.,Britain in Europe(London, Heinemann,1980)
S.J.Warnecke ed.,International Trade and Industrial Policies. Government Intervention in the Open World Economy(London,Macmillan,1978)
S.J.Warnecke & E.Suleiman ed., Industrial Policies in Western Europe(New York,Praeger,1975)
Roger Williams,Politics and Technology(London, Macmillan,1971)
Viscount Wolmer,Post Office Reform,its Importance and Practicability(London,Ivor Nicholson,1932)
Hugo Young & Anne Sloman,No Minister(London, BBC,1982)
Stephen Young, Privatisation,Planning and the Public Sector(London,Croom Helm), forthcoming
Stephen Young & A.V.Lowe,Intervention in the Mixed Economy(London,Croom Helm,1974)
John Zysman,Political Strategies for Industrial Order(Berkeley,University of California Press,1977)

OFFICIAL PAPERS

Cmnd 4149 (1932)Report of the Committee of Inquiry on the Post Office
Cmnd 1337 (1961)Financial and Economic Obligations of the Nationalised Industries
Cmnd 2211 (1963)The Inland Telephone Service in an Expanding Economy
Cmnd 2764 (1965) The National Plan
Cmnd 2889 (1966)The Industrial Reorganisation Corporation
Cmnd 3660 (1968)The Computer Merger Project
Cmnd 4506 (1970)The Reorganisation of Central Government
Cmnd 5710 (1974) The Regeneration of British Industry
Cmnd 6850 (1977)Report of the Post Office Review Committee.
Cmnd 7937 (1980)Report of the Committee to Review the Functioning of Financial Institutions
Cmnd 7779 (1979)Innovation,R&D in Japanese Science

SELECT BIBLIOGRAPHY

Based Industry
European Commission,9361/80 (com(80)421 final) Proposal for a Council Regulation (EEC) Concerning Community Action in the Field of Microelectronic Technology
   Council Resolution of 15.7.1974 on Community Policy on Data Processing.Official Journal of the European Communities,No.C 96/1,20th July 1974

PARLIAMENTARY COMMITTEES

Defence Committee,Minutes of evidence,Ministry of Defence Organisation and Procurement. HC 22i & iii(1981-2)
   Memoranda,Ministry of Defence Organisation and Procurement.HC 22iii (1981-2)
House of Lords, Report of the Select Committee on the European Communities,New Information Technologies (1981)
Expenditure Committee, Sixth Report (1972)
Public Accounts Committee,Fifth Report(1967), Third Report(1981-2)
Select Committee on Nationalised Industries,First Report on the Post Office(1967)
Select Committee on Science & Technology,
   Minutes of evidence,HC 137, Sub-committee D (1969-70)
   Appendices,HC 272,Sub-committee D (1969-70)
   Fourth Report,The Prospects for the UK Computer Industry in the 1970s,Vols.I-III (1970-71)
   Minutes of evidence,UK Computer Industry Sub-committee,HC 63-i,December 1973 (1972-3)
   Minutes of evidence UK Computer Industry Sub-committee,HC 199-i,June 1974 (1974);
   Minutes of evidence Japan Sub-committee,HC 105(1976-77)
   Second Report,Innovation Research and Development in Japanese Science Based Industry. HC 682 (1976-77)

INDEX

AT&T, 80, 82, 99, 236
Baker, Kenneth, 169, 170, 190
Banks & government, 38-9
Benn, Tony, 60, 63, 115-7, 125, 143, 156, 160, 185
Britain
    & industrial capital, 31, 38-9
    & inward investment, 56-7
    & R&D, 21, 64-5,
British civil servants
    & industry, 51-3
    & technical expertise, 145
British Telecom Bill, 122
Cable TV, 66, 191
Callaghan, James, 205-6, 215, 218
Canada, 36-7
CCITT, 87, 239
Cross-bar, 78-9, 131, 136, 144
Central Computer Agency, 162-3, 186-7, 270
Chataway, Christopher, 119, 135
Computer Advisory Unit, 156, 159
Conservative Government
    Heath, 58, 60, 63, 119
    Thatcher, 57, 63, 67, 163, 169, 200-201, 270

Defence Policy & R&D, 19, 36, 64-7, 158, 244, 275
EEC & industrial policy, 12-16, 40, 69, 229-30, 233, 236, 239-40, 255, 265, 276-7
Employment in IT 10-11, 55, 61
Ericsson, 83, 85, 121, 137
Export/Import Ratios 88, 96-7, 105
Ferranti, 63, 67, 91, 94, 96, 103-5, 164, 180, 198, 202
Fifth Generation Computer, 66, 269
France
    & computers, 22 25, 93-4, 169, 226
    & ideology, 32, 234
    & microchips, 23, 231-4
    & R&D, 64-5
    & telecomms, 88, 237-8, 243-4
GATT, 2, 13-16, 27, 40, 255, 265
GEC, 67, 84, 86, 103-5, 121, 124, 132-6, 141, 143-4, 164, 176, 180, 201-2, 208, 210, 215-7,

INDEX

Honeywell, 25, 93-4, 97-8, 159, 164, 167, 180, 192, 225-6, 229, 231, 242-3, 271
IBM, 25, 53, 63, 67-8, 91-8, 101, 122-3, 157, 159, 162, 165, 225, 242, 271
ICL, 25, 53, 63, 67-8, 91, 95, 98, 158-65, 168, 170, 172-3, 178-80, 182-6, 243, 270, 272-3
Ideologies, 4, 17, 28-9, 31, 35-6, 54
Inmos, 206-19, 221
IRC, 59, 60, 62, 69, 128, 133, 143
ITT, 82-3, 103, 106, 204-5, 209, 211, 216
Japan
   & banks, 246-8
   & computers, 24-5, 227-8
   & ideology, 28, 32, 35
   & industrial success, 3, 87, 253
   & microchips 233-4
   & MITI, 18, 24, 245-53
   & non-tariff barriers, 26, 229, 240-1
   & peripherals, 231
   & software, 232
   & telecomms, 237-8, 243-4
Joseph, Sir Keith, 181, 213, 215
Labour Government
   1964-70, 57, 104, 115, 128, 133-4, 153-4, 199
   1974-9, 60-61, 63
Mercury, 80, 123
Multinational Companies, 10-11, 17, 19, 21-2, 29-30, 54-6, 61, 69, 161
Microchips,
   general, 100-101, 197-8
   & R&D, 101-2, 198-200, 203, 205-6, 220, 230, 235-6
NEB, 62-3, 69, 152, 168, 174-5, 182-4, 188-9, 206-7, 220, 271
213-4, 216-7, 256, 267, 273-4
NEDC, 40, 65, 67, 70-1, 115, 119-20, 169, 171-2, 186, 199, 204, 206-7, 209-10, 212, 221, 256, 271, 274
NRDC, 63153-5, 174, 203
Overseas investment, 11, 31,
Philips, 83-6, 103-4, 137-8, 207-9, 211, 216, 226
Plessey, 83-6, 103, 105, 132-3, 135-6, 137, 139, 141, 176, 207, 210, 271
Post Office Acts, 114, 117-8, 120
POEU, 115-7
Public Accounts Ctee., 127, 163
Racal, 67, 105, 180
Reed Relays, 79, 136, 144
Regional aid, 19, 37, 57, 61
SBS, 80, 123, 237
Select Ctee on Nationalised Industries, 116, 118, 125
Select Ctee on Science & Technology, 160, 166-7, 178, 185, 187, 202, 256
Siemens, 104, 158, 213, 226, 229, 242, 263
Sinclair, 204-5
STC, 83, 85, 121, 124, 132-3, 135, 141, 271
Strowger, 78, 124, 130, 136, 144
System X, 66, 84-5, 137, 139, 140-2, 144-5
Tariff barriers, 4, 12, 15, 17, 33, 37, 39, 68
Treasury, 50, 53, 71, 111-2, 114, 157, 160, 165-6, 271
Univac, 25, 95, 165, 181-2

290

INDEX

UPOW,118,121
USA,
    & banks,38-9
    & computers,
    225,240-1
    & ideology,28,
    32,37
    & microchips,
    233-4,241,264
    & R&D,20,31,
    64-6,101,245,254,
    265-6
    & software,232-3
W.Germany
    & banks,38-9
    & computers,93
    & ideology,32
    & R&D,20,64-5
    & software,232
    & telecomms,88,237-8,243-4